The

Geography

of Love

The

Geography

of Love

A Memoir

Glenda Burgess

Broadway Books

New York

PUBLISHED BY BROADWAY BOOKS

Copyright © 2008 by Glenda Burgess

All Rights Reserved

Published in the United States by Broadway Books, an imprint of
The Doubleday Publishing Group, a division of
Random House, Inc., New York.
www.broadwaybooks.com

BROADWAY BOOKS and its logo, a letter B bisected on the
diagonal, are trademarks of Random House, Inc.

*While this is a true story, some names and details have been
changed to protect the identities of those who appear in these pages.*

"The Human Heart," used as epigraph, from PAX ATOMICA by
CAMPBELL McGRATH. Copyright © 2004 by Campbell
McGrath. Reprinted by permission of HarperCollins Publishers.
Excerpt from Edward Abbey's NORTH RIM is reprinted by
permission of Don Congden Associates, Inc. © 1994 by
Clarke Abbey.

Library of Congress Cataloging-in-Publication Data
Burgess, Glenda.
    The Geography of love : a memoir / Glenda Burgess. — 1st ed.
        p. cm.
    1. Burgess, Glenda. 2. Grunzweig, Kenneth. 3. Novelists,
American—20th century—Biography. I. Title.
PS3552.U71419Z466 2008
813'.54—dc22

2007023619

ISBN 978-0-7679-2859-5

PRINTED IN THE UNITED STATES OF AMERICA

1   3   5   7   9   10   8   6   4   2

First Edition

a Barolo, amore mio

The Human Heart

We construct it from tin and ambergris and clay,
　　ochre, graph paper, a funnel
　　of ghosts, whirlpool
in a downspout full of midsummer rain.

It is, for all its freedom and obstinance,
　　an artifact of human agency
　　in it maverick intricacy,
its chaos reflected in earthly circumstance,

its appetites mirrored by a hungry world
　　like the lights of the casino
　　in the coyote's eye. Old
as the odor of almonds in the hills around Solano,

filigreed and chancelled with flavor of blood oranges,
　　fashioned from moonlight,
　　yarn, nacre, cordite,
shaped and assembled valve by valve, flange by flange,

and finished with the carnal fire of interstellar dust.
　　We build the human heart
　　and lock it in its chest
and hope that what we have made can save us.

—Campbell McGrath

The

Geography

of Love

Physicists say we are made of stardust. Intergalactic debris and far-flung atoms, shards of carbon nanomatter rounded up by gravity to circle the sun. As atoms pass through an eternal revolving door of possible form, energy and mass dance in fluid relationship. We are stardust, we are man, we are thought. We are story.

"It's always a story, my girl," my father told me one summer evening when I was young. "Falling stars, rings in a tree trunk, the river as it swells by, all stories."

We were camping in the wilderness north of Vancouver, Washington, along the pebble shoals of the Lewis River. It was an hour after sunset, and the sky was deepening to an inky lavender at the edge of the black canopy of trees. We crouched beside the water, washing up after a quick dinner of cowboy stew. I asked him what made stars shoot. At nine years old, I was ready for real explanations, heavy truth, clues and answers to bigger mysteries than long division. My father had studied physics as a young man. I knew he would take my question seriously.

He reached behind him to loosen a flat river stone and skipped it out across the burbling rapids. *Please,* I begged silently, *tell me the truth.* I knew with deep inner conviction that the way my father answered my question would somehow affect the way I asked and answered questions the rest of my life.

He tossed out another stone as he considered the darkening sky.

"Just a bit of chance and chaos, Sunshine," he said. "Atoms that dance."

I think back to that long-ago conversation as I ponder the effects of luck and disaster on the human heart. A child then, I had no real awareness of human fragility, but I absolutely knew shooting stars pirouetted across the universe. Life, my search for truth, seemed dusted by a dash of magic.

Only now in the wake of fortune, do I truly understand.

Part

One

Quintessence

SUMMER, 1988

I awoke to the sound of the unfamiliar. Disturbed by the rustle of feathers and harsh caw of a crimson and teal parrot
perched on the balcony railing four feet from my nose. The
bird sidled along the railing toward the balcony patio table,
eyeing the remainders of a late-night fruit plate. A brilliant
green slug curled at the bottom of an empty champagne glass.

I lay still, coming slowly awake, registering another unfamiliar sound: the muffled snores of the man sleeping beside
me. The sheets were crisp, expensive linen—hotel sheets. And
the bright sunlight streaming in through the filmy drapes was
the hot sun of Rio de Janeiro. The man was my lover. I was
thirty-one years old, and this was happiness. I had nothing to
compare it to, but you know the sweet from bitter, and this
was most definitely sweet.

I slipped out of the sheets careful not to disturb Ken and
pulled on his dress shirt from the night before, walking
through the sliding glass doors to the balcony. A breeze salty

and cool whipped in from the sea, carrying the lush green smell of the jungles and bluffs that shouldered the white sands of Ipanema. The beach was visible from our room, a scimitar of glossy heat that ended in a sparkling sea, rimmed by high rises and hotels, exotic gardens as far as the eye could see.

I hugged his shirt close, inhaling the musk and sweat of the man, memories of thrilling guitars and Latin drums, the salsa dancing of the night before. Who travels an entire continent in order to salsa dance in Rio? Ken Grunzweig. "Nothing comes from nothing, nothing ever could"—the phrase from "Something Good" by Oscar Hammerstein drifted into my head and I hummed the lyric with a smile, flicking a rind of kiwi toward the parrot now hovering in the tree canopy below. My grandfather had sung the song to me as a child. He and my grandmother, on one of their periodic visits east to New York, had booked in at the Plaza, picking up tickets to Mary Martin in *The Sound of Music*. Broadway, 1959. I was not yet three at the time, but I remember the song, the way Grampa would twirl me and plant a big kiss on my neck as he sang, "Somewhere in my youth or childhood, I must have done something *good*."

I looked back over my shoulder at the man sleeping rumpled under the sheets, one arm flung over his forehead in vulnerable disregard for the world. For our many mistakes, the unexpected tragedies, the sadnesses rounded with time, life had produced the unfamiliar. Something good.

* * *

If you were to ask me what three things I know to be true of life, I would tell you these three: what you dreamed of yourself at fourteen reflects your purest wish; don't marry the first person you kiss; and all the great questions bounce back from God.

Fourteen is the first time we ever really ask our future selves, "What do I want to be?" and the self answers back, pure and free of rationalization. And love. Romance plops the macaroni salad right beside the ambrosia. Grandmothers tell us not to marry first crushes, unless we're the type of person who has only ever liked bologna sandwiches and always will. And while the question of God himself frames the universe, the great mysteries exist in the human heart, unsolved. What is faith, intuition, if not human sonar—hope that pings the universe, mapping life? Sometimes gut instinct is the only way to answer the big questions for ourselves.

I've learned to listen for the echo of small answers.

My father taught me that science was the puzzle play of God, that the mysteries and theories of all creation were understood in levels of revelation, degrees of understanding. There was no wrong answer, but there were inadequate questions. The scientific path to God, my father believed, was the pursuit of "Why?"

I grew from a child to a young woman, and the question "Why?" seesawed for dominance within my life with the bleakness of "Oh well." Short on answers but long on questions, I learned to protect myself, to avoid the complicated detours in favor of more well-traveled paths. For me, these paths were particularly barren in matters of the heart. Dating the guy sitting next to me in class, on the subway, in line at the Department of Motor Vehicles, I encountered a profound lack of imagination and magic.

Needless to say, I made a pretty good hash of things learning about love. I know now that first loves are scooped from reflecting pools, mirroring back to us, as the cool waters revealed to Narcissus, how greatly we yearn to perceive ourselves as lovable. The self, in its innocent quest to survive, takes no prisoners. I think back to the sweet high school boyfriend who just seemed to *like* me, the pothead intellectual in college whose sense of independence taught me to think for myself, the business graduate student from Wyoming who stepped in and kept the world steady after my father died. What was wrong with me? Why were they all so good and so not right?

Eventually I constructed a layered exoskeleton, a coral reef instead of a life. The structure was there, but the essence was missing.

Quintessence: the essence of a thing in its purest and most concentrated form. *Quinte essence.* The fifth and highest element in an ancient and medieval philosophy that permeates all nature and is the substance composing the celestial bodies. Stars are not quintessence, but space, believe the physicists, must be. Quintessence, like faith, remains unproven: a deductive belief. A scientific theory suspended between the idea of dark energy, the static glue thought to be three-quarters of the universe, and dark matter, the inevitable clump and form of structure within these fields. Quintessence was the possibility of spark, dynamic vibration suspended at varying levels within time and space.

The smallest bombardment might jostle us from lax energy to subtle vibration. Possibility was everywhere.

Possibility dipped me over his arm last night on the salsa floor, requested one room key for two, snapped my thong as I brushed my teeth at the sink.

*   *   *

Bronzed and athletic in pressed khakis and a white shirt unbuttoned at the neck, Ken waved over a cab. Brazilian conga music spilled out of the open windows as the Land Rover pulled over to the curb. Ken lifted our bags into the taxi and we tumbled in, reaching for sunglasses against the noontime glare.

"Good-bye Rio." I smiled back through the palm avenues of the Intercontinental Hotel as the taxi pulled away from the curb.

"Where to now?" I asked. I really didn't know. This was the kind of mystery I loved best.

"Argentina." Ken smiled, in his dark shades every inch the movie star.

"What's in Argentina?"

"The tango."

Red Wagon

In the summer of 1987, the year before I met Ken, I returned home to visit with my mother on her small farm in the Palouse Hills of eastern Washington. I flew in from Washington, D.C., on the red-eye, taking a long weekend away from my management analyst work at the State Department.

An ache had settled into my life in the capitol city. I felt confused and uncertain about the goals I had set out vigorously to achieve and now found so wanting. I had a career in the government, traveled the world, and lived with a hole in the center of my being that ambition could not fill. My instincts were in disarray. Life felt tenuous. I wanted something, a nameless something, that mattered. What was central to work, to life, to love?

Unraveling these threads backward, I began to think about my childhood.

Seeking comfort or something like wisdom from the woman who was the only constant in my life, I left behind

Washington, D.C.'s sweltering humidity, and with it my naive failures navigating bureau politics and the ex-boyfriend who would rather drink than be with me. I would visit with my mother and try to forget that I could see every exact day of my unfolding life from where I stood today.

I felt a fierce loyalty to my mother, but she was also my central conundrum, a question with a conjectural answer. The terrain between us was defined by conflict and tumultuous consequence. We lived in a constant state of one influencing the other, bound by the act of observation and intention. I admired her but could not comprehend her reasoning. I rebelled from her law but sought her approval.

The farm marked the great divide in the timeline of my childhood. What formed me, and what drove me away. It had been several months since my last visit, on the somber occasion of my grandfather's funeral. My grandfather had been the cornerstone of strength in our family, his rich Scottish laugh the joyous bell tone of our happiest family gatherings. His decline, in the wake of burying my grandmother, had clearly been a very great burden for my mom. She lived for her parents; one of the oddities of her nature I never fully understood. Most people lived forward through their lives, growing and changing in the company of their spouses and children, celebrating the next generation of grandchildren to come. My mother lived backward. Childhood was the only song in her ear. Her parents were her identity, her sense of security.

We are autochthonous, formed of the familial earth. Was my mother becoming my sense of security?

In my child's eye, my mother opened and closed the curtain on love. Watching her, I observed what it meant to be married and happy, what it meant to be married and not, and what it meant to be alone, living with something in between. I learned that good things that came together might also break apart, and that the joy of loving might ultimately total less than the pain left behind.

My mother held the lead role in her own two-part play. Act I Mom was the Beautiful Blonde swirling on the arm of her officer, my dad. There were cocktail parties and muggy summer evenings. Backyard barbecues I watched in shorts and flip-flops from the top step of any of an endless succession of look-alike bungalows on military air force bases. Young and energetic, Mom organized the endless military relocations, aced real estate, packed and unpacked her wedding china. Life was both adventurous and magical. I remember as a child of four or five, watching my parents ready to leave for a Christmas ball. Enchanted, I reached up to touch the stiff undernetting of my mother's scarlet cocktail dress, thrilled at the sparkling rhinestones on her red high heels. She had her hand curled around my father's arm, dark and handsome in his uniform, smelling of Old Spice. Act I Mom seemed always to be laughing.

The last move my mother organized for the family, the last house she shipped boxes to, was here, the home in eastern Washington. A prolonged decoupling had occurred in my parents' lives somewhere between the Officers Club and the farm: My father's drinking worsened, initiating a period of forced smiles and declined social invitations, late-night arguments in the basement family room on the other side of my bedroom wall. Moving back west from suburban Maryland and buying the farm represented the last effort my parents made to save their marriage.

At eight I didn't comprehend what was happening, but it was clear something was. The magic was splintering. I responded as any child might, I suppose. I loaded up the red wagon with my white, long-eared stuffed dog and a box of Cheerios and ran away. When my father caught up with me three blocks from home, heading toward the highway, he bent down, took the handle of the wagon away, and asked, "Where were you going, out here like this?"

Back to how we were before, I remember thinking.

Eventually my younger brother, Tim, and little Judy were to follow my example. It wasn't until the State Patrol knocked on our door, informing my parents they had picked up Tim and Judy walking along the Interstate, that the red wagon was decommissioned.

An American landed on the moon; Richard Nixon resigned.

Act II Mom emerged, the Lady Rancher. Gone were the golf clubs, the party dresses. In their place a collection of motley horses and whitewashed wooden jumps hammered together by my father, a riding ring of soft spring mud. Each year, orphaned lambs to be bottle-nursed were brought down by the neighboring farmer, the lambs soon dead of milk disease. Each lamb was a love affair, each death inconsolable. Stray dogs wandered to the house and seemed to stay, and just as unpredictably vanished the nights the coyotes hunted. The beginnings and endings of connection felt rough and random.

My father slid deeper away. Somewhere in the military, between Greenland and the Pentagon, his quiet nature had dulled into a vodka haze. The detox centers failed and the last-ditch move to eastern Washington, from military to academic civilian life, seemed to remove what vestiges of his self-discipline remained. What my mother demanded my father do for love became what disillusionment did to love. The fighting between my parents grew harsher, and the empty hills only magnified our isolation. There were four of us after Helen was born, and what as children we might have wanted or needed fell away. We were casualties of war.

Within two years, my father was gone. The ensuing divorce battle crossed six states, the bitterness vitriolic and invasive. A teenager, I saw that love could fail, and even within families, bludgeon hearts. Visitations, loyalties, even the mention of my father's name, became conflicts. Tim and Judy, and Helen starting kindergarten, were moved to another school district. I took the bus alone to the old school where "everybody knew us."

My mother stopped answering the phone and answering questions. She worked strange small-town jobs, and of necessity, was often gone. At night, when I made dinner for the five of us, it was either fish sticks or a 49-cent tub of beef liver from the Safeway, fried crisp in a pan with white onions, rice with a dollop of margarine, and reconstituted dried milk, sometimes with the lumps still in it.

My younger siblings learned to love the farm, the apple tree, the orphaned animals. Tim, tall and sunburnt like the late summer wheat, made friends with the other farm-town boys, getting into fast cars and *Star Trek* and baseball. And although five years apart in age, Judy and Helen, leggy and freckled in matching pigtails, seemed identical in their love for the creatures that came to live in our barn.

My mother found the peace she craved, finally, in a life she commanded alone.

I was the one unable to adapt. I missed our Act I life. I missed my father's quiet hands and crinkled half smile. I missed hitting the streets with the neighborhood kids, romping through the green city parks, how we shrieked and doorbelled at Halloween. I missed swim team. French in the second grade. School trips to the Smithsonian. In this treeless, blustery, ice- and mud-covered farm country, the pride of school science was the awed distribution of a frozen cow's heart. My life was over. I knew it. I put my head on my desk and plotted my escape.

In high school I realized college was my way out. I learned French and world politics, took Spanish and German, captured the state debate trophy. With a check for the application fee mailed from my dad in Indiana, I applied to the best state university that would take me, and to which I could apply without having to enlist my mother's support. Mom, lying on the floor in the darkened living room between afternoon shifts working the phone banks at the. sheriff's office and night shifts at the nursing home, did not feel like telling college officials the details of the travesty of her personal finances. She wasn't filling in any forms, nothing thank you, go away. The college money sent every year from my paternal grandmother had been rerouted to farm taxes, and before that, detox clinics. There wasn't a dime.

The faculty offered a scholarship, and I penciled in my Social Security number to take out my first student loan. I had a new bike from my Mom charged to my grandfather's store account, a used typewriter from my dad. I was going to college.

The beginning of freshman year, fall term, Mom loaded the kids into our teal Chevrolet station wagon and drove across the state, unloading my boxes outside my dorm room. She sent me off to the student cafeteria alone—my meals were paid for—and fed the kids and herself from a one-dollar bag of Dick's Burgers. That night my family slept in the back of the car in the parking lot as I looked down from the empty space of my seventh-floor room.

This was the only family I knew, and the last time I belonged at home.

* * *

The farm felt unchanged, remote, and inescapable. Pulling up in a rental car, I opened the chained gate and drove up the long gravel road to the house. I relived again the shock of being carted as a teen so abruptly into the country: into a life without high school friends or activities, the end of piano lessons, of track and debate club. A teenager marooned without a car, surrounded by acres of wheat and buckets of horseshit. Horses. So many horses. I might have wanted a high school dance, or even a bookstore. My mom wanted horses.

The house and stable looked the same to me as they always had, a bit more worn perhaps, but the pastures were mowed and the house bore a new coat of brown stain and green trim. Tim and Judy and Helen were grown, gone away to work and college, but the old chicken coop was still outside Tim's window, and the bees and horses still feasted on the rotten apples at the foot of the old tree. My father had died, and although the old arguments were gone, there remained a blackened burn. For the last twelve years, my mother and I had shared only the occasional visit, letter, or holiday card.

Standing near the four-stall barn in the hot August sun, I watched Mom pull on her work gloves, boost an eighty-pound hay bale across one hip and toss it down the low hill. She clipped off the twine binding with a pair of needle-nose pliers and forked apart the leaves of hay. Lifting two fingers to her teeth and emitting a piercing wolf whistle, she brought the horses up from the lower field. She was happy. You could see it in her stance as she watched the horses nudge apart the green alfalfa flakes.

"So I take it you don't approve of me leaving the government," I said quietly.

I jammed my hands in my jeans, squinting at her through the direct sun. I felt as I had at twelve, tall and gawky, an ordinary girl in a brown ponytail, wondering if my mom loved me.

Mom shrugged, stroking the neck of the old bay.

"Don't see why you would," she said with a grunt. "Good jobs are hard to find."

But this wasn't about a good job.

"I've thought about writing. Trying seriously."

Mom said nothing.

In a burst of sudden courage, I cleared my throat. "I'm so lonely. Did you know that? Traveling all the time . . ."

"You've done all right."

"I'm thirty, Mom. Thirty. Still hoping for a true love."

I kicked a dirt clod.

"You should keep your job."

"I know."

My mother twisted slightly, shading her face with her gloved hand. Her eyes were bright blue, nested in crow lines; the muscles of her forearms tanned below the line of her old blue T-shirt. Sighing, she poked the pliers into her back pocket and bent to scoop the twine off the ground, balling it in her hand as she headed back to the barn.

"Changing your life . . . well, different isn't necessarily better."

That's all she said. I collapsed inside.

"Look, Glenda . . ."

Her silhouette cast a long shadow down the slope from above. I felt my body bend instinctively toward her, needing so much.

"Thirty's young. You have time."

You have time. The kindest thing she had ever said to me. Reluctant, to be sure—anything emotional for her was. But there it was, a mother telling a daughter to wait on hope.

One year later I was in Rio, in the arms of the man of my dreams.

The Mystery of Geography

Spokane was the unexpected thread that connected us.

Kenneth Grunzweig had relocated to Spokane in the early fall of 1987, a new executive with a local technology company. I resigned from the government, returning to Spokane Christmas of that year with all my worldly belongings in the back of my white hatchback, finding low-level work as a tech writer with a local company. We met for the first time a few weeks after the new year, meeting in the cheese section of the Four Seasons Deli, a small grocer tucked inside an old brick coffee roaster's building. Our hands collided reaching into a cold case. His coat was bunched beneath his arm, and he wore a pastel polo shirt, coral pink, the collar turned up.

Not from Spokane, I thought.

We exchanged smiles, and then I asked the clerk if she carried Montrachet cheese. She gave me a blank look.

"I just asked that!" the guy in the polo said.

Still grinning, he remarked off-handedly that he was organizing an opera party at his house and needed something special, a good cheese to accompany chilled Semillon wine.

"Opera? In Spokane?" I suppressed a chuckle. "Better you should like Van Halen. Better yet, monster trucks are coming to the coliseum."

I smiled at Montrachet Guy and we parted ways.

*　*　*

Months later, walking the sandy spit along Lake Coeur d'Alene on a hot, end-of-June afternoon, someone called out my name and I turned around.

Montrachet Guy. And more darkly handsome than I remembered.

His entire face lit up in an infectious smile.

"Remember me? The cheese shop? I think we work together. Ken Grunzweig."

He extended his hand.

Of course I remembered him. But I had never connected the face to the name. Each day I passed by the suite of executive doors as I clocked in to my cubicle. Kenneth Grunzweig was my boss's boss, a corporate vice president. In fact, rumor had it he had been responsible for my hire against the advice of the midmanager, who had his eye out for the lesser, less-threatening candidate, one that would not compete for his job. Ken had flat out instructed the man to hire the best candidate he could, and that happened to be me.

Still smiling, he invited me inside the cool resort lakeside bar for a drink.

"So you're really not gay?" I asked. I laid my floppy straw hat on the cocktail table, easing my feet out of my sandals and tucking them under me in the roomy rattan chair.

"Say what?" His face crinkled.

"That's the rumor at the company. Pastel shirts and pressed jeans? Last known origin—San Francisco?"

"My God, this *is* the provinces." Laughing, Ken ordered a bottle of Edna Valley chardonnay.

He impressed me as smart, that sexy kind of smart that makes conversations lift across whole continents of subject matter.

"So how did your opera party go?" I inquired, eyeing him over the rim of my glass.

"Oh the fat lady sang, all right. Later seen having fries at Dick's." He referred to a popular drive-in greasy spoon.

The sunset over the lake washed into an indigo summer night. The waitress, busting out of her white sailor hot pants, came to the side of our table. She stooped low, lighting the candle at our cocktail table. "Anything more for you, sir?"

She flicked her lashes at Ken, openly flirting.

"How about a large Caesar for two, and steamed clams?" Ken looked at me for agreement.

I nodded. The bar had begun to fill with the boat crowd straggling in from the docks.

"Not gay. Not married?" Ask early, especially with the cute ones.

He began to shake his head, and then stopped. His blue eyes darkened in the flickering light.

"Widowed, actually. Twice."

"Whoa. Bad luck." *On both sides,* I thought.

"Is that supposed to be funny?"

"No! Look, I'm sorry. Sometimes I just blurt things. I only meant that such a double loss doesn't seem fair some-how. . . ."

"You're right."

Without missing a beat, Ken moved on, refilling our glasses. "You're in tech writing, correct? Formerly with the government, if I remember rightly. Big career change. What brought you here? Family? I've been here a year. My daughter, Jordan, just finished high school. But she's back in California with her boyfriend now."

I could see this was the fresh wound, the one that still caught him by surprise. Ken talked about California, how he missed the sophisticated coastal culture, his bicycling friends.

"So what on earth brought you to Spokane?"

"One last attempt to give myself and my daughter a new life—and she left. We see how well that worked." He dipped a piece of French bread in the clam sauce, took a bite, and handed the rest to me. "Here, try this. The dill and wine sauce is superb."

One thought. I had one improbable thought. *I was the one to love this man.* I recognized my future in the sparkling eyes of this Californian, handsome as an Italian seventeenth-century Caravaggio with clam juice on his chin.

As the hour grew late, Ken touched lightly on his marriages, describing his early first love and her tragic loss in a car accident, and his later relationship with the woman who would become his daughter's mother. Already a widower, Ken had fallen in love for a second time with a stunning Choctaw woman with shining coffee bean–colored hair. They settled in Oakland, California, and a few years later, Jordan was born. But the marriage remained a combustible union, and after years of escalating arguments, Ken had finally moved out and the couple filed for divorce.

Ken took a breath, leveling his gaze on me. "I don't know why I'm telling you this. I never share this part of my life. It gets a bit . . . grisly. Sure you really want to know?"

"Absolutely, if you care to share. You and I, we seem to keep running into each other in the oddest places. If we're going to be friends—"

"Brave girl," he murmured. "Not everyone would."

The facts were, as Ken had warned, unexpectedly brutal. Prior to their divorce, Beckah was murdered: stabbed to death late at night in their home in Oakland, December of 1981. The same charming Tudor cottage Ken had remodeled by hand, laying in each decorative tile, painting the walls a bright and cheery yellow.

"Murdered? Your wife was murdered?"

Ken flinched. The word itself inflicted pain.

"I'm sorry," I said, fumbling for composure. "It's just—shocking."

The waitress slipped our tab across the table. The lakeside bar had nearly emptied.

His voice soft, Ken explained that lacking any solid leads, the detective in charge of the investigation had calculated that the soon-to-be ex-spouse must have committed the crime—the statistics always pointed to the family first. Despite prominent evidence of a serial murderer in the area at the time, the Oakland PD hounded Ken. Living under constant suspicion had made his and Jordan's life an unending nightmare. Ken was never formally charged, but neither was Beckah's murder ever solved.

"Yet you stayed? In San Francisco, I mean?"

"No one was going to drive me out of town." Ken's lips tightened. "I was innocent. Innocent people stand their ground."

Ken described the fight to protect Jordan from the trauma, and at the same time, clear his own name. Beckah's family had turned bitterly against him, and unsuccessfully sought custody of Jordan. One sister-in-law stalked Ken through the streets of San Francisco, screaming accusations.

"You can only imagine." He shook his head.

My throat grew dry and I fiddled with the last of the

chardonnay in the bottom of my glass, swirling it around and around, avoiding Ken's eyes. My thoughts were racing. *Whatever are you getting yourself into? What if everybody is right and he did murder his wife? You can't get interested in this man. He's disaster in a great-looking package. And, you work together! You need this job.*

I glanced outside at the dock gaslights, noting how each lamp cast brilliant golden ripples across the dark lake. I felt suddenly unable to think. On the face of it, his story seemed unbearably tragic, and yet he exuded genuine warmth, an infectious love for life that appeared unstoppable in his determination to live beautifully and as deeply as possible. Was he mad, or merely the most complex and astounding human being I had ever met?

I could barely breathe. I sipped my wine, feeling the world as I knew it, shift.

Glancing up, I met the quiet ironic awareness in Ken's gaze. I forced a smile. I felt both fear and free fall.

I believed in his innocence.

The atomic weight of the man was goodness. I simply knew it. I felt as sure as I'd ever been in life, separating the real from the unreal. It was intuition with the force of conviction.

"And your daughter? Losing her mother? How did she cope?"

"Jordan? Jordan was Mommy's girl."

Ken sketched out the years of trying to raise Jordan on his own. It was a tough history for a kid.

The therapists he and Jordan visited in the aftermath of the tragedy had blamed her seething adolescent anger and frightening self-destructive behavior on one thing: tremendous repressed grief. The therapists explained to a bewildered Ken that his daughter needed to pin her traumatic overwhelming loss on the one safe person in her life, her father. Ken accepted this. He tried to both love her and contain her escalating bouts of rebellion, to detach from her verbal attacks.

But nearly eight years later, things had not improved. Jordan had placed herself beyond his reach, yet Ken wouldn't, or couldn't, quit trying.

"Honestly?" Ken sighed, rueful. "Neither of us was much good at the father-daughter thing. I was trying to restart my own life and at the same time set ground rules for hers. Total fiasco." He shook his head, sliding his credit card over the bill. "About five years after Beckah's death, I returned home from a symphony date . . ."

He had opened his front door to discover two teenage couples entwined on opposite ends of the sofa, necking in the dark, bottles of vintage wine uncorked on the coffee table. The couples broke apart as Ken flipped the lights on.

"Jordan! What are you doing?" Ken had demanded in shock.

Jordan stood up, smoothing down her shirt. Across the room, her girlfriend stared at the floor, her face flaming. And two boys slunk out from where they had darted into the back bedroom, making a beeline for the open door.

"Not so fast, boys!"

Ken collared the nearest and handed him the phone. "First you call your father and tell him where you are. And then you tell him what bottles of wine you have with you, because these are most certainly not mine."

The color drained from the teen's face as he blinked from under a dark fringe of hair. He whispered into the phone, and a deep voice on the other end exploded in anger, bellowing out from the receiver: "Jackson, those are two-hundred-dollar bottles of wine!"

The teenagers left moments later under the escort of their parents.

"Well, Jordan?" Ken demanded of his sixteen-year-old daughter, closing the front door.

"Well, what?" Jordan smarted back. "Like *you* haven't been out doing something?" Her eyes darted toward the edge of her father's rumpled shirt collar, unbuttoned and bent up at the back, the telltale flush still on his cheek. *"Dad?"*

I said nothing.

"I tried the best I could." Ken appeared tired suddenly. "Well, she's made a choice, and it seems to be final. It's just me now."

Unfinished business, closed circles.

One thing I knew for certain, what tears apart a family is *never* final.

* * *

Two days later, Ken called me at home and invited me to the movies. There was both hesitation and intent in his voice.

In equal, measured tones, I said yes. We drove to the theaters on the far side of town. And I said yes again, to long weekends at a distant lake resort, followed by a holiday in Napa, discreet vacations to Europe, South America.

We met, we danced, and we loved.

We lived within our own moment in time, knowing how genuinely improbable it was that we should meet—Kenneth Grunzweig, the Jewish boy from Cleveland, born in the wartime forties, and me, the cold-war kid born on an air force base in New Mexico, smack in the middle of the "duck and cover" fifties.

Falling back and forth through geography and history, the

two of us had our feet firmly planted in different decades of the last century.

Ken had come of age during the Bay of Pigs, doo-wop, the Beatles, Kennedy, and Vietnam, while I walked to kindergarten through snowdrifts outside the military base near Rome, New York, *The Jetsons* painted on my metal lunch box. Ken was already a senior manager in the financial district in San Francisco when I graduated from high school in the seventies, my bedroom wall taped with pictures of the Apollo missions and the moon walk, the daily papers filled with details of the Watergate scandal. On our family television—the tube set my father had built from a kit newly replaced by the big color console purchased on time payments from Sears—Michael Jackson slid backward across the stage, his white gloves flashing. Paper millions were made and lost on Wall Street.

As children, Ken and I lived vastly different American lives. While my brother and I swung from rope vines, playing Tarzan in the Vanetti's backyard outside Andrews Air Force Base, Ken and his brother jumped tenement roofs, dodging alley gangs. Under broken street lights the handsome brothers stole kisses off the Polish girls—fire-escape love—until a low draft number shipped Ken from Ohio across the North Atlantic, and into the company of military power generators and remote Icelandic women.

In the days that followed, I learned more about Ken's past as bits and pieces floated to the top of conversations—most often in the quiet after making love, moments of sharing we treasured as both safe and private. Ken seemed to need me to know the absolute harshest facts, as if protecting himself and me, by giving the worst up front. Where he was unwilling to go, I did not push. I knew instinctively that some questions had no answers, that some feelings had been simply boxed because survival depended upon it.

It was so wide, the landscape of this man's life. The details were sketchy, but their significance was unforgettable. What I knew seemed far too much, and yet ultimately too little. How do you know a heart? The life only tells the journey.

The littlest details accompany the biggest hurts. I learned that after the air force Ken returned to California, and while still in his early twenties, married his first love, a smiling girl named Diana. Within the year, Diana was killed in a collision with a drunk driver, a wreck that Ken survived. Devastated, Ken lost himself in Mexico. He joined a traveling band, burying his broken heart in jazz. He played nights without end on a dented, second-hand flute for tourists on exquisitely beautiful Mexican beaches. "Wasting away in Margaritaville" was no joke for Ken. He was a man with an ache greater than the sum of his being.

Returning from Acapulco to the United States after thieves stole his flute, Ken met Beckah, his second wife and Jordan's mother, at a cocktail party. Besides her dark beauty, he had felt drawn to her because she understood all that he didn't care to explain, as she herself had lost a spouse in the Vietnam War. After Beckah was murdered, when Ken was in his late thirties, his life was swept up in the scandal of a violent crime that would haunt his every waking moment.

During Ken's years of heartache and survival, my naive world was just unfolding. I lazed on a midwestern campus green, listening to "Sugar Magnolia" and reading Rousseau. After graduate school I moved to Washington, D.C., a bright-eyed executive-in-training, an analyst with the U.S. State Department bearing my first passport.

And I gave it all up to begin again at the beginning. Who

did I want to be, what did I want to do, who would be my one to love?

Quintessence. I waited on the possibility of spark. My one extravagant heart's desire to live large, to find love, to know joy.

Ken arrived in Spokane looking for a new future. Me, I was just passing through.

The mystery of geography is that you can both find and lose yourself in latitudes familiar and strange. We stumbled into romance with few questions, knew what was necessary to know, and hoped, yes, hoped the best was yet to come.

Barolo

Ken and I sat touching elbows, deep in the shadows of the Italian café on Bernard Street. The cozy side-street trattoria had become our Friday-night haunt. We would arrive late, after the work crowd left the small bar, and order a plate of calamari, entrees of eggplant parmigiana and the seafood pasta the chef was famous for. Candlelight flickered across our faces as we talked softly. We had found a place in Spokane where we could be a couple, but a private one.

Barolo.

Ken lifted the Italian bottle out of its coarse canvas caddy and broke the black wax seal. Carefully, he poured us each a glass of the deep garnet wine, handing me mine.

"To you," he said, his eyes full of depth in the candlelight.

"To you," I answered back.

Barolo is an elegant wine; a red, aged in oak barriques deep in the sheltered valleys near the village of Barolo in northwestern Piedmont, in northern Italy. The smoky, chocolate violet flavors were the seductive daughters of the Nebbiolo grape and the proud winemaker. The Barolo red was a song, a myth, a mystery on the palate.

Ken Grunzweig the man was like his wine, I decided. Distinctive, deep, and worth the second look.

"To the tango," I offered suddenly.

Ken smiled.

We toasted to the pleasure of that warm Argentina evening when we had strolled the wide boulevards of Buenos Aires, "Fair Winds," the city of beautiful air, coming away from a night of dancing the tango in the company of dark Argentine men and their jeweled mistresses. That Ken was fourteen years older than me had allowed us to slip in among the couples on the dance floor unnoticed. Enthralled by the rhythms of the orchestra, we danced the story of the tango, flirted in the confines of each other's arms. The dance was a romance, and we were having one, and in the quiet closeness of that midnight walk home, we both knew we had experienced the unforgettable.

We had uncorked a Barolo that night with thick-cut Argentine steaks. Ken telling me the history of the Italian immigration to Argentina, the transplantation of the old vine stocks, the Argentine respect for the Italian masters. The next morning he left our room early to find breakfast—croissants and coffee from the Lebanese bakery on the corner. I awoke to a note and a rose by my pillow. *Remembering your warm brown eyes, the feel of your soft lips, Barolo.* The wine became the secret signature of our affair.

I winked at my Barolo.

The waiter delivered the calamari, lightly breaded in cracked pepper and sea salt. He moved to refill our glasses but Ken held up a finger. "No. Let it breathe."

"Certainly, sir." The man moved off to another table.

"You still have my watch on?" Ken reached over and fingered the brown leather band of the Cartier tank on my left wrist.

"I like having something of you with me all day long. Do you mind?"

"Not at all."

It was the middle of October and I had just come back from a five-day vacation in Europe, visiting friends in London and Munich. Ken had been gone at the same time; part business, part family vacation with his sister, Abby, and his brother, and their families. I knew he had flown his daughter, Jordan, out from San Francisco to meet them in Hawaii as well, but did not inquire as to details.

At the airport, Ken had given me a soft kiss and held me back a foot or two as he studied me.

"Have fun." He sounded a bit melancholy, as if this reminder of our separate lives were something he would choose to ignore.

"You won't forget me?" I teased.

"Not a chance."

He unstrapped his watch and fastened it around my wrist. "Keep this. Remember me while you're gallivanting around over there."

I grinned. My girlfriend in Munich was a six-foot-tall, redheaded stage dancer, her friends given to wild parties, spontaneous trips to clubs and other countries. I had packed light, not much more than a lipstick and a passport.

I stroked the smooth leather, examining the face of the watch. "Ken, I can't take this. It's Cartier!"

"A ten dollar Cartier, sweets, bought off the streets of New York. I keep it as a memento. Wear me while you're gone." He tweaked my chin. "In the *hope* you'll have little else to remember."

I laughed. Ken had worked for Chase Manhattan Bank in New York in his late twenties. The lean years: one suit and an apparently fake watch bought from the Nigerian vendors.

I came home from Europe and the watch remained on my wrist.

Ken had been traveling a great deal lately with work, and although my job paid the rent, the dullness of life in a cubicle had moved me no closer to beginning to write. Restless, I desperately wanted us to disappear together again. To stay where there was no complicated past, no uncertain future, only the intoxicating present.

"Do you remember the three old men in straw hats by the wharf?" I asked, brushing salt from the corner of my mouth. The calamari was delicious.

"In Buenos Aires? Playing the guitars?"

"Yes! I can't forget how the three of them sat on that bench by the docks, making music as if they had all day."

"Probably did."

"They played something bittersweet, do you remember?" I hummed a line of the melody, an old Spanish folk song, I guessed. Something of girls, the sea. "I miss that feeling, having all day."

Reminiscing, we finished our appetizer, and when the big plates arrived, the conversation wandered to work, our weekend plans to go north to Priest Lake, Ken's search for a house.

"I think I found a place." He nodded, satisfied. "There's a house for sale that belonged to Whitehouse—you know, the local architect that built St. John's Cathedral? I've looked at it twice. Small, but well-designed, and made of the same stone block and wood beams he imported for the church. It's empty, been on the market awhile."

Ken lifted his wine, gazing at me over the rim of his glass.

"Want to come see? After dinner?"

My heart flipped. Of course I wanted to see where he would be living; but this business of house hunting also defined the distinctions between us. Not just that we had different domiciles, but different destinations as well. I had an apartment on a month-to-month lease, Ken was buying a house. He had come to Spokane from San Francisco to grow a tech company into global markets, and I had come back only because the town was familiar. Mine was an open ticket: my job at the company a bridge between my old career and a new life. I was constructing my future out of both dream and ignorance, but Ken was punched in. He had responsibilities, command.

"Sure. I'd love to see it."

"I have supplies." Ken winked. "I brought along the tape you made, a music player, good French champagne, and of course, a Santo Domingan cigar."

"You brought the Jane Olivor?"

"It's become unforgettable." Ken glanced at me oddly, as if this shared love of music surprised him, and I had surprised him as well. "No one has ever given me anything quite like it."

"Thank London. I heard Jane Olivor perform at the Palladium. Totally packed concert. But when she was done, you could have heard a pin drop. It was as if the entire city had fallen in love." I took a sip of wine, abruptly embarrassed. "That was how I felt then, missing you."

Ken reached for my hand. "G, stay the night?"

"Stay the Night," the title song off the album I had given to Ken, became the song that linked one day of our romance to the next. Ours was the love affair that wasn't likely, couldn't last, but those soft words kept one or the other of us coming back.

A short while after dinner, Ken let us into the vacant house using a pass key from the realtor. The house was chilly, and there was no light, or heat. Grabbing a Presto Log from the trunk of his car, Ken lit a fire in the living room fireplace and spread his "provisions" on a plaid stadium blanket across the exposed cement where the carpets had been ripped out. Within moments firelight flickered across the copper mantle, danced against the empty walls.

Ken opened the champagne, pouring us each a glass in a juice tumbler.

Sometime later, Ken sat cross-legged in front of the glowing embers, his cigar in one outstretched hand, the smoke drifting up the flue. His bare chest glistened in the light.

"Being with you feels like an open horizon," he said suddenly.

I stirred, rolling over in the blanket, tugging on my bra and panties. I looked at Ken with idle curiosity. He seemed lost in some inner summation of his life and dreams. I had rarely seen him so relaxed. Ken's energy was famous at the office: The man moved in a rush, as if the past nipped his heels and the future was slipping away.

"Remember the night I came back to your apartment after that conference in Seattle?" he said. His voice fell in the lazy hiss and pop of the fire as it crumbled into coals. "I had that late-season sauterne from St. Michelle, poured us a small glass, laid my head on your lap, and fell asleep."

"Old lovers need naps." I chuckled.

"No, I never sleep like that. Zonked. Like a kid."

I remembered perfectly. The late-afternoon sun had thrown long bands of light across my apartment, striking gold the African masks and Bolivian weavings on the wall. I was sitting on the couch with Ken's head in my lap as he kicked off his shoes and stretched out after the long drive from the coast. The sauterne had tasted of peaches and golden grape: a heavy, intense sweetness on the tongue.

Before drifting to sleep, Ken had said something I thought I might have whispered, because the words were so nearly my own. *Found you.* Just "found you."

Ken looked at me in the empty living room, his eyes gentle. "It's good with you."

There were so many reasons a man like Ken might not sleep. We both knew what wasn't being said.

I ran a hand through my hair, trying to untangle it, before finally giving up and leaving well enough alone. "Ken, do you think your parents would like me? Will they mind I'm not Jewish?"

"I'm certain they'll like you. My mother will ferret everything out about you and then share it with the community center, which is to say, greater LA. She'll tell you all my odious secrets, and if you haven't run away by that point, she'll make banana bread and knit you slippers. So you're a shiksa—we're not very Jewish, G, as those things go."

"She sounds sweet!"

"Deadly as an anaconda, love that hugs the breath out of you." Ken glanced sideways with a smile. "We'll have them up for Thanksgiving. And Jordan, if she'll come. And about time you meet my friends, next time we're in San Francisco."

I said nothing. Jordan was a topic I was apprehensive to broach. What girl her age wants to meet her dad's new lover? And if she had made Ken's life so miserable, I could only guess what she might bring to mine. As to his friends, Ken's friends were legendary. They went back years together, stayed close through the rough and ugly. I anticipated they would be protective of Ken, curious about me, but always, they would

35

be Ken's friends. Like Jordan, his daughter. Never mine, never ours. I was walking in on the man's life midstanza, and principal parts of the story were set.

"What about *your* mom? Will she run me off with a gun?" Ken asked. "Can I meet your brother and sisters?"

"Seriously, what's not to love? Mom will flirt with you. You're not *that* much younger than her." I reached over and poked him in the ribs.

"*Ow.* I broke those ribs. Bike wreck."

"Poor baby. Sports challenged too?" He flipped the champagne cork at me. I caught it. "My sibs. What's to say? With Tim in Seattle and Judy in Texas, we've not stayed terribly close. I've been away too long."

"All this talk about family and friends . . ." Ken smoked his cigar, deep in thought. After some time he looked up. "You never did say. Do you like the house?"

I laughed, pulling on the rest of my clothes. "Uh huh. Think so."

"Maybe you'd keep me company here."

"Stay the night?"

"Every night."

Foreign Lands

"If we're going to be together, we can't actually *be* together,"
Ken had said to me quietly.

We stood bathed in the mercury halo of a streetlight,
alone in the parking lot outside the company loading docks.
It was dark and cold, the black early dark of a northern winter.

"What do you mean?" I asked, confused. I pulled my collar up, shivering. "Not be together?"

Ken pulled his leather gloves on, shifting from one foot
to the other. "I'm an executive, G. You work in a division below me. The personnel office has made our, um, personal-
professional conflict quite clear—"

"You're saying I have to choose one or the other? You or
my job?"

"Well, no. I could choose not to work, I suppose." Ken
grinned, trying to lighten the mood. He squeezed my elbow.
"Wish you were still working for the government in Europe,
babe, then I could quit! Nothing I'd like better than to sit at a

café sipping wine, while you slaved for our foreign interests abroad. But with the two of us in Spokane . . ."

"I get it," I muttered, secretly stunned. How had I not seen this coming? "Spokane's a one-horse town and this is the only company big enough to need us both. Your salary's about seventeen million times more than mine. You wouldn't want to live on latte change."

"You could write, G. You've said you always wanted to."

"Write? You're kidding. I'd be broke by lunch."

Ken took a deep breath, leaning in to kiss the tip of my nose.

"Let me take care of those worries. We live together as it is. Let's make it official—move in and we'll cut expenses by half."

"Have you pay my way? I don't think I could ever be fully dependent on any man. No offense."

"As my *wife* you would have things to do. We could travel together." His face stilled, earnest and gentle.

"You're proposing to me?" I squinted up at him in the poor light, uncertain.

Ken smiled. "Well, for months I've been propositioning you—this is definitely more honorable! Would you want that? I mean me? Marriage?"

* * *

If I had given it much thought, I might have hesitated to marry a man for whom at the age of forty-five much of the past was too painful to consider, for either of us. Truthfully, thought had little to do with it. Instinct did: the instinct to seize a sure and ebullient happiness, or go down trying. And as we grew entwined, I felt the edges soften in the strange unbalance between us, the young/old. I was all old history and dead-end decisions, clear as glass and untempered. Ken was new story, renewed again with me and begun fresh, possessed of the unmeasured depths that might sustain a genuine and unending infatuation.

Through his eyes I saw myself as someone better—the someone I might be. What there was of my small life he fully understood. What we wouldn't talk of in his was agreed upon by the both of us.

Travelers in foreign lands begin with simple translations. Our words were three, *stay the night.*

What those heartfelt words left out of our affair was almost everything. Jordan, and the question of children of our own. The career and work I had planned ahead of me, Ken's "frequent flier" status through the echelons of global technology development companies. Already there was talk that the Spokane company was to be sold, and the new international owners would downsize. Ken was talking with a recruiter about a position in Boston.

I had stepped on the carousel and the only thing to do was to hang on tight, or take a header into the bushes.

We set a wedding date in February, the day before Ken's birthday. "So I won't forget our anniversary," he joked, "and you won't either. Spectacular excuse for romantic getaways, don't you think?"

We traveled to Los Angeles for Thanksgiving and I met the extended family, including Jordan, who had driven down with her boyfriend. She shook my hand politely, promptly breaking free to go hang with her cousins. While in LA, Ken and I secretly took a trip down to the diamond markets and Ken negotiated with an Arab broker for a spectacular one-carat stone. He slipped the diamond, wrapped in tissue and brown paper, into his inner jacket pocket and took me out for dim sum. "I want to design something of our own," he said.

Twice in the following weeks, we visited Jordan. She was

in college, living north of San Francisco. She had broken up with her boyfriend, but otherwise seemed a normal, carefree college student. Yet Jordan remained an unanswerable riddle. It was clear she both adored and rejected her father. She was beautiful, dark like her mother, funny like Ken, secretive and moody. Her attitude toward me veered from coolly cordial to emotional ambush. I held to a stoic goodwill, figuring it was neither mine to engage or comment, but to stay completely away from Ken's often combustible arguments with his daughter.

It had to be difficult for her, I said to Ken. I would never be someone *she* chose, and I would always be the successor to her mother in her father's life. I would forever represent the end of her childhood, the symbol that her father had "moved on."

In a nutshell, I was doomed.

* * *

An open bottle of Chianti sat on the table between us in the little Italian café on Bernard. It was the Christmas before our wedding and we had just announced our engagement to the family. Word spread like wildfire at the company as a result of a secretary's avaricious reading of the Official City Records. In the back of the paper, she had spotted our names in "applied for a marriage license."

One of the scary, perfectly coiffed women in public relations marched up to me and seized my hand, scrutinizing my engagement ring.

"Well, if I had known he was looking!" She dropped my hand and spun around on her heel, disappearing into the cubicles.

Meeting Ken at the café after work, I pushed away my

wine, in my thoughts an awkward conversation that had occurred early in our relationship, one of those necessary "housekeeping" chats that defined the relationship protocol of the modern age. Specifically, we had discussed his aversion to vasectomy and my private concern regarding the practical long-term odds of pregnancy prevention armed with rubber shield and killer gel. When merely a kiss or a word led to the wholesale shucking of clothes faster than pumps primed Texas oil, we had taken some risks.

I had then asked the man I was in love with whether he would ever want to have children again—the unspoken hope in my heart, *with me.*

"Can't do it, Glenda," Ken had answered decisively. "I just can't become a dad again. Jordan has flat-out taken the heart out of me these last years. Giving and giving, and getting nothing but hurt in return. Kids—mine, at any rate—are a one-way street."

Ken reached across the table and took my hand, squeezing it tightly.

"You and I. We're the best thing I've ever experienced. That's enough, isn't it? For both of us?"

I remember I nodded. Who was I to question his personal experience, or doubt his honesty? It was all I could think of.

We gave the waiter our order for margherita pizza and tossed green salad. Closing my eyes I asked myself again if anything that felt so right could ever be wrong. The answer was simple. I had to choose what was right for me, and trust Ken would do the same for himself. Perhaps—I felt myself wish for it—the choice would be the same.

"I have something to tell you," I said.

"What?" Ken asked, relaxed and curious.

"Do you believe in the two percent?"

"What do you mean?"

"When the statistics say ninety-eight percent are doing x or y, that means the rest are doing something else. Something spectacular. That's the two percent."

"G, what *are* you talking about?" Ken looked bemused.

"Our two percent. The flyboy that made it."

In the champagne celebration of our first home together, Katy had been conceived, part of that sweet night's "surprise." The unexpected would force us to face the question of children square on. Behind the funny face I felt strangled inside. Driven by something primitive, I knew I would choose the baby, even if it meant giving up Ken.

I looked away, pleating my hands in my lap, and then straight into Ken's eyes. "I think I'm pregnant."

Ken blinked. He swooped across the table, hugging me close, a tender delight in his eyes.

"You're serious? Our baby? G, that's magnificent news!"

Ken dragged his chair next to mine and took my hands. He was grinning, oddly proud and equally stunned. "When we first talked about children, I was certain that for me the answer was no. But I know that I can't bear to lose you, and I see from your eyes that not having this child . . . A baby! And ours—imagine that!"

Ken chose Katy, not bearing I might leave him. What I thought would cost me everything had brought everything into my life. My darling. My amazing, courageous man.

Until my last day of work, the vice president of marketing threw cartons of 2 percent milk over the wall of my cubicle as he walked by on his way to executive meetings.

* * *

No one knew about our pregnancy except our closest friends. Ken had decided it would be best to publicly welcome Katy *after* his family adapted to the reality of our marriage. There had already been a few raised eyebrows and low-voiced Yiddish remarks at the news of the impending third wife. And I suspected the cousins were laying bets on my "survivability." In a sweet, protective gesture, Ken wanted to shield our baby, and me, from impolite speculation.

I left it to Ken whether or not to tell Jordan, but at that time they were arguing about her getting passing grades and staying in school, and she was frequently out of touch for long periods of time. It was complicated. Our private love affair had become not only very public, but quite "life altering" as well. Ken decided to wait to tell Jordan she was going to be a big sister until after our marriage. One hurdle at a time.

A few hours before our wedding ceremony, Jordan and I stood in the living room of Ken's new home in Spokane, watching snow pile in muffling layers upon the ground. Jordan, in a white suit, wore open-toed California sandals, her lips painted an adult, brash red. She turned obliquely toward me, a daring challenge in her eyes.

"I'm really torn having you and Dad together, you know. On the one hand, I don't want to share him—he's been mine all these years. On the other hand, I'm glad you'll be there and *I* won't have to be the one to take care of him when he's old and feeble."

The easy, dismissive laugh. Anger wrapped in icy language.

Flustered and rendered silent, I was both in awe and shaken by her honesty. I had understood, I thought, what it must be like to gain a step-mother nearer your age than your father's. I had accepted that we stood forever on the broken glass of her mother's death and her uneasy relationship with her father. What I did not expect was that Jordan's long entrenched anger had gained a new focus: me.

Although Jordan was now nineteen, her ambivalence weighed on us both. I didn't expect an open embrace, but surely, I thought, her dad's happiness must mean something? Her words foreshadowed an emotional seesaw: She was anxious to be gone and reluctant to let go. That I absolutely understood.

Ken's friends had warmly embraced our plans to wed, as had my family. The wedding was planned as a small, intimate ceremony to be held in front of the same fireplace Ken asked me to forever "stay the night." The best man and his wife arrived from California, and two other of Ken's friends traveled in from the East Coast, arriving in the midst of a heavy February blizzard. Judy arrived from Texas, and Tim drove over from Seattle with his wife and baby daughter. Helen came in from college to stand as my best maid, and the minister caught a ride in from Idaho, driven by a friend with four-wheel drive.

Mom surprised me and braved the snowy roads, arriving in a new garnet-colored suit. She gave me a tight squeeze at the door.

"Told you." Her eyes twinkled.

I hugged her back. She was thinking back to a hot August afternoon. *You have time,* she had said, and I seized it.

Only Ken's sister, Abby, seemed less than enthused. There was something there I could not quite put my finger on. She had certainly been welcoming at Thanksgiving, hosting the large family gathering in her home that included her parents, Ken, his older brother, the spouses, children, and cousins. She was herself divorced with grown children—Jordan's closest cousins—and dating someone of her own. But I felt the assessment behind her smile, recognized the language of inside jokes that are code for who belongs and who does not.

In her bright red hat, Abby stood limply in our living room as we said our vows, supported on the arm of her older brother's wife and best friend: the posture of a woman at a funeral. And while Ken's mom and dad, with their wizened apple-cheeked smiles, hugged us and cried openly, her face was careful, watchful. What I saw there was a cautious distance. She had come to honor her brother; they were close that way. But in her mind I was a given disaster. I was *the next wife*. And, hell yes, a shiksa.

Together we joined candles and lit the Unity flame and Ken slipped the ring he had designed onto my finger. Three points of diamond, he said. One small diamond to represent each of us: and the solitaire, a bridge of *forever light* in between. His eyes glistened. "May we be as strong as the diamond, as truthful as the light, and as happy as we are now."

His dad cried, burying his head in my chest.

* * *

We returned from our honeymoon through Southeast Asia—Hong Kong, Bangkok, and the island of Phuket—recuperating with a few days' sleep on the sands of Kauai. We had cut our trip short: Back in Spokane the company was in the crucial stages of a merger, and the executives commanded "all hands on deck."

Ken navigated the politics of corporate change as I navigated those of my own. I closed out my work life and turned to the joys of making us a home. And as the seasons changed, I navigated the changes within my body.

As I rounded into pregnancy, summer lingered in golden shadows in the old maples of Manito Park. We took long walks through the park, hand in hand, talking about our future. Our love affair possessed this intense timeless quality, yet time itself was very compressed, as if there were few moments to lose.

"Do you think I'm too old to be a father?" Ken asked

abruptly one evening as we walked the few blocks for frozen yogurt.

Surprised, I glanced at him. Too old? How much time does anyone need? We had a whole future to be together. The strangest thought entered my head. *I'd feel blessed to have fifteen good years.* A whole lifetime could be lived in fifteen years. A child raised, family albums, holiday ornaments that were "just ours." The strange and magical number seemed like a luxury of years.

"Come on. Look at you," I teased. "Fit, athletic, all cuddly and wise. You'll make a fantastic dad."

And then I stopped, putting a hand on his arm, looking into his eyes.

"Are you sorry? About the baby, I mean?"

Ken patted my tummy. "You can't say no to a good thing, G. And you, having a family—*very much* a good thing."

Katy made three, and within a matter of months Ken had flown east for a second set of interviews, and I sadly put a For Sale sign on the lawn. I would miss this sanctuary, this house that had so beautifully sheltered us and become our first home.

Ken took the position as president of a software company in Boston and our little family moved to Massachusetts. For six months we lived downtown on Commonwealth Avenue in a corporate rental—a cramped, *Architectural Digest* gay man's summer pad. Adrift, I spent lonely days climbing the circular captain's stairs up and down from the basement galley kitchen, balancing the baby on one hip. I became good at scheduling delivery services, finding the best cleaning price on boxed shirts.

Our social life in Boston pivoted exclusively around the men and women of Ken's executive circle. No longer a professional myself, I felt abruptly exiled into that category of indulged "significant others," those well-polished young women and some older men costumed in cabaret beads and wild ties, drinking too much at the company Achievers Club gatherings. Overwhelmed and deeply heartsick for my former independence and ambition, I resolutely organized my domestic shop. *I would make this work.*

A son followed our daughter twenty months later. David, named for Ken's grandfather, was born in Boston's Brigham and Women's Hospital. Apparently, we had kids who loved afternoons. Katy arrived in the world at 12:20 p.m., and David at 5:41 p.m., following a leisurely Saturday brunch. For each of our babies, their first kiss into the world came from their father. He scooped them from the doctor, folded the tiny infants close to his heart, and waltzed around the room in slow motion, counting toes and tiny ears, overjoyed as their fierce wrinkled hands wrapped tightly around his large finger. The nurses let him go, smiling gently. I fell back, exhausted and content, watching my gorgeous man fall in love with his children.

* * *

Three years in Boston changed to life in California, which became two winters in Seattle, and then back to California again. One day, while supervising a moving truck in Los Altos as Ken met with investment bankers in New York City, I realized I had indeed become my own mother—setting up house in one corporate camp after another.

But Ken and I were a team, and as our lives together deepened, so did our appreciation of each other. The delight we experienced as a couple continued as we took advantage of birthdays and holidays to plan romantic getaways.

Jordan stepped in and out of our family life, at times openly enchanted with the brother and sister she had always wanted and the normalcy of a boisterous, noisy house. She grew kinder to me.

But graver things were happening in her life.

During our frequent relocations she had remained in the Bay area, but dropped out of college to complete a resort management program. The world of hotels seemed to suit her. Yet for months at a time, Jordan disappeared into life as a single in the city. There seemed to be so much she would not share, so much we could not understand. Ken and I would ask her home for birthdays and holidays, and, excited, the kids would wait by the door. As the hour grew late, Ken would become sad, making up excuses to Katy and David when she did not come.

Over time, California grew familiar for me, comfortable, full of friends. The village of Los Altos was family-oriented. Everyone turned out for the Pet Parade, the winter Festival of Lights, Art Walk. We loved the easy stroll from the library to the ice-cream shop, browsing the children's bookstore in between. Katy and her friends went to ballet together, and David and his pals launched squirt gun wars in backyard pools. The local vet called us up when our Yorkie was found sprinting around the El Camino.

"Looked like your dog," he said.

I felt a sense of home.

Katy and David started elementary school. I was class mom, a reading tutor, a volunteer librarian. I shaped their lives, but Ken seemed to hold their hearts. I remember how Ken wrapped Katy in his arms in the aftermath of her first tirade, the two of them nodding off exhausted on the living room sofa after hours of tears at the indignity of giving up her crib to a brother, the unfairness of having to stay in bed when it was so convenient to jump out.

Grown to be a sweet third-grader, with long blonde hair and a passion for drawing with crayons and designing fashions for Barbie dolls, Katy went with Ken on a "Dad and me" trip to Southern California to see Gramma and Grampa Grunzweig. Ken stopped in the Danish village of Solvang to buy his little girl her first strand of old-fashioned freshwater pearls from a German granny in a starched apron; led her through the Hearst Castle to admire the spectacular fountains and mosaic tiles, giving Katy a taste of the architecture and play of light and dark he loved.

Ken had begun to delve into fine art photography again, and set up a darkroom in our garage. He photographed Katy often, enchanted with the clarity of light from her face, the wide openness of her expression. When Katy turned ten, we celebrated her birthday in Napa Valley with friends at the champagne cellars of Domaine Chandon. We spread a gourmet picnic on the estate grounds and danced to a Fourth of July zydeco band. Katy was all light and ebullience, a diva in her father's lens.

Ken and David formed The Boys Club—car shows, Legos on the floor, visiting the Tech Museum in San Jose. In the quiet streets of Los Altos, Ken and David rode their bikes together, Ken rushing David twice to the clinic for stitches after he wobbled first into a mailbox and then into the bumper of a parked car. All of that paled in comparison to the day David, just a toddler, took a header down the stairs when he and Ken were home alone. Ken scooped him up, raced to the ER, and charged through the hospital doors straight to the nurses. "Someone save my baby!"

I remembered the summer Ken and I watched David hit his first grounder in Little League, hopping to first base and then rounding to second. We were deep in the happy hours. Our family memories were of joy and magic. As perfect as the Napa Valley birthday party magician, who, yes, pulled a dove out of his hat.

Shift

There are certain moments, sometimes just words, that part time. *Who we were then,* from *Who we are now.* The words that changed everything were uttered over a pastrami sandwich at a curbside deli in Los Altos, California. Katy, eleven, was fiddling with her pickle, mincing it and tossing it to the sparrows hopping from curb to chair back, eyeing what was uneaten on the table. David was away at a week of summer basketball camp.

My husband of twelve years sat perfectly still in the hot midday sun, his eyes closed. As on most days, Ken wore elegant business attire: his favorite blue nubby silk jacket, gray tailored shirt, and Italian silk tie.

His pastrami on rye sat untouched, still wrapped in wax paper.

"Glenda?" Ken said, opening his eyes. "I don't think I can do this anymore."

It was early June, the summer of 2001, and the technology bubble that had fueled Silicon Valley's multimillion-dollar deals had unexpectedly burst. Ken's stewardship of a cutting edge technology company collapsed, along with the financing for the company, one week short of an acclaimed initial public offering. All his arduous work gone in a flash—just so much paper on the floor of the New York Stock Exchange. Such losses had occurred before, but we had always absorbed them with optimism. There would be another company, another opportunity. But this time was different: the corporate board was hostile, the venture capital investors pushing for cuts and technical breakthroughs even as they forced bridge-loan financing diluting share holdings for the leadership team. Work that once had been about creativity and leadership had been tortured into a quest for fast IPO profits, Ken's ethics set in defense against the pirate ethics of shifting investors. Betrayals, firings, broken promises.

Timing, they say, is everything.

"I need to leave this place," he said. "I'm done."

I remember Ken's tired eyes, the blue washed out by the harsh sunlight glancing off the sidewalk. I laced my fingers together tightly. *Done? How can you be done in the middle of your life?*

"Are you serious? It took ten years and three career moves to return to San Francisco, Ken. Start again. Build another company. This is home to you!"

To all of us now, I was thinking. So many companies, so many changes at the drop of a hat. Our life in California had successfully weathered the most corporate shifts. We had roots here, friends, the kids were in schools they loved. I thought about the mortgage, the car payments, private school tuition. We lived on salary. Taxes nearly swallowed us up. But in the Bay Area, work was readily available. There was always another company in the investor-rich high-tech valley.

Ken reached over, unlocking my hands, playing with my fingers.

"I just can't do it anymore, G."

There was truth in his eyes. For years this man I loved had put all that he was out there in the world. A bold businessman and irrepressible optimist, he was a man accustomed to incisive, high-risk decisions, unafraid of the wildness of life. This decision had nothing to do with corporate frustrations and losses. This time the shift was personal. In his eyes I recognized a new intensity, a self-awareness that craved change, the kind that shakes your bones and realigns your DNA, breathing room to limn new green on frames of exhausted thinking.

Ken was done. He had captained his last new company.

"What will we do? How will it all work out?" I said. I was still the young woman who had laughed with her lover in Brazil—"Where to now?"—but adventure was no longer simple. Our little ship of two had become a boat of four.

He smiled his familiar smile, one corner of his mouth turned up. "Have a little faith, kiddo."

Faith, he said.

* * *

A few days after our conversation at the deli, we breakfasted on tea and melon in our California backyard. We had been idly discussing where we might live if we wanted to live well, and on far less. Ken tossed a quarter on the table.

"Santa Fe or Spokane?"

I set down my teacup, surprised. "Well, all we love about

art and landscape is in New Mexico. Not to mention I was born there. But family is in Washington. And *you know who* is near Spokane."

"She who shall not be named?" Ken chuckled.

"Yes. Mom."

I shuddered as Ken spun the coin on its edge, remembering our last summer trek to Priest Lake, Idaho. Our annual August family camping trip with my mom had ended—no, not even begun—disastrously. Priest Lake was Mom's piece of heaven, the place she had water-skied, hiked, and camped since childhood. Unfortunately, her wilderness heaven was sixteen hundred miles from Los Altos, California. But every year we found a way to make things work. For Katy and David, Priest Lake was "Gramma time."

Ken, the kids, and I had holed up in a Spokane motel a few miles from the airport. We planned to drive the remaining hundred miles north to the lake after breakfast. Jammed with bags of beach gear, food supplies, fishing rods, floaties, and school art for Gramma, the rental car sat parked and ready outside the motel.

At six in the morning the telephone rang.

"Glenda?" There was no outcry of emergency at the other end, just my mother's chipper no-nonsense voice. "I'm sorry to say you're one week too late, dear. I'm on my way home. Camped all week at Osprey, so lovely this year—but have to get back to feed the animals. They'll only last a week, you know, on what pasture is left."

I pinched the bridge of my nose hard, still half-asleep. "What do you mean too late? You're not at the lake?"

"What I said. Just left."

"But we came all the way from California! Six suitcases by airplane . . ." I threw off the sheet and sat hunched over the edge of the bed. "I wrote and called, even e-mailed the dates at least three times, Mom. The same week as always! Same cabin, same week."

Mom sucked at her teeth. "Sorry. But really, nothing I can do."

Was she losing her mind? Had she not read her mail these last months? And then it hit me. *My mother was ditching us.*

"Mom!" I wailed. Forty years old and I wailed. "You can't mean it? You won't stay even a day?"

"I can't fix it now." Her tone grew impatient. "But I'm sure you'll enjoy your vacation—the water is perfect."

A hot rage roared up my core.

"Eff you!" I spit out, slamming down the phone.

Ken bolted upright and clutched me to his chest as I burst into tears. "No Gramma?" he murmured, stroking my hair as I sobbed.

"No Mom."

Shaking off the memory, I watched Ken toss the coin. The many years on my own and attempts to reconnect with my mother knotted in my throat. The missed holidays, wrong dates, the unattended childbirths and christenings, even the endless ringing of unanswered telephone calls, distilled within the spin of a coin in the sweet morning air.

To choose my mother represented real risk. The smart money would be on Santa Fe.

Heads. The quarter gleamed in Ken's palm.

"Spokane it is then."

Part

Two

Fable of Things Past

By summer's close, we were gone.

Ken officially became a consultant, leaving his card on the desks of the venture capital partners he had worked with on Sand Hill Road. *Call if you need help. Spokane has an airport.*

We handed the key to our house to its new owners, a pair of dour Belgians, and left the crush of Bay Area humanity on a surge of sadness and anticipation.

It had taken just two months to undo nine years. The decision to move north was ridiculously facile, naive even. There is little left to decide once you decide to change your life. Everything else is detail.

Somewhere in Oregon the gray Volvo blew out a tire, but when we finally reached the cliffs and wide waters of the Columbia Gorge crossing into Washington, my pulse quickened. Miles later we crested the plateau on the Interstate to embrace our first sweeping views of the Spokane valley, and I knew instinctively we were home. Not to Mom and the farm. Not a return to the arguments, the divorce, the hard and lean years. But to Spokane, the city where the chaos in our family distilled in sweetened family reunions and holiday visits. Spokane, where my grandparents had lived, and where Ken and I had fallen in love. The geography of love.

My Spokane was a snow globe of magic holidays, a swirl of memories of winter and summer vacations. If I closed my eyes, I could easily recall my grandmother's delectable baking, the Dorothy Dean recipes clipped from the *Spokesman Review* spilling from her cookbooks. I learned to dance on the toes of my grandfather's wingtips in the marble lobby of the Davenport Hotel—a child of eight at the Viennese Ball, surrounded by elderly doll-cheeked ladies clutching Roosevelt furs.

Memories of summer evoked the sweet burnt-leaf smoke of Havana cigars and the perfume of lilacs. I read Nancy Drew mysteries with a flashlight in my grandfather's study, listening to the chink of ice in tumblers as the grown-ups chatted late into the night, often recounting stories of my grandfather's famous hole-in-one, shot through the fog at the Manito Golf & Country Club.

Summer belonged to the lake. We were just a pile of cabin kids sleeping on the docks. My brother and I, and our sunburnt friends from around the south shore shrieked and giggled, ducking under our sleeping bags as the bats swooped low, hunting the glassy surface of the water. I remember the creak and rock of old wood, and falling asleep to the haunting call of loons. So many memories.

I gazed eagerly out the window as we exited from the Interstate. A rusted station wagon had pulled off at the edge of the road. A mother and four children waited by the side of the car, steam hissing out from under the hood. There was surrender on the face of the woman, and hunger in the way the children stood, bone thin against the buffeting highway winds.

We drove slowly past, heading through town. My heart contracted. Everywhere, from the vacant department stores to the clusters of homeless on the streets, there were unexpected signs that this region had become not so much a destination as a derailment.

How could this be?

"I don't recall things this—decayed," Ken remarked carefully from behind the wheel as our eyes met. Had we not noticed the economic decline, year after year, on our way to the lake? During last month's house-hunting weekend, in the flurry of touring homes for sale and school visits, had we not been paying attention? Where was the Spokane I remembered? The Spokane where Ken and I had fallen in love?

"Me either," I muttered, thinking *Oh my God, what have we done?*

Saying little, Ken navigated the freeway exchange and headed south on Highway 195. Behind us in the backseat the kids remained fast asleep, exhausted from the two-day drive. Our Yorkie lay nestled in blankets between them, entwined in Katy's long braids.

Ken reached over and clasped my hand.

After a series of switchbacks up the bluff, we turned into a neighborhood of quiet homes set within stands of tall pine.

"We're here," he said. "Feel like home?"

Overwhelmed, I nodded.

I was lost, completely lost. Home as a landscape of the mind had become a virtual trickster.

Home was not, then, as I had believed, an idea synonymous with simple geography, the nuts and bolts of addresses, neighborhoods, and classrooms. But if not cached in logistics of placement and locale, I reasoned, then surely home could be defined by history—the history of people, of the years growing up. Home was the front and back flap on the Book of Self. Wasn't the first question asked of any stranger, "Where are you from?"

All my history led back to Spokane. This ponderosa landscape was my provenance, my fable of things past. Roots. Perhaps all you had to do was dig to find something to stand on.

I stepped out of the car and tilted my head back to accept the sun. What were the lessons of my father? That science was the web of principle, the vade mecum of equations that comprised the prime calculus of the universe. My father believed the laws of dynamics affected all relationships. There was momentum and inertia in the play of human events. Science could explain heartbreak and misfortune, even the fractured drift of family. We were all just a degree away from the falling star.

I looked sideways at my husband, scooping the kids from thes backseat, laughing and tickling them awake.

Thank God for Ken. In every way, he was my true home, my center of gravity. If I could ever just begin to understand the physics of life, of hearts meeting equal and opposing force, I could protect this gift.

* * *

Later that afternoon I drove up the bluff, swinging by my mother's city house on Fortieth before running some errands. Perhaps she would be in the city. Perhaps she would agree to come to dinner. Perhaps she would tell me how glad she was that we had moved closer. Perhaps.

I knocked on the door, but the drapes remained drawn and there was no answer. *Still at the farm,* I thought.

Back in the car, I drove along the southern ridge, aware of thunderclouds massing at the mouth of the valley.

Holding a bag of peaches outside the small corner grocer's, I paused, my attention caught by the open smile on the face of a boy bicycling by in a fury. His feet, tar-stained and summer bare as mine had always been as a child, churned the pedals of his bike, the spinning spokes smacking against a seven of diamonds clothespinned to the brace of the front wheel.

Tat-tat-tat-tat, he flew by.

Tears blurred my vision as I suddenly realized the enormity of my loss, my yearning. I would have to follow the face of that child to find a Spokane I could love again. Childhood had long since spun by.

* * *

Over the next few days as we unpacked boxes, set up beds, and placed dishes on the shelves, I told the kids stories of Spokane. Today the three of us were tackling the kitchen and dining room. Boxes, stacked randomly, cluttered the floor, and summer heat beat through the tall, bare windows.

"Your great-grandfather Glenn, born in 1903, came from nearby Tekoa." I held up a blue glass pitcher that had been my grandmother's, blowing off the packing paper lint. "Imagine growing up in a farm town, a settlement of six hundred."

"Counting the cows?" David asked. Just ten, he wasn't entirely kidding.

"And the sheep," I said.

A towering man with a hearty laugh, my grandfather had possessed a flair with a good story. His Scottish mother, Icey Dainty, had stood less than five feet tall in a rough Western world, and Grampa would amuse us, even as I held my own kids spellbound, with stories of how Icey could kick a six-shooter straight out of a grown man's hand.

Glenn Byron Waugh had moved from the farm to the city, where he met my grandmother, Ellen Agnes Gerhauser, Jerry to her friends. Jerry married her flamboyant Scot at eighteen, carrying a bouquet my grandfather assembled of flowers from his mother's garden. The bride wore handmade German lace, her groom a fedora pulled low over one eye, a pocket watch his late father William had given him tucked in his silk paisley vest.

Locating a shipping box marked "Family Rm Closet," I unpacked a dented cookie tin and fished around until I found a creased, black and white photograph of my grandparents on their honeymoon. My grandfather stood one foot astride the running board of a shiny Model T Ford, my grandmother leaned out from the passenger side waving gaily, her copper hair cut in the saucy curls of the twenties flappers.

"There were roads back then?" David examined the photograph in wonder. "Cool car."

"Mom, who's this?" Katy asked. She held a gilt-framed picture of a couple dressed in wedding finery. My mother and father, June 18, 1954.

"That's Gramma Louise. And somewhere she has that Chantilly lace dress—for you someday."

My mother married my father, a college boy she met life-guarding at Liberty Lake, in a grand affair of tulle and tuxedos spilling down the steps of the stone church in two rows of six-teen bridesmaids and groomsmen, all sorority and fraternity friends.

My mother wore pearls and French lace. Thomas, my dark-haired father, a physics graduate and newly minted military officer like his father before him, stood at her side, dashing in a white tux. Following a country club reception of savories and champagne with butter mints tinted the color of the bride's lace, the newlyweds caught the transcontinental train for a military base in New Mexico.

Theirs was a life on the move. But without fail, my parents returned with their growing family to eastern Washington for the Christmas holidays and hot summers spent at the lake, memories that shone for me like nickels at the bottom of a pool.

Gazing over Katy's shoulder, I absorbed the innocent brightness of my mother's wedding-day smile. Youngest child of a successful self-made man and his wife, the only daughter of German Lutheran farmers who mule-tilled the wheat fields near Fairfield, my mother was born to both privilege and earth. And it was to the fields she returned when life became difficult.

I thought about the fractured geography of those early years, the promise of "tomorrow" only a lifetime of relocation could breed. On my own I had continued the pattern: eighteen addresses, all before the age of twenty-one.

Yet Spokane remained my idea of home. From anywhere in the world I could shake that glass ball and stand in my own flecked swirl of memories, see again my grandparents welcoming us in with apple pie and laughter, hear the cuckoo clock chiming in the night. Spokane was the magical city in the pines, where my brother and sisters and I rode sleds down long lawns of diamond snow.

Gently, I placed the wedding picture of my parents on the fireplace mantle.

Faith

"I'm finished," Ken said, dropping my pages on the desk.

We were in my new study, a small room divided by two tall windows that overlooked the front garden. Outside, honey bees swarmed the Russian lavender and the fragrant Lincoln roses that lined the walkways. A few brief weeks had passed, a crazy time of settling in.

Ken leaned on one elbow against shelves filled with inked and taped paperbacks of poetry and stiff leather-bound books of art. He thumbed aimlessly through *Nickel Mountain* by John Gardner, the topmost book on a stack of fiction beside my chair. I knew that absorbed inward look; he was thinking of the exact thing he wanted to say.

Ken, my brilliant critic. A dark-haired, aging athlete with the looks of 007, the Connery model, wedded to the mischievous wit of Mel Brooks.

I tapped off the computer, set down my glasses, and

leaned back in my chair. *My God, what if he hates it? He won't exactly say so, but it will be there in his eyes.*

"The section where Zoë plays that French cello for the first time? Brought tears to my eyes."

He gripped my shoulder gently and slipped out the door.

I picked up the well-thumbed pages and folded them to my chest, smiling as I looked out the window at the hot sun, the dizzy bees.

Have faith, my husband had said to me on that afternoon that changed our lives.

Faith. What was that anyway? A philosophical place of being? An act of will? The inside out of hope?

I set the pages down on the old Scottish pine desk. How different we were. To Ken faith was a verb, and to me an untrustworthy noun. As a writer I worked within: My dedication was to the search, the seduction, the frustration of language. Words were keys that opened locks to all I needed to know and understand. I was a daydreamer, an introvert, a traveler circling the universe in boats of good poems.

But rarely, if ever, was I certain.

Ken was always certain: certain that something was better than nothing, and that any choice was better than none at all. He offered himself as my champion, a nonreader who read for me, upholding my faith in my work, my faith in myself. He built the bookshelves on which I stacked my burgeoning piles of manuscripts, and as I struggled with the new novel I was writing, I gave much thought to the faith Ken had in life, in me.

* * *

In the following months we embraced a new rhythm of days. Seasons in the Northwest appeared to interleaf seamlessly.

Summer lingered into a mellow fall, until one morning frost bruised the roses and the green and garnet hummingbirds were gone. Late geese beat southward across the sky and we knew winter was coming.

Ken sometimes traveled, consulting, working in his advisory role on corporate boards. He was invited to join the mayor's civic art committee, and began to mentor new entrepreneurs in our adopted city. The kids were enrolled in a new school, and I was slowly making headway in the work of the novel. The tone of our days had become playful, the hours long and full. In a coin toss, time had become our friend rather than a thief and taskmaster.

* * *

In the aftermath of 9/11, every separation carried with it a new awareness, and I found myself especially anxious when, near the end of September, Ken headed to New York. On his return, all three of us went to the airport to bring him home.

"Dad! Dad!" David tore across the smooth granite flagstones of the airport lounge. He slammed against Ken's broad, strong body and Ken dropped his briefcase and overnighter, lifting him high into the air before crushing him in a big hug.

"Hey, what's up? Miss me?"

"Oh, yeah!" David grinned, showing off the new space between his first and second molars. "Duffy ate the house yesterday!"

Katy, grown into a serious and watchful twelve, hugged her father tight and slipped her arms around his waist under her brother's flailing legs.

"The puppy ate the house?" Ken asked over Katy's blonde braids.

"He did, Daddy." David giggled.

Ken lowered David to the ground, tugging one of Katy's braids playfully. I retrieved his briefcase and linked my arm in his as we headed out of the Spokane airport.

"We came home from piano lessons to discover McDuff had gnawed his way around the baseboards in the dining room." I sighed. "We have brand-new *dental* molding."

Ken looked at David solemnly. "That dog is going to need more serious fiber in his diet, my son. Or a muzzle."

"Did you bring anything from New York?" Katy asked. I guessed she hoped it would be a book, or a costume sketchbook from the Museum of Modern Art.

I looked up at the night sky. Here we were, a kiss away from Canada, the green and bluish flares of the aurora borealis flickering amid a thousand stars. I shivered, and tucked my hand in Ken's warm one.

David skipped ahead toward the parking lot. "We missed you *so much*, Dad!"

The day ended over cocoa in our four poster bed, the children tunneling in beneath the covers as Ken and I half-listened to the late-night news. The old snoring Yorkie, and the puppy, the brash Scottie, McDuff, lay flopped across the frayed Chinese rug. Ken's bag leaned against the doorjamb, unopened.

Our eyes met and hinted at things to share later. For the moment, it was enough to touch each other lightly, small strokes of reassurance and reconnection, and to breathe deep the warm clean smell of children in socks and jammies tucked up close to their father's chin.

In this hermitage of chaos, with these wise and funny and sometimes furious faces tangled up in the bedclothes, I celebrated life in the equinox of love—my family. The daily miracle of us, the life I led with this generous, warmhearted man and our two tumbling children and equally mad dogs, might be proof enough Ken was right. *Have faith.*

We were mapping the unknown universe, trusting in the instinct that had brought us together, held us together and kept us together still.

What Love Is

On a blustery winter day, the sky a fistful of iron clouds, Ken and I walked the bare gardens of South Hill's Manito Park. The pond willows shook in the winds, the naked tangles of twined branches tapping in the winter quiet.

"Why, the pond's completely frozen!" I said. The duck pond had glazed over, thin ledges of ice clinging to the shoreline. Mallards, their caps of peacock green and blue fluffed up against the wind, huddled at the icy edge.

"I see what they mean by 'Cold Duck,' " Ken murmured.

"That's cold *butt.*" I elbowed him.

A bounding Labrador broke through a clump of pines above us on the hill. "Rex! Rex, come back!" The man who had been walking the dog shouted, shaking the leash in his hand. But Rex plunged on, disturbing the swans on the island in the pond's center. The birds unfurled their wings and spread them, graceful and full of threat.

Arm in arm, Ken and I followed the snowy path to the

edge of the pond. In one hand I carried a paper bag of day-old crumbs.

"When I was a kid, my grandparents brought us down here to toss bread crumbs to the swans," I said as we pitched bits of crust and bagel to the birds. "I was always a little afraid of them, but Grampa held my hand and showed me a good side lob so I didn't have to get too close."

"Still trying to figure out where you're from, kiddo?" Ken squeezed my arm. "Your memories sound pretty bucolic. I'm from Cleveland."

"But you have lovely memories! You were the apple of your grandfather's eye."

"Someone had to be. We were one crazy fruit salad."

The mood was light, airy, twisting like spun candy between us.

"Imagine," Ken said, "two extremely loud eastern European families living in a four-room row house. There were eight of us."

"Bit tight?"

"Not a thought to call your own. I remember hiding in the basement, usually drinking beer with Grandpa David."

"A beer? How old were you?"

"Eight? Nine, maybe?" Ken chuckled at my shocked expression. "And Grandpa snuck bacon too, on Saturday. Some kind of kosher." He shook his head, amused.

He ripped a bagel in quarters and tossed a piece toward the pond, watching the crust skid across the ice as three ducks squabbled after it.

"They said Grandpa David was the best tailor in New York City. So good, the mafia wore his suits. Good enough he lived to sell suits to their sons."

"Extra pockets, that kind of thing? Weights in the cuffs?"

"Reason enough to retire to Cleveland, I guess. As a kid,

I really thought Mom would poison my grandmother. Such a racket between those two! My grandmother was a chef, but Mom could only make this God-awful banana bread, heavy as a brick. She lorded it over her, my grandmother did. Now, none of us live in Cleveland."

I turned to Ken, blowing on my hands in their bright blue knit gloves to warm them. "I still can't believe we met in this city," I said. "All those years ago, the two of us just passing through . . ."

"More of a major detour, G. And one we keep repeating."

"Slow learners?"

"Just can't get enough marmots, and myopic old folks driving Buicks."

"In the fast lane."

"In all lanes."

I was suddenly flooded with a powerful memory of Ken and me, standing by this same pond on a soft July night the summer we fell in love. We had come to the park for a walk following a date of Thai food and the gallery opening of a local photographer. The two of us barely acquainted, Ken had grown suddenly very quiet and I touched his arm.

"You all right?"

"Just suddenly thinking about Diana." He looked at me, gauging something. "To be honest, I'm feeling unexpectedly sad. And it's confusing. When Diana died, I had just realized how much I loved her, how much she loved me. I had just told her so, moments before we were hit. And now I'm looking at you and thinking about her. . . ."

"Thinking what?"

"Does love belong to the people loved, or continue on somehow? Get folded into something . . . new?"

Ken had always skimmed over Diana's death, stating just the facts. But as we strolled by the pond that evening, he revealed some of the more personal details of his first love, the young wife he'd lost so long ago. They had been singing along with the Top Ten of 1963 on the radio—The Ronettes, in at number three with "Be My Baby," Ken's hand resting lightly on Diana's knee, the other on the steering wheel of the little sports car as they zipped along through the warm California afternoon. He had felt so happy to be alive, he told me. Twenty-two, and feeling loved for the first time, he looked sideways, telling his new wife she was beautiful. That he adored her. Diana, laughing in the seat beside him, had brushed the windblown hair out of her eyes. "Well, I love you too, baby."

At that exact moment a drunk driver careened around a bend in the road, crossing lanes at eighty miles an hour, and smashed into their car. Diana, just twenty, had died in Ken's arms by the side of the highway.

I took a deep breath.

"I don't know where love goes, Ken. But to me, love feels as unique to each of us as our fingerprint," I said uncertainly. "Never duplicated, never plays favorites, never borrowed. Your love for Diana belongs with Diana, and hers with you. But I have to believe the future is born new."

What I held from this memory was the dented optimism Ken had worn pinned to his sorrow; and how much I had wanted to smooth that scrim of sorrow away, offer something better to believe in. Me. How much I had wanted to offer him *me*.

And here we were.

"This *is* a place for new beginnings," I whispered as I pulled in close to Ken's parka, my breath frosting the air.

"Has to be." Ken's eyes twinkled. "We live here now."

I lifted his gloved hand to my lips and kissed the cold

leather. This was what it meant to love someone, I thought. To be *home*.

On our walk back, what floated to the surface of my thoughts was a fragment of memory of a young woman I had met years ago at a writer's conference; a writer devoted to the quest for love, or at least, to the satisfaction of its illusion. She had been a plump, bright little thing with bad skin, completely giddy as she embarked on her first book tour. Hers was a tale of an abandoned marriage and a vacation liaison with a chain-smoking married cynic; a Frenchman who, even as he wooed her, expressed his constant need for massive amounts of alone time.

Her book had been filled with her French lover's clever put-downs of American women, and I had found myself wishing she had done more to defend the species, or at least sent him packing back to his own philandering wife. But I said nothing as the author scrawled her name in my book, rattling on about her plans for future travelogues about Italian men, Russian men, men around the globe. Blithe, confessional, detached. A woman chasing fragments of fantasy.

As Ken and I crunched homeward over skiffs of old snow, our breath trailing behind us, I realized how often love swept in on waves of sudden happiness, an unexplained joy tangled up in the ordinary. We might entice love, hold dying love in our arms, or pen it away with sharp, witty one-liners, a broken heart in the pocket of a French cynic. Love might reside, forever, untended in memory.

Love could leave you with absolutely nothing to say.

Ladders

One year had passed in Spokane, an uncertain but hopeful time. Weeks of heat burned the yellow grasses dry and the creek dwindled to a trickle. In the cool, silver blue nights, deer slipped through the shadows across the lawns, hunting for succulents and water. These were the days people disappeared to the lakes.

Ken and David began packing for Montana, preparing for their "boys only" fishing trip to Flathead Lake. The truck was stocked with jerky and licorice, iced root beer, camping gear and fish hooks. Ken threw in a necessary compass, several padded bags of camera gear, and for David—a new pocketknife and a bag of colorful plastic Legos to occupy the long, empty miles.

Eleven now, with a few new summer freckles across the bridge of his nose, David loved our new life in the Northwest. After school he and his friends would ride their bikes for hours in the woods behind our house. And David loved this time with his dad. He absorbed the spooling hours just palling around with his father—this new, mellow guy who was around much more, relaxed and goofy, ready for adventure.

My boys, the big one and the small one, left Monday morning in the gray predawn with little idea of where they were going, but confident they would get there. I tried not to worry, and squelched recurrent images of roadside breakdowns and back-country scenes out of *Deliverance* from my mind.

Katy was due later that same day at Eastern Washington University to attend a youth symphony music camp. Excited, she packed up her cello case, every bit as tall as she was, and we drove out to the university under the shade trees of the winding Spokane-Cheney Road.

Music was Katy's consolation that summer. In September she was beginning the eighth grade, a second year at the cliquish new middle school that had none of the heart of her beloved Castilleja School in Palo Alto. I was aware that everything important to Katy had been left behind when we departed California—her gang of friends, her adored Russian music maestro, her sense of mastery over her environment. Katy had given up the most for the family move to the Northwest. She knew it, and so did I.

But for now, there was the cello.

I smiled at my newly thirteen-year-old daughter as I dropped her off in front of the campus music building. She no longer wore twin Pippi Longstocking braids, but had brushed her blonde hair straight to her waist and sported a baseball cap, twisted sideways, with "Mostly Mozart" glittering on the bill. Beaded bracelets tangled around her wrist, and on her feet, a pair of Paul Frank monkey flip-flops. My budding teenager.

" 'Bye, sweetie." I leaned over to kiss her cheek.

"Okay, Mom." Katy quickly scooted out of the car, flashing her braces.

I raised my hand in a half wave. I had almost broken the rule. No public display of affection, *please.*

"I'll pick you up at four."

A whole day to myself. I savored the drive back home, rolling down the car windows and letting the breeze flip my hair. Humming to the radio, a bit of Springsteen from the eighties, I breathed in the woodsy fragrance that was both astringent and toasted, of pine bark and fallen needles mixed with hot dust that is a mountain summer. As I swung into our neighborhood I passed the Cochran twins setting up their lemonade wagon and waved. Sprinklers ratcheted slim nets of light across lush lawns.

Out back in my small garden, I picked the ripe tomatoes, and then drove the short mile to my mother's city house.

Located off High Drive, my mother had inherited a sixties era house from my grandfather Glenn. The house was a simple brick structure, kept precisely as my grandparents had left it. Here lived my grandmother's lamp with the frilled shade like a French woman's party dress, and Grampa's office with the shiny black and white photographs, the newspaper clippings of awards and activities yellowed and crinkled with age, still thumbtacked to the wall. My mother's unwillingness to alter so much as the layout of their linens suggested both homage and security in the unchanged: She remained fiercely sentimental to her childhood.

The previous week, she had left a voice message on our telephone, the rare call informing me she would be up for the weekend from the farm. So I left a note with the tomatoes, inviting her to dinner. This was how we saw each other: her last minute appearance, and my ability to fold her in, no questions asked, the penalty for slamming the telephone down five summers before. She would see us but never with a plan.

Each day that week I followed the same routine, dropping Katy off and picking her up late in the afternoon, chatting with Ken as he and David drove through Glacier National Park.

On Friday my sister Judy telephoned.

Pretty, with an infectious giggle, Judy was a big-haired cowgirl. She had recently moved with her husband and two children from Texas to Moses Lake, Washington, a farming area a hundred miles west of Spokane. Moses Lake bordered the edges of a shallow lake, a small retirement community in the center of the warm sage desert, miles from nowhere. Judy was a physical therapist at the local medical clinic, her husband, Jake, a physician's assistant.

My sister was breathless. "Glenda, Mom's here. In Moses Lake!"

"Say what?"

"We're both at the clinic. Mom was sawing tree branches at the farm and fell backward off the ladder. She's got a hematoma on her left upper trapezoid. . . ."

"Please, Judy! English."

"Mom's got a nasty fat pocket of blood on the back of her shoulder that's getting bigger not smaller."

"How?" I sank into a chair at the kitchen table.

Judy explained that Mom's fall had created deep-tissue bleeding, and a pocket of blue blood had blossomed on the back of her left shoulder, following gravity down her bony spine.

"And when was this?"

"Days ago. She called yesterday when she couldn't stand the pain anymore and asked me to come get her."

"She asked you to drive her from the farm to Moses Lake?"

"Yes."

I absorbed the oddness of that, confused. I was the closest family, Spokane the nearest city. Judy explained that Mom believed Judy's medical connections were her best bet. And there was always the thorny issue of anyone who might know my mother knowing her business. But why was Judy only calling now, a full day later? Why not contact the family during the three-hour drive to Mom's farm or the equally long drive back?

I could guess why not. A requested moment in my mother's presence, a chance to be needed, to help, was rare and worth hoarding.

"I'm worried, Glenda." Judy paused. "Things don't look right. Lots of things. Mom's middle is weirdly swollen. She looks seven-months pregnant yet skinny as a chicken."

*   *   *

The doctors ordered more tests. Mom would have to stay in Moses Lake a few days longer with Judy. But far from seeming put out by this sudden turn of events, Judy seemed to be in full swing, energized and marching toward the Alps. A born rescuer, Judy.

"Well, let me know if I can do anything," I offered, feeling at a loss. Mom was *never* sick, never in need of assistance or medical attention.

The following afternoon Judy called again, her voice quiet. "It's not good. Mom's got cancer."

Stunned, I asked her to repeat everything she had just said.

Judy sighed. "Mom doesn't get it either. She just wants to

take something for her pain and go home. It's hard to keep her here."

"But I thought she had a bruise? She's got cancer?"

"Chronic myelogenous leukemia, to be precise. And the kind for which there isn't a cure."

"Do you want me there, Judy?"

"That would be nice. Mom's a handful."

Ken was still somewhere in Montana with David, so I quickly arranged for Katy to stay overnight with her cello teacher and left that day for Moses Lake.

Judy and I sat with Mom through her final diagnostic tests and a bone biopsy, trying to interpret her nearly unintelligible doctor.

"The prognosis?" Judy asked.

"One year likely. But medicine fail, no one know for sure," the Korean doctor pronounced with a shrug. The clinic oncologist was a small, doughy man with pocked skin and smudged glasses, who addressed my mother as if she were an ignorant, dusty farm wife, in town for animal feed or food stamps.

Mom listened through a haze of pain and medications, treating the oncologist to a curious stare like that of a bird watching fresh roadkill from the fence line.

"He's the best," Judy assured me privately. "The clinic is lucky to even have an oncologist."

"He's a jerk, Judy. Mom's totally tuned him out."

"That's because she hasn't listened to anyone! She's made it clear to everyone, *in the most polite way,* that she doesn't want to be here."

"Well, would you?"

Judy sucked in her breath. "You should see her MRIs— her inner organs are a mess, Glenda! The staff is only trying to help."

On staff at the clinic as a physical therapist, Judy and the nurses she worked with helped "manage" Mom, who was given tranquilizers and pain pills. Her eyes, filmy and red, held a queer, inarticulate alarm.

I agreed to look after Mom the next morning while Judy ran errands, and immediately Mom and I fought over what to do next. "Fine," I said. *Cancer,* my mind bellowed, *Mom, you have terminal cancer.* "Leave it in God's hands. In the meantime, see a lawyer. You have to think about the future, Mom." I sat next to her as she rested on Judy's fold-out couch, my hands filled with Medicare numbers, clinical trial data, and prescription orders.

"No." Her chin rose. "I don't need anyone organizing my life or sticking their noses in my business! And when Judy's done with me, I will *not* be coming to stay with you. You two can forget that. I want to go home."

Caring for my mother had become a frustrating exercise in futility. For a week Judy had given every waking moment to caring for her and attending to her medical needs and appointments. I watched Judy coax and box my mother into things she didn't want to do, hem her in with one sturdy hip as if she were one of her own balky physical therapy patients.

Mom's resistance and misery grew more entrenched, culminating in a lecture delivered by Judy's husband, bluntly pointing out the burden her stubbornness created for those trying to help her. He and Judy now felt only a dose of tough love would shock Mom into acknowledging the grimness of her diagnosis, force her into accepting help, and in the face of her dependency, make an effort to be part of the family. This crisis was Mom's chance to step into the grandmotherly shoes of her own mother. Sweet, pliable, and attendant. Good with pies.

I remember my mother, doped and shrunken on the

couch, as Judy's husband carefully and kindly lectured her. How fiercely her inner will blazed from the stillness of her hands.

The next day the clinic doctor instructed my mother on the necessity of living with one of her daughters, and further, he suggested she join an experimental drug program in Seattle at the University of Washington, six hours from where she lived, south of Spokane.

"As if," I whispered to Judy.

"He's right," Judy said. "For now, one of us keeps her."

I drove back to Spokane.

* * *

Ken returned a few days later from Montana with David. The two arrived in the late afternoon, sunburnt and mosquito-bitten, the truck full of dirty socks and wet shoes. Laughing, they launched into stories of Pepsi delivery trucks off-roading in the remote wilderness, of getting lost hunting for deep mountain fishing holes, of gun racks and Gummi Bears, bad fishing advice from crimped, dour-faced locals, and a cadre of new fart jokes.

David smelled like the cooler full of fish and had bits of chocolate stuck in his hair. Giving him a great hug and praising his treasure of lake trout, I sent him inside for a bath. Ken and I began to unpack the truck, alone in the garage, when I stopped. "Mom's sick, Ken. She's got leukemia."

Ken dropped the sleeping bag and pulled me into a hug.

Only a few years before, we had buried his own mother, a rosy-faced woman appropriately named Rose, a Latvian who had loved to crochet and devour steamy romance novels even as she carried on a good yak. Rose had passed away a few months after Ken's father's sudden death, both parents in their late eighties. One entire generation, gone in a year. My mother remained as the last grandparent, and my only parent.

"She's tough, honey. Your mom's a true Steinbeck character," Ken encouraged gruffly, knowing perfectly well how hard that kind of crusty character was to love. "She'll be all right for a while."

Within the week Judy called a second time, her voice tight and ragged. "You need to take her. I can't stand it anymore. I've got to take care of my daughter, the horses, work . . ."

"She's told me to my face she's going home, Judy. And you just said they've stabilized her white blood cell count on that low-dose chemo pill. So let her go—at least to the Spokane house." I was afraid I was about to be sandwiched between Judy's expectations of full-time nursing and my mother's alligator hisses.

"No way. She needs round-the-clock care. The medications alone—"

"But Judy . . ."

The next day Judy drove Mom to my house and we argued on the sidewalk, tense and polite, as Mom sat on the steps, saying nothing. Moments later she got up and climbed back into Judy's truck.

"You go to that Disney show with your daughter, Judy. Take me to Grampa's. I've had enough."

"I'll look after her there," I whispered to Judy, ashamed. I eyed the paper bag full of medications. "I just can't have her *here*."

Judy's eyes held no expression as she backed out of the driveway and headed up the hill to the Spokane house.

Mom left town that night and disconnected her computer at the farm. The phone rang unanswered for nearly a month. What could we do but give her more time? Letters piled up in the foyer of the city house, plunking in through the slim mail slot in the door—cheerful colored Hallmark cards from each one of us, her adult children, begging her to write back.

The first hint of the coming winter was carried in on the brisk Canadian winds.

Desert Solitaire

Early in October the kids began plans for a Halloween party, cutting out black cats and three-dimensional pumpkins, adding names to the guest list as the middle of the month neared. Too old for games like bobbing for apples, Katy had hit on the idea of everybody making caramel apples on a stick. I had a flat of crisp Jonagold apples, handpicked just the last weekend in Green Bluff, already sitting in the garage. Another box had been left on the doorstep of Mom's house in Spokane.

As the kids cut and glued, Ken and I began packing his duffel bag in the bedroom. Everything he might need for a photography trip to the Southwest. The floor was covered in haphazard piles of clothes, maps of Utah and Arizona, packets of film, his Black Lizard Ale cap, talcum powder, and extra hiking socks.

Returning from the garage with Ken's rain jacket under my arm, I brought along two apples and handed one to Ken.

I rubbed mine to a polish on my jeans and had just bitten into the sweet juiciness when Katy darted in, and giggling, stole the apple from me. She took off downstairs, where she and David were now untangling twine and attempting to construct intricate spiderwebs.

Ken laughed at the startled expression on my face, my mouth still open for another bite. Apples were Katy's absolute favorite food and Ken teased her she would someday have apples for cheeks and a little crab apple for a nose.

"Have a bite of mine," he said, proffering me his.

"You have clean jeans, socks?" I handed over a stack of folded long-sleeved T-shirts.

"Check."

"Anything else left to do here?"

"Just a fax I have to send to the company."

Ken had just wrapped up a six-month series of working board meetings for a company in Michigan and was eager to take a break on a long-anticipated photography expedition with his good friend Jim. The two amateur photographers planned to explore the red canyons of southern Utah and northern Arizona. Ken had spent weeks readying his gear, had ordered fresh film, and devoted long preparatory hours in the darkroom planning his development chemistry.

Lately I noticed Ken unobtrusively sink into the bedroom chair and close his eyes for a few minutes' rest in the afternoons. Odd, that. Yet Ken was fifty-nine, I reminded myself. However fit and athletic, maybe it was time to do less, or do it more slowly. Perhaps he had always yearned to take a midday siesta but had never been able to do so.

At the moment, however, he was full of energy, completely focused on the expedition. This was everything he had wanted out of his new life in the Northwest—time for family, time for his photography, time for friends.

"Heard from your mom?" Ken asked, sorting through a lens case.

"Not since September. She sent me a birthday card. Ken, I don't get it. She's smart, educated, no dumb bunny. But she's acting as if this isn't cancer and everything will just go away on its own. We came all the way to Washington to be close to her, and she won't leave the farm!"

I felt so guilty. I should have taken her in and kept her when I had the chance. How was it I could be so knotted up inside around her and still need her so much?

"Did she say how she's feeling?"

"Okay, I guess. She's taking the baseline cancer drug the clinic in Moses Lake prescribed. Promises she'll get her blood levels checked when it's time to renew. But Judy thinks she'll avoid that and skip her meds as long as she's feeling okay."

"She's a grown woman, kiddo. You can't tell her how to handle this. She's had the best possible input from her doctors, and you and Judy. Without knowing how she really looks at this, I'd give her the benefit of the doubt. The farm is where she's happy from all you've told me. Fresh air and rest never hurt a soul."

I shrugged, packing sunblock into the duffle. Ken made her choices sound so reasonable. *But if she's dying, if she's really never going to get better, then every day that passes is one we can't replace.* It was the wail of a child, and I knew it.

On the nineteenth of October, Ken departed on the early flight to Phoenix. From his cell phone he called from Arches National Monument, and again later from the Escalante Wilderness to describe the hypnotic pull of the long distances, how he set up shots flanked inside tight, striated box canyons of colored clays and sandstone, climbed over and under twisted weathered arches, capturing black and white images that spoke to him of the shape of nature and its silences.

"Listen, G, listen to this poem." I heard sounds of pages turning as he shifted things in his hands, balancing the phone under his chin. "This is Edward Abbey, from *Earth Apples*, part of a poem called 'North Rim.' Listen to this. This is what it's like out here. 'Everything conspires to haunt me here with memory and thought and sense of you: the fragrant lupine and the quiet deer, the hawk that soars against the icy blue of noon, the silver aspen on whose bark I carved your name and mine within a heart. . . . My darling girl, is there no end to love which lives despite all loss, regret and tears? That flourishes on mountain rock, above the plain, and grows against the wind and years? Let it be so, I'll consecrate my days to loving love, and you, and all I praise.' "

"Ken, that's beautiful. You're a romantic, you old dog."

"Wish you were here, G. The wilderness, the sky, everything I see is like this poem. I'll call again in a day or two. Love you."

Ten days later Ken returned from the desert, tanned and deeply content, if tired. He and Jim had hiked the wilderness hefting fifty-pound packs of bulky camera gear. Heading immediately to his darkroom, Ken worked for days in a row, winnowing the promising shots from the hopeless, completely absorbed in his work. But late at night, when I was already in bed with a book, the sounds of a deep cough carried upward from the darkroom through the heating vents to our bedroom. *So much for camping! I'll give that cold a week,* I thought to myself.

Halloween brought Spokane's first light snow and a deep cold snap. The big blowout Halloween party had been a noisy success. Bits of caramel remained stuck in the basement carpets and wedged in the crevasses of the easy chairs. The dogs chewed leftover popcorn under the sofa.

Over breakfast, Ken sentenced David to a half-serious

grounding, light punishment for a "trick or treat" prank. Somehow the neighborhood's carved pumpkins had gotten switched around, so that the Calhouns' five happy monster faces sat where the Clarks' cats and whiskers should be, and the Clarks' pumpkins had swapped places with the Vishanramas' geometric white and green gourds.

Wrapping up a business call after lunch, Ken leaned back and rubbed his neck, stifling another sudden spastic cough.

"Damn, I'm tired," he muttered.

He headed to our bedroom and slept two or three hours, and later that evening declined his dinner, saying he was too exhausted to eat.

This was more, much more, than a few minutes' siesta in the chair, I decided.

The next day, I intercepted Ken on his way to our bedroom, laying my hand on his arm.

"You all right?"

He halted. "I'm more tired than I realized, I guess. I'll be fine if I lay down awhile."

I searched his face. He appeared pale, but we were northerners now and nearly always pale—people the color of pallid spaghetti. Heavy shadows underlined his eyes, however, so I lay the back of one hand against his forehead, measuring the slight warmth.

"You're staying too late in the darkroom. And that cough. More cough medicine, maybe?"

"I'm not, and I did." Ken's voice grew terse, catching the creeping impatience in mine.

"Then perhaps you should see a doctor? Get an antibiotic."

"I'll be fine—just let me rest."

I dropped my hands to my hips.

"Ken, someone's got to pick the kids up from the North

Side this afternoon and get David to piano lessons, not to mention the bank sent notice we're overdrawn on that last trip to Michigan. Did you forget to file your expense report?" I sighed, distracted. "And as usual—we're out of milk."

Ken rubbed his hand along the side of his face, pushing the skin into loose folds that fell back slackly down his jaw. There was a fatigue in his features I had not noticed before, a gray agedness.

"Honey," he begged softly, "just let me lie down for a few hours. I promise I'll get the business stuff squared away to-morrow."

I frowned, wrestling between concern and frustration. Ken simply looked back at me, his entire body surrendered to exhaustion.

I kissed him on the cheek grudgingly. "Fine. I'll do the kids and the milk-and-music run, if you'll keep an eye on the chili pot. Don't let it burn?"

He nodded, and slipped away to the bedroom.

Before I left, I glanced in to say good-bye. Ken lay fast asleep. There was something in the way he lay on the bed, curled on his side, his arm drawn up over his head in a gesture of protective vulnerability that caught my heart.

Call it instinct, call it a feeling. But something in the mute language of his body, in Ken's unearthly exhaustion, was not right. Something felt terribly wrong.

Part

Three

Last Chance Road

Ken and I looked first at the X-ray, then at each other.

"I'm sending you directly for an MRI, Mr. Grunzweig. Your right lung appears to show a hilar—that is, a bronchial obstruction of some kind. Right here."

The doctor tapped the X-ray.

An unspoken question hung in the air as the three of us gauged the enormity of the white geometric shape on the ghost gray field, a mar on the image of an otherwise perfect lung.

Our slender family physician turned away hurriedly, leaving us alone in the privacy of the exam room. Ken and I sat frozen, salt white, alert, holding our breath in the space of what wasn't being said.

Ken began to button up his shirt cuffs, but his fingers fumbled from one small white button to the next. I focused on the X-ray. How could a cough picked up after a dusty hiking trip be a 7.5 cm tumor, so immense to have hobbled the best athlete, yet until this very moment a complete unknown? How?

Knocking on the door before letting himself back in, the doctor, engulfed in a soft weariness, handed Ken the paperwork for an MRI exam. He ushered us toward the cluttered front desk and gave the attending nurse Ken's file.

That simple gesture of handing over Ken's medical record burned the moment in my mind. A life, Ken's life. He was now a case. He had become both a statistic and a probability. A medical narrative written in a heavy short-hand scribble. *A tumor has progressed to cause persistent cough in the chest of a fifty-nine year old Jewish Caucasian male of Russian-Hungarian descent. Patient is married, a newly-retired chief executive officer, currently employed as a corporate board adviser in the high tech industry. Active photographer, new member of the local art board. Intelligent, competent. Patient appears physically fit—former marathoner, bicycle centurion, fund raiser for the American Lung Association. Nonsmoker. Dad.*

The physician shook Ken's hand. "We don't know anything yet for sure, Ken. Remember that."

I felt the center of my chest collapse into a tight dark space without oxygen. What floated in this compressed square of darkness was fear.

*　*　*

The house was silent when we returned home from the clinic, the children still at school. McDuff followed Ken along the hallway toward our bedroom, his tail thumping against Ken's legs. I heard the door creak close.

I needed to think.

"God never promised life would be fair or even that life

would be pleasant—only that you do not have to go it alone."
These were the words that came to mind, Rabbi Kushner lecturing at a writer's festival in Aspen. The rabbi, with kind and benevolent empathy, declared that God the Omnipotent, possessed of all the fiery genius necessary to create the universe, offered humanity no more than a shoulder to cry on, companionship in our darkest hour. Kushner closed his talk with a reminder that a loved one's death was a challenge to undertake wise governance of a beloved's legacy, the life not lived. To live the full potential of the life the dead could not. "Live!" the Rabbi proclaimed. "Celebrate every day for yourself and those you have lost!"

I stared at the MRI appointment sheet stuck to the refrigerator door under the "Got Milk" magnet. Angry, I slammed my hand against the refrigerator door. First my mother and now Ken? Mom's diagnosis I could grapple with. At sixty-nine, illness was not wholly unexpected. But my husband? Ken was my life.

I closed my eyes. We needed solutions, not platitudes. Science, I thought, not God. Despite the chaos—the spectacular madness of cellular cytokinesis, of cells replicating without reason—science offered us a chance. For even chaos had a pattern, and in any pattern there was an elemental organization. Organization reflected order, and, in order, the rule of wisdom.

And in wisdom, solution.

There was but the smallest probability for a miracle in the unexplained. Give me the physics of shooting stars.

* * *

The dumpy pulmonologist chewed his mustache, telling Ken and I not to panic, optimistic that the lump in the lung could very well be an infection, even an aspirated watermelon seed (he'd removed them!), or some benign blockage. Dr. Pugh, attired in a baggy tweed jacket and loud green tie, inspired confidence only because he told us what we wanted to hear. *No worries.*

Pugh scheduled a bronchoscopy for the following morning. Seven sharp. He hustled out the door.

Ken tucked his shirt back in. "Some breakfast! Roto-Rooter down the lung, fiber optic up the nose."

"Did you hear the guy say he buys LPs, the old vinyl kind, and those awful ties from Goodwill? Don't they pay him enough?" I was thinking *second opinion.*

Silently we crossed the parking lot. I offered to drive, and Ken hunched down in the passenger seat. Abruptly, I made a detour out of town and turned down the long country roads. "This okay?"

Ken nodded, his face averted.

I concentrated on the soothing mechanics of driving, resting my eyes on the road ahead.

Out on the Palouse Highway, I followed the empty sky and soft brown of the late autumn hills. Road signs to small farm towns flashed by. I made turns following side roads with names like Old Baltimore Road, Hangman Valley, Valley Chapel Road. Beckoning horizons promised the kind of solace I had sought all my life . . . escape.

Only this time there was no choice in this anguished uncertainty but to stand and face the facts.

"What are you thinking?" I reached one hand over to touch Ken's knee. He had been quiet a long while, his head thrown back against the car seat.

Ken glanced over, his eyes the color of slate. "No matter what, Glenda, we fight like hell."

I gripped the steering wheel. Yes, yes, we would. It felt like a prayer.

Memories I believed forgotten jumped from the roadside shadows, echoes of my twelve-year-old heart pouring out impassioned prayers to my mother's gentle-eyed Jesus, prayers for my father to get well, and prayers for my mother to stop yelling. Yet my father moved away, and a few years later, died in an alcoholic coma. My mother, that buoyant blonde tomboy, the Skating Queen of my childhood, retreated within a bitter anger.

No answers, no mercy, no miracle. *This is about science.*

The car crashed over a cattle guard, jarring my teeth. We drove through the lavender shadows of the early winter afternoon, passing under bare locust trees festooned with pompoms of withered leaves. I gunned the accelerator, following the signs from Mount Hope to Rattlers Run, on northward to Elder Road, Paradise Road, and taking the fork at Stevens Creek for Last Chance Road.

Last Chance Road. What was this? A God-gram?

"Do you believe in God?" I asked Ken suddenly.

"You think God's interested in my lung?" His mouth tightened.

"Well, do you?"

"I haven't seen a whole lot of God up close and personal, Glenda. The way I was raised, Jews don't just slap God on problems like Band-Aids. And my family didn't exactly get the temple thing down well."

Ken's words brought to mind the wedding of Abby's youngest son, Stan. A shallow, blond pretty-boy from Los Angeles, her son had recently and rather abruptly plunged into colonized Jewish Orthodoxy, first living in Jerusalem and then in upstate New York. Now thirty, he had undertaken an arranged marriage as part of his new life in the heart of an ultra-Orthodox Jewish community in upper New York State.

Abby had called Ken, confused and upset by her son's radical conversion, and most especially, by his criticism of her and his relatives as lax Jews.

"Nothing says 'lost' more than fanatical choice, Abby," Ken said. "This religious conversion is about basic belonging, I'd guess. Maybe that part *is* our fault, but the problem seems bigger than keeping kosher. Give him until he's forty."

"And then what?"

"He'll want out. He'll want more. Even if he remains Orthodox in his practices, he'll want to make his own decisions someday. I'd bet on it."

All the not-so-good Jews flew back to New York for Stan's wedding. Afterward Ken penned a letter to me. He stuck the pages of folded yellow notepad paper in an envelope and mailed the letter from his hotel.

Dear G,

For me, this celebration was a window on the past. What's the deeper issue here? My Jewish state—what happened to that?

The wedding brought to a head my lack of a Jewish education, or even an adequate understanding of my heritage. I didn't attend Yeshiva, my training was simple—a number of lessons reading Hebrew text in preparation for my Bar Mitzvah. I learned to read Hebrew phonetically, but not the language itself— what the beautiful old words meant. I just learned to recite the sounds of the ancient past.

Mom's father was a rabbi, Rabbi Goldman—and a crook and bastard from all reports. Mom grew up in an orphanage; the good rabbi put her there when he

remarried after Mom's mother died. We rarely saw
him. We always lived with my dad's parents growing
up.

My family didn't attend shul, although we kept
the holidays, the laws, and lit the Shebbes candles
every Friday night—at least my grandmother did. We
didn't celebrate or acknowledge the American
Christian holidays, not even Christmas, but neither
did I feel a part of a larger Jewish community. I knew
the holiday names and some of the celebrations, like
the traditions of Passover Seder at Grandpa
Goldman's. I do remember some of the sweeter
rituals—my grandfather David hiding a mitzvah for
us to find, a bit of gelt or a coin.

We lived next door to a temple, and I could go
over during Saturday morning services to see the men,
and look for my grandfather or father. My friend
Paulie was with me. The men made a big deal of us
boys and were very loving and inviting. I miss that
feeling of belonging. My place. A sense of belonging in
the soul. I think my nephew Stan has found a place to
celebrate his heritage and share the joys of his
Jewishness with these others who are also walking
back to their heritage and covenant with Hoshem.

It is hard not to know what you are but to know
only what you are not.

· I wouldn't know where to start to find my place
again in Jewishness. My choices have been made in so
many ways. I am afraid of going to temple. But maybe
there is a way for me to explore this? Even as little as
he is, our David seeks to know his heritage. Perhaps
this is a way to enter back into that space, in Yeshiva.

Glenda, I always wanted a son, a son named

David. I told you this before our son was born, and I
tell you this again. Named for my grandfather, the one
I loved, Dad's dad, who shared beer and stories with
me in the basement while the flour fights flew among
the women in that tiny two-family house. And you, G,
named him for King David, the greatest warrior and
poet of his time, who as a boy, wooed the world with
courage and music. "David Playing for King Saul,"
wasn't that the name of the Sunday school finger
painting you made as a child for your mother?

Ken's letter was a clear-eyed assessment of the state of his own Jewish soul.

Ken returned from New York with extraordinary photographs of the wedding. In one remarkable moment captured in dance, Ken had made an image of the men of the village whirling furiously in wild emotion, dancing in a circle arm in arm. In the center of this tornado of black coats danced a rabbi, who in sheer ecstasy had lit his hat on fire. The rabbi laughed as he twirled, and the songs of the men surrounded him. The image was haunting, a blurred ecstasy of fire and dance.

From that one simple image I understood how much Ken missed his identity as a Jew—the joy, the belonging, the longing. How much of an outsider he felt himself to be.

I turned the car toward home.

"What do you think the dancing rabbi would say?" I asked Ken gently.

"Your hat's afire," he answered wryly.

*   *   *

I prayed for that watermelon seed.

I recalled the cold bright Easter mornings my mother,

brother, sisters, and I would climb the muddy hill behind the farm to welcome the miracle of the Resurrection at first light. A simple observance of Easter dawn, accompanied by a quotation from the Bible.

"God hears us." My mother had smiled, offering out a fistful of brave new daffodils bobbing in the chill wind that reddened our cheeks.

That night Ken held me as I cried. I wanted back the time I could take my love for granted, fall asleep to the steady rhythm of that unstoppable heart.

I wanted to know God saw the damn daffodils.

*   *   *

I awoke the next morning, Ken sleeping heavily beside me. A pool of gray colorless light fell through the window onto the floor by the bed. It was chilly, and as I lay warm under the blankets, I puffed out little breaths of air, experimenting with the idea of getting up and making a cup of tea.

Forgoing the notion, I nudged deeper under the covers and my foot brushed against Ken, his limbs warm and solid. I rolled over and curled into his back, wrapping my arm loosely around his chest. He sighed in his sleep, taking a turn deeper into his dreams.

I remembered then. The strange dream, an unfolding scene in which time seemed to have stopped and every single thought and word shimmered, perfectly enunciated.

Ken was alone, wandering aimlessly from one white box-like room to another; all of the rooms unidentifiable, entirely empty, each smaller than the one before. His disorientation was profound and I felt his fear rising, his need to escape.

A shadow appeared at his elbow. The shadow was calm, purposeful: a being smaller, older, yet slim and erect. A guide,

I thought, someone who knew Ken and loved him. The shadow directed Ken out of one room and through another, not allowing Ken to stumble, become confused, or linger. On and on they walked, moving purposefully. Where were they headed? I did not recognize this shadow taking my husband farther into the distance.

At last Ken crossed out of the smallest and final room and I breathed a sigh of relief. Ken stood alone now, in pale, empty light.

"It's going to be all right."

I heard this distinctly. Who said this? An infusion of great peace overcame me. I did not understand, but I trusted.

Shaken by my dream, I woke Ken and described for him the images, asked him if he recognized my description of the mysterious guide.

He smiled. "You've got to be the poster child for an over-active imagination, G. But your ghost might be my uncle Ben, my mother's brother. He always loved me."

* * *

Today was the day. I pulled the bronchoscopy appointment card out from under the "Got Milk" magnet. We kissed the kids and set their lunches out by their backpacks for the last school day before Thanksgiving break. Katy was already boss-ing David around, as it was her job to ensure they caught the school bus at the appointed hour. The two of them knew Daddy was to have a procedure to check out his cough, but Ken and I had agreed that until we knew otherwise, there was no need for details.

Fog clung to the bluff, feathering in through the trees as we passed through the empty streets on our way to the hospital.

In-patient was efficient. I stood beside Ken, stretched out

on the gurney, holding his hand nervously as he joked with the staff. Sticking her pencil in her iron gray bun, the intake nurse explained the bronchoscopy was just another form of endoscopic investigation: a surgical biopsy guided by fiber optics. Ken thanked her for the explanation, and the nurse tucked in a stray hair, smoothed the hip of her polyester white slacks. I suppressed a smile. Ken exuded such warm masculine magnetism. He had, as my mother said, *such charm.*

Ken and I, the nurse, and Dr. Pugh crowded into a tiny curtained space banked on three sides with electronics, medical monitors, and optical equipment. Static hummed in the air, which, oddly, lacked any smell: the room so frigid and sanitized there was not even the familiar whiff of antiseptic. Administering Ken a light anesthetic, Pugh fed the thin fiber optic down his nose, chuckling his way through a repertoire of endless blonde jokes, carping about a sexual harassment suit a nurse at the hospital had recently filed.

Ken winced, fighting a gag reflex, willing himself to remain immobile. Unnerved, I focused on the camera images of Ken's lung displayed on the monitor as the fiber-optic camera twisted down his right bronchial passages. No horrid, black, or pustule nodes emerged as the optics probed his airway. The inside of Ken's lung was as sweetly pink as the sole of a baby's foot.

"Look at that beautiful tissue!" I exclaimed, astonished by the beauty and wonder of the inside passages of the human lung.

The fiber-optic snake reached the obstructed airway, where it could go no farther. The passage was completely blocked by a bump of swollen tissue, a dimpled button of flesh. There was nothing to see—and worse yet, there was clearly no "seed" to remove.

Snip, snip.

Pugh made a series of lymph and tissue biopsy cuts, and the whole ordeal was over. Lymph nodes, he explained, were the early warning system of the body. Toxin drains. When cancer cells migrated, they used those same protective glands as a wayside inn, homesteading the neighborhood, sending new cells onward. Accordingly, three of the biopsies were taken from lymph nodes located near the lump in Ken's lung, one of which was clearly enlarged, a sign of possible infection.

I waited, studying the chart on the wall as the surgical assistant printed out color pictures of Ken's lung to accompany the biopsies to pathology. Examples of lung tumors were identified on the chart in glossy color. I studied them, surreptitiously examining each for any similarities to what I might have seen on the monitor.

There were so many kinds of tumors. Lumps that swelled in from the sides of the bronchial walls; odd growths that erupted like honeycombs in the lung passages; thick masses that annealed the walls of lung and chest tissue together, cells soldered together in one anaerobic mass, and some truly scary growths, black like gangrene. But nothing, not one image resembled the sweet pink flesh of Ken's lung.

Encouraged, I smiled brightly at Ken.

"How long until we know?" I asked the doc in his Disney tie.

"Sometime after the long Thanksgiving weekend, I would imagine," Pugh responded cheerily.

If the biopsy results were normal, Ken faced an excision of the midlobe to remove whatever had caused the blockage. But if malignant? The biopsies would provide the doctors an initial staging of the type and spread of the cancer. Pugh said the word *cancer* lightly, as if such a thing were hardly possible. *No worries.*

Thanksgiving

I rose early Thanksgiving morning.

We had set the table the night before with Mom's mother's anniversary china and the good Irish crystal, and laid out the old polished silver flatware, the combined set from both Ken's mother's and my father's families, crafted in the same pattern, oddly enough.

I set to work. Soon, sausage and celery and onion sizzled in the fry pan as I chopped apricots and oysters for the stuffing. In the background, the Macy's Thanksgiving Day Parade flickered on the TV, my only companion as I cooked in the quiet early hours.

I took ferocious pleasure in the labor of chopping and stirring, managing the details and the complicated timing of the meal. There would be sour cream–and–rosemary mashed potatoes, a raspberry-walnut whipped-cream salad of my grandmother's, green beans in Szechuan sauce—lightly sautéed with bits of browned bacon, apricot oyster stuffing, and three pies. Pumpkin, apple, and pecan, my mother's favorite.

For this one day I would not worry about Ken's cough.

Moving the pecan pie to the back of the buffet counter, I worried instead about the easier scary thing—chronic leukemia. My mother and I were a parenthesis to each other, mother and child. Our bodies sharing the same history and, ultimately, interleafed destinies. If I were to lose my mother, it was somehow in the natural order of things, the shift from one generation to the next.

But Ken was my lover, a gift, key to all life might offer. His sudden vulnerability was a fist around my heart. His uneven beat, my own.

Thanksgiving would be the first social contact Mom had granted the family since the days following her diagnosis. Four months had passed. Dinner would be just our family, Gramma and Uncle Joe. My brother was with his in-laws at their ranch, and Judy was keeping her distance awhile longer, still stung by the medical fiasco. My youngest sister, Helen, remained in New Mexico, and called even less than Mom.

Mom had decided to bring her bachelor brother to dinner. Joe, in his midseventies, lived alone in a one-bedroom apartment in a spotty, scabrous neighborhood in east central Spokane. Lincolnesque in posture and pooch-bellied, Uncle Joe dressed in my grandfather's threadbare clothes, which he considered too useful to give away—along with the broken-down Cadillac parked under his carport. My uncle was accustomed to speaking in innocuous monosyllables, brief Germanic truisms in keeping with the Bible.

On the television Santa Claus floated down New York's Broadway in a snowstorm of confetti as I finished spooning stuffing into the bird. I patted garden herbs across the turkey's pale, pebbly uncooked skin, trussed the bird, and slid it into the roasting pan and set the timer.

Gusts of wind rattled the windowpanes as I sat at the oak kitchen table with my tea, aimlessly watching twists of clouds scuttle through the tips of the pines on the upper ridge. Eventually the kitchen smells grew too good to resist and the rest of the family awakened to join me. David, half-asleep in plaid boxers and a Stanford sweatshirt, put our favorite holiday DVD, *It's a Wonderful Life,* in the television, and curled into the nook chair, cuddling the dog.

Wrapped in his flannel robe and leather slippers, Ken, my Gregory Peck in the morning, settled at the table. His glasses slid half-down his nose as he perused the quarterly report from one of his companies. I set a cup of hot tea at his elbow, and, standing behind his chair, rubbed his cheek gently with my hand, warmed from the tea. He reached up and pressed his own hand over mine, our eyes meeting.

By afternoon, the clouds had cleared and the sky shone hard as blue enamel. The doorbell chimed and the kids rushed to answer the door.

"Hello, hello!" My mother greeted us shyly, bringing in a grocer's bag full of close-out bin plastics—novelty straws, red and blue cereal bowls—and bars of candy for the kids. "Presents!"

Behind her Uncle Joe sniffed at the good aromas, stooping to swipe gently at the bounding puppy.

Wiping my hands on my festive pumpkin apron, I reached up and gave my uncle a kiss. I recoiled slightly, having forgotten his musty, undisturbed scent, the way cases in museums sometimes smell. Uncle Joe cast his eyes vacantly about for a place to sit back and watch some television. I guided him toward the family room, taking the bag from my mother's arms.

"You look good, Mom!"

"And I am. Much better! I'm resting, and faithfully taking my pills," she said.

In the earnest brightness of her eyes, I understood how badly she wanted this visit to go well. I handed her a glass of champagne and reminded her softly that she still needed to find a new doctor.

Katy was in the kitchen, mashing boiled potatoes. As she beat in the cream cheese, sour cream, and chives, Mom soon had her tasting spoon in the bowl, her eyes sparkling mischievously. "Delicious! Just wonderful, Katy. Must be the old German in me, but I love potatoes!" She smiled, the first in many months; a gap-toothed granny in a gaudy patchwork sweater, whipped potatoes on her cheek.

Those missing teeth. I felt a sear of remorse. Mom had recently lost teeth in odd and strange ways, one a year for the last six years. A tooth cracked on a frozen chocolate bar, another dropped out while she was laughing. During our visits at the lake, we'd teased her about those missing teeth. Sometimes the jokes were nudges. Once I discreetly offered to pay her dental bills.

"Thanks, anyway, but no. More trouble than it's worth," she'd replied tartly.

"Fine." *Look like a stupid hick,* I thought.

Mom blamed her old dentist for an infection in her jaw, followed by an even bigger bill, and flatly refused to go back. She adapted. Missing teeth had yet to impact her lusty appetite or deter her love for cheddar cheese and candy. Although her smile nipped in on one side now and had developed an upward hook, like Disney's hound dog Goofy, around the family or in town purchasing farm supplies, Mom hid the widening gaps with more compressed expressions, less laughter. Among ourselves, Tim, Judy, and I fumed in frustration. Why would Mom indulge this lapse in hygiene and appearance? She was a Phi Beta Kappa college grad, a Spokane socialite! Katy and David never seemed to mind, however. They loved Gramma's gap-toothed wolf whistle: She could whistle loud enough to scare off a poacher or a wily coyote angling for her chickens.

Hugging Mom's thin shoulders, I put the mashed potato bowl by her elbow. The Mayo Clinic Web page I had just read stated that tooth loss was often an early consequence of undetected leukemia.

Thanksgiving proved unexpectedly festive. Mom and her brother bickered and fussed at each other like small children as Mom showed her brother around our house in the manner of a grand dame. "You never return my calls!" She poked his arm. "Well, how can I, Louise? Your answering machine's shut off. I can't leave you messages, and you don't answer your phone," he responded, mildly offended. They never mentioned her illness.

After dinner, Katy helped me dry dishes, and then she left to watch the end of the televised football game with her dad, cracking open her book as she cuddled next to him on the sofa. Off to one side, David played chess with Uncle Joe: the two of them a study in contrasts, the young boy and the old man focused on the wooden pieces on the board.

As I put away the china, I contemplated my mother from across the room as she rested in the soft chair in the kitchen nook. Her head was sunk back against the cushions, and her eyes were closed in unmasked weariness. Vulnerability gathered in the deep lines of her face. I stood still, observing the unfamiliar birdlike thinness of her hands as they lay folded in her lap. Bluish veins pulsed under the callused parchment of her skin. Were her low-dose chemo pills still working? Was her white blood cell count down, the massive kidney and spleen damage arrested? Her chest rose and fell with light breaths as she napped.

Was Mom really, simply, going to die?

Yes, her doctor had been excruciatingly blunt in Moses Lake, his small eyes beading into my mother's soft, swimming gaze. "You nearly die *already*. You not have curable leukemia—no Gleevec, no new medicine for you."

"What do doctors know, anyway?" Mom had muttered.

You lived life, you did not talk about it. A competitive athlete throughout her youth, Louise Waugh played to win, and this perhaps was the kingpin of her personality. She aced the putt, won the skating medal, dove in and lapped the cold waters of the lake no one else would brave. She spent three weeks laying down ice in our snowy backyard outside Rome, New York, for the pleasure of practicing camel spins and teaching her toddlers to skate. My mom did not play Barbies on the floor or pull up a chair to help with math homework, and there weren't sleepovers. She did not understand the importance of a best friend. When I was ten she told me the birds and the bees were a part of the Bible. I spent an entire year looking through scripture for sex.

Mom dismissed my file of research and list of pharmaceuticals. She would take on the challenge of life and play to win, her way.

Crossing the room, I draped a wool throw around her shoulders, stroking her hands as she slept. For this one day, this lovely Thanksgiving, I was profoundly grateful.

Work Party

After Thanksgiving, Mom returned south to the farm, and on the following Saturday, everyone rose early to execute Plan B. Judy had taken the lead organizing a family work party at the farm, a concerted effort she hoped would give Mom the practical help she needed. All of us had agreed to gather there. Even Helen was flying in from New Mexico for the week, largely because Judy had insisted she deal with the issue of her old horse.

"No way Mom is going to be hauling water and hay out to the barn in January," Judy all but snarled into the phone. "You need to come out and deal with what you've left behind."

Helen was infamous in the family as the kid who brought home foundlings of all species, usually pregnant, and left them behind for Mom to care for when she headed off to college and married life in New Mexico. The farm was littered with

Helen's "projects." Rabbit, chicken, dog, and cat kennels of all sizes.

"Why? What are you planning to do?" Helen had demanded, suspicious.

"If Mom won't stay with one of us, or in town, then we absolutely have to make it safe for her to stay at the farm, Helen. Mom's sicker than she'll admit, and weaker too. The slightest cold or accident could trigger pneumonia, or another hemorrhage. We're going to do whatever's required to ready the place for winter. Wood, food, hay—you know those roads can be socked in for weeks with snow!"

"Fine. I'll be there." Helen hung up.

In truth, the diagnosis of Mom's leukemia had shaken us to the core. Even as we organized what we hoped would be a comfortable few months for Mom, we discussed amongst ourselves the inevitable emergency call in the night. We debated how best to interpret and manage her long silences, the weeks without a sighting; even the macabre possibility of discovering a corpse, weeks old.

Saturday morning we formed an urban caravan of flatbed trailers heading south through farm country, loaded with heavy equipment, pruning tools, flats of dried and canned goods, animal feed, and a pallet of pressed sawdust logs for the farm's wood-burning stove. The day loomed gray and cold, the field canes rattling in the Palouse winds as we followed the rural roads toward the Snake River.

The caravan of vehicles trundled up the long drive to the upper gate.

"What's this?" Mom called out, venturing out of the house to unlock the gate, a mixture of shock and apprehension on her face.

The kids and their cousins burst out of the cars, delivering a flurry of hugs.

"Surprise!" Tim boomed out as he parked his truck. "It's a miracle! Your kids are here to do chores!"

The mood grew exuberant, fueled in part by doing something positive for my mother as well as the joy of the four of us kids reuniting after so many years spent in different states. Laughter floated on the cold air, as within minutes, enough equipment was unloaded on my mother's front lawn to launch an Arctic expedition.

Our daughters set to work in the farmhouse while the younger boys snuck off. Moments later they were spotted in the field trying to drive the old pickup across the pasture, whooping loudly as the clutch jammed and popped. The truck's front end hit one pothole after another, frightening the old mare into racing the fence line, kicking up her heels.

Ken, Tim, and Jake set to work outside, hauling several loads of heavy metal salvage and debris the five miles to the county dump. They employed riggings of chains and ramps to pull loose from the frozen earth the framing of an old camper and the carcass of a bee-infested Chevy Caprice. Called in from the pasture, the boys were put to work chopping down dead tree limbs and clearing the long driveway of three-foot grasses. The rest of us formed a human chain to shift the pallet of pressed logs, one at a time, from the flatbed to the storage room. We lay in food stores and scrubbed the dog smell from the pens in the back rooms.

Helen, younger than me by twelve years, and like my mother in her rigid expressions and aloof reserve, headed out to the barn to assist the local vet as he vaccinated the remaining horse—her horse, the old mare Judy had insisted she either ship back to New Mexico or find alternate stabling for the winter.

It was, I sincerely hoped, the last horse my mother would own. They came, they stayed, they aged, and they died. She loved her horses, my mother: She rode the pastures through the blazing heat of August and the wind-whipped snows of February. She worked like a numb brute for their welfare: repaired fencing and hauled water by the bucket out to the barn when the deep freeze hit; pulled a coat over her pajamas to fire her handgun into the hills when midnight poachers mistook her animals for elk.

I stood at the sink, scrubbing pots. Within sight of the kitchen window lay evidence of the plywood and tarp grave of the pony that had just died. Why did the old ones always die in the winter, and not out in the barn, or behind the trees in the back pasture, but smack in the front yard? In twelve-degree winds and snow, Mom bundled up and pickaxed and scraped at the frozen earth to scrabble out the best grave possible nearest to where the horse fell. How had she dragged the beast even those few short remaining feet? Better to have called Claudsen Rendering and had the ingrate hauled out by the hooves.

I felt a familiar weight on my heart. The shamed, fierce love I felt for my mother.

Somewhere in the back rooms, a radio blared country music over the roar of the ancient vacuum cleaner. Puffs of dust floated down the hall toward the kitchen past the telephone nook, where as kids, Judy and I raced each other for the phone, only to hang up disappointed by a party-line ring.

Here we were with our daughters, aged eight to sixteen, cleaning the rooms of Mom's modest ranch house, an echo of the home I remembered as a girl. This house was an efficient, if plain, structure, rebuilt to replace the rambling rancher our family had first moved into, destroyed in an electrical fire. An architect in Seattle, my brother had spear-headed the reconstruction. Mom, and Helen, still in high school and living at home, had holed up in a camper through two seasons of summer heat and bitter cold, making do until the rebuilding was done.

I wrapped and packaged individual-size meals for the freezer, watching, curious, as Helen silently went about her work outside hosing out the dog and cat cages. What must that experience have been like for her and Mom? Living tethered within four feet of each other for two years, dependency and resentment entwined through every silence, every short burst of impatience.

Ken had joined Tim and Jake in the backbreaking work, cheerful and determined. I watched him throughout the busy morning, my chest tight with our dreadful secret. How could I prioritize each and every moment between the two of them, my mother and my husband? One worry I shared openly with my family, one I could not bear to breathe.

Done in the kitchen, I stood at the back door and tugged on work gloves, preparing to tackle the overgrown yard. Sometime in the last two years, the bing cherry tree had died, and lay split in two across the lawn. Tim had the chainsaw and ladder already unlashed from his SUV, but clearly needed help hauling cut branches and debris.

I froze. Across the yard, Ken suddenly doubled over, coughing in deep-chest spasms, clinging to the fender of our truck. Recovering, he shook it off and climbed into the driver's seat. Jake secured a chain attached to a heavy salvage pile to the truck hitch, waved his hand, and Ken slowly engaged the clutch.

I felt my throat clench. What if Ken had another coughing fit and couldn't control the truck? Ken shifted into low gear and the wheels bit into the frozen ground, straining to pull out a rusted six-foot propane tank. The tank had once been used to heat the camper, but had been left half-buried in the ground for fifteen years. The tank shuddered, and then gave free with a hollow groan, rolling on its side.

"Whoohoo!" Jake slapped his thigh and the boys danced.

Clapping shoulders, the men began to winch the tank wreckage onto a trailer.

Off to the side under a towering spruce, the same one I had given my mother on Mother's Day as a seedling, Mom stood silent, her face closed in a kind of devastated acceptance. She straightened her shoulders stiffly, her thinness buried under layers of sweats and a muddy barn coat.

"What's wrong with Mom?" Judy demanded, hands on her hips as she came up beside me from the back bathrooms. Her face was sweaty and she had rubber gloves on that came up to her elbows. "See? She just started walking out to the barn." Judy pointed one blue rubber finger toward the pasture. "She's headed toward the road! Is she mad? You'd think she'd be hootin' for joy to get rid of that hunk of junk."

"I don't know what's wrong," I murmured, feeling a knot take hold in my stomach. "Too many memories, maybe? Too many people? This must be overwhelming. Our showing up *was* a surprise."

Judy scowled. I took a breath, anxious to protect Mom suddenly, afraid we had gone too far. Afraid our good intentions had crossed the line into a jovial unstoppable bullying. "Um, I'll ask Ken to go speak with her. She'll talk to Ken."

After a hike out to the far pasture, and a few moments of conversation as they faced the far hills, Ken returned to the front yard. We gathered around.

My brother set down the power saw and wiped the dirt from his brow. "Well?" he asked. "Everything all right?"

A year and a half younger than me, Tim had a strapping build and an open, honest face that radiated concern and responsibility. His wife was dark-haired, a reserved, carefully distant woman. She laced an arm around her daughter, and then drew Katy into her other arm as Judy pressed Ken for details. "Why won't Mom come back to the house?"

Ken opened empty hands philosophically.

"It's everything and nothing. Apparently our presence has breached your mother's personal space. She feels we are insulting her independence, criticizing her ability to take care of her own life. She feels . . . patronized."

"Shit," Jake muttered, kicking the sod as he walked off.

After a quiet dinner in which we enjoyed only the satisfaction of tired muscles, we gathered our things and prepared to depart the farm. Mom had managed one strained "thank you" at the table; grateful, she said, for all the supplies and food. But she just as clearly didn't want to be. Ken was right; she felt violated.

We stood together at the kitchen sink.

"Why are you so mad, Mom?" I asked helplessly, my hands in soapy water, finishing the last dishes from our meal.

She snatched the wet glass from my hand, dried it, and thrust it back in the cabinet. She slapped the cupboard door closed with a bang and turned to me, her eyes blazing. "How would *you* feel if I marched into your house and took over everything?"

"But we're cleaning, doing chores—trying to save you the work and the burden!"

"Did I ask you for it? Did I? I *already* cleaned my house, thank you. What are you saying, it's not clean enough for you? I have things just the way I want them, the way things work for me."

"But, Mom, cleaning the house—doing the hard stuff— that's exactly what we did together for Grampa after Gramma got sick, remember? We're just trying to help. We haven't wrecked anything—only the junk is gone, the weeds and the garbage. Aren't you glad?"

"Who asked you? That old camper was fine out there, gave me my privacy from the road. The trees I can get around to myself in the spring." Her lips drew into a thin line. "Of course, I am grateful for the wood and the food, but you all just marched, just *marched* in here like you had every right. And I—" Her face pinched shut and she seethed silently, full of outrage.

I took a shaky breath, my head full of a tempest I would *not* let loose. I would not let her goad me into it. Not this time. It was right to have done what we had done for her. This fury was about power, I realized. She was taking back her power. Her right to not be pitied.

"Fine, Mom. We'll go."

I dried my hands, and collected Ken and the kids. Silent, we followed Judy's family out the door. Mom remained in the kitchen with her back to us, finishing up the dishes. Not even a good-bye to the grandchildren. Helen stood apart, watchful.

Judy and I hugged outside in the dark. We held each other, numb with shock. Had we really been so very wrong?

After my grandmother had begun to fail with Alzheimer's, Mom had spent nearly every weekend for three years enforcing a family work posse at their home. All three of us older kids had helped cook and clean, or taken turns watching Helen. Each weekend Mom stocked up on groceries, did the yard work, small repairs—anything that needed doing. Uncle Joe had somehow always been in training for table tennis, away at a chess meet, or sleeping on a cot at the barbershop.

The weekends took their toll. Chores complete, and exhausted after the difficult winter drive to Spokane at the end of her own workday at the County Courthouse, Mom would fall sound asleep on Grampa's living room floor, her head on her crossed arms, still in her work clothes. Mom had taught us that to help family was not just our Christian duty, but the simplest commitment owed by adult children to their parents.

This same woman rejected our efforts on her behalf?

Judy sniffled in tears as Jake finished tying equipment onto their long trailer. I could see that this was almost more than he could take, this "in your face" castigation. Under his breath he vowed to *never* come back, to never again work so hard for someone so damn graceless and abusive of his wife's gentle heart.

Pulling on a coat, Helen stepped outside to join us and we conversed quietly. She had decided that she would stay a few days more with Mom at the farm to arrange for the transfer of her horse after the new year to another ranch run by a friend of hers. She still had a few days' leave from the Los Alamos school district, and her teenage daughter and husband would take care of things back home.

"Come to Spokane with us for the night," I urged. "Let's at least have this one complete day together. Everybody's crashing at our house—there's plenty of room. You can drive our Volvo back down tomorrow, and use it while you're here."

"Louise might like the night to herself," Ken added.

"Okay." Helen shrugged. "Let me go tell Mom."

We finished loading the cars and trucks in the dark. After a few minutes, Helen came back out and climbed in beside Tim and his family, and our caravan of headlights rolled back down the gravel driveway, headed for the main road.

In the passenger seat beside me, Ken shook his head as I drove toward Spokane behind my sister and her trailer full of work equipment.

"What?" I asked puzzled, glancing at Ken's face in the muted glow of the dashboard lights.

"Just thinking. What a truly amazing reunion for the four of you after so many years—and all the chopping, hauling, and hard physical work accomplished for your mother. The house just sparkled. What a job everybody did!" He looked over his shoulder, smiling at the two kids zonked out in the backseat.

"Damn meal was great too." I sighed. "Who the hell knew you could Crock-Pot a ham?" I ached inside, hurt and puzzled by my mother's unaccountable, almost spiteful anger.

"Your mom is just not able to accept love, honey," Ken observed as he closed his eyes, worn out. "How sad."

That instant embraced a moment of great clarity. I had been dancing this dance of reach and rejection with my mother all my life. And yet here beside me in the gently illuminated dark rested my husband, who had always met my slightest reach with a steady, accepting hand. My mother, my marriage: What did I care for and what were these things truly worth to me?

Back at our house, the kids and their cousins bounded downstairs to watch movies, and Ken, the fatigue plain in the soft roundedness of his shoulders, excused himself and retreated to our bedroom.

The rest of us lounged around the kitchen table, drinking beer and wine and cracking pistachios, trying hard to enjoy what good had come of the "work party."

"To being together!" my brother toasted, and we raised our glasses.

I looked down and then away, gulping half my glass of wine. These laughing, dirt-smudged, sweat-stained people were my family. Angels with Crock-Pots, chain saws, and trucks. My God Squad. I closed my eyes, cradling my glass. The angst on my face must have been pregnant with significance, as within moments, everyone around the table fell silent.

"You all right?" Judy asked.

I set aside the glass and lay my hands on the table in front of me, offering them all, these beloved faces, a wavering smile.

"I have some news to share with you."

"Ho!" my brother exclaimed, slapping down his beer. "You're not pregnant?"

"Good God, no! Not that," I said, genuinely taken aback.

The sudden delighted smiles faltered.

I tried to speak up, but my voice seemed stuck in my throat. Finally, in short dry sentences, I explained the sudden appearance of Ken's cough, the recent tests at the clinic.

"I know I'm the closest to Mom geographically," I apologized, "but with Ken's looming medical situation, I don't know if I can be very available to keep an eye on her beyond clinic appointments—if she agrees to them—and maybe looking in on her now and then." Oh the sick ordinariness of words used to describe medical appointments, diagnostics, biopsies. "I thought I should tell you, so, you know, we could plan."

Judy's husband, long since over his anger, sat nursing a beer with one protective arm slung around his wife.

He looked down the length of the table at me and said very quietly, "Ken must be your first priority."

Circles

Dr. Pugh bustled into the examining room, crimping the edges of Ken's file. The lung doc shifted his shoulder, facing away as he cleared his throat.

"Preliminary diagnosis is an atypical adenocarcinoma of the lung. Unfortunately, Kenneth, a cancer. And, the cancer has metastasized from the tumor to the lymph nodes we biopsied. The pathologist found cancer in three of the six sites."

Ken blanched. Clearly we weren't talking aspirated watermelon seeds.

"There's still a bit of a question." Pugh pulled fiercely at his mustache. "The radiologist thinks the tumor is lung in origin, but the pathologist believes the cell typology might indicate, um, pancreatic origin." Pugh hesitated. "We have to be certain where the cancer comes from to correctly treat it. So we've scheduled you for an abd/pelvic CT scan today, a bone scan tomorrow, and I'll refer you to the hospital lung clinic on Thursday. There you'll meet your oncologist."

Ken would not look at me, but from the thinning of his lips I knew he was stunned. Two more major tests and another doctor. An *oncologist*.

"But Ken doesn't smoke!" I burst out. "How can he have lung cancer?"

"I did once," Ken interjected quietly. "Forty years ago in the air force. And, I used to like a cigar now and then." He bent over and cupped his mouth against another deep cough. "Good God." He panted, recovering.

The pulmonologist sniffed. "Not relevant, Kenneth. Cancers from smoking develop around an eight-year window around the time of smoking—and you quit decades ago. As for cigars, well that's mouth cancer." His tone softened. "You were smart to quit when they realized it was bad for us in the seventies. Not many did. No"—he tapped Ken's file—"this malignancy is not a cell typical of lung cancer. You just happen to have this bad boy in your lung."

"But how?" I asked. "How could my husband have grown such a large tumor and not known it? Ken runs marathons, he rides two-hundred-mile bike races. He has the lungs of a goddamned horse!"

I glared at the doctor. *Show me the seed.*

Pugh glanced sideways at Ken. "Those great lungs are no doubt why you've lived unaffected by the tumor for so long."

"What do we do?" Ken asked.

Pugh looked down at his notes. "If the tumor is some atypical lung cancer in origin, well, that's one thing. We treat your cancer as a lung primary. But if this has spread to your lung from elsewhere, well, that's different treatment altogether. I suspect, given the size of the tumor, any treatment will include both radiation and chemotherapy."

I squinted down at my clenched hands, feeling my face flush as tears welled up. *Dear God,* I breathed.

When Ken asked his next question, his voice was very soft. "How do I manage this? I'm a Daddy."

The fat little doctor was sweating now and his eyes slid away as he showed us out the door. "Go kick ass."

*　　*　　*

"I'm a Daddy," Ken had said to Dr. Pugh.

After we returned home Ken went straight to his office, saying nothing to the kids about our appointment. It was not in him to tell them the truth; he would die trying before he accepted failure. I knew from the way he looked at David and Katy over dinner that he felt that by becoming sick he had let them down, had failed as their father and protector. I saw for the first time how terribly afraid he was.

The next afternoon Ken left for a meeting at Gonzaga University, where he served as a volunteer leader and a mentor in an entrepreneurial business undergraduate program. He moved slowly as he dressed, pulling on his suit, a nice Hermès tie, took the time to polish his shoes.

"See you in a few," he said, kissing me on his way out the door.

I picked up the kids from school, but instead of coming home, detoured to the Manito duck pond. I pulled into the parking lot and turned off the engine, and we sat in the car for a few moments in silence as snow tapped gently on the windshield. The kids said nothing: They knew something was coming.

Lying awake the night before, my gut instinct had told me I needed to step in where Ken could not, to create a safe space for Katy and David to question, and to understand the next steps in treatment. They shouldn't be forced into knowing too much too soon, but encouraged to spend time with their Dad.

Taking a deep breath, I shared the facts with Katy and David.

"It's a tumor. And not in a good place. We don't know yet if it's something to be removed, or just a blockage. But Daddy is otherwise very healthy and the best thing to do is get on this and get it fixed."

"Is Daddy sick like Gramma?" David asked.

"No, honey. This is different." I twisted sideways in the driver's seat looking at them squished together in the backseat, loving their quiet faces. "We're a family, we're still okay. I'm here for you, and so is Dad. And no matter what, we will always take care of you."

I felt the steel harden within me.

* * *

At home the phone rang. Abby, Ken's sister in Los Angeles, was on the line. "Any more news?"

Two weeks ago, after Ken had shared the news of his troublesome X-ray, Abby had begun to call daily.

Knowing this would be a tough conversation, I left the two of them to chat and slipped into the kitchen, intent on preparing a roast chicken for dinner. Abby, like Ken's daughter Jordan, remained one of the closed circles in our marriage—a tight, impenetrable chamber that did not include me.

Seeking solace in the simple chores of cooking, I seasoned the chicken, adding a finishing braise of rosemary and lemon, thinking about the painful question of Abby. There had been cordial get-togethers over the years, but Ken had fallen to visiting with his sister lately as he did with Jordan, alone. After the tension surrounding his father's hospitalization and unexpected death before we left California, and the fight between Ken and me that had followed the funeral about the time away from home at Abby's and the backseat role the kids and I played in the services, it seemed clear to me that I lived in a part of Ken's life that was not equally "family." Not intentional—conflicts in loyalty pained Ken greatly—we were nonetheless set aside when "his" family needed him. I bowed to the hierarchy of childhood over marriage, although everything in me objected.

The oven timer went off. Pouring myself a glass of wine, I sat down at the kitchen table, suddenly bone weary. I felt worn down trying to buffer Ken, especially from Jordan. Her reaction to the recent news of his illness, like Abby's, had seemed to drain him.

For years Ken's eldest daughter had chosen to limit contact with our family. Before Kurt, it had been her practice to arrive at the last possible minute for the holidays, and always with a friend in tow, someone to place between herself and the rest of us.

"Is it me, Ken? Is it me she won't accept?" I had asked him, distressed after our particularly hard first Christmas when Jordan and her then boyfriend, whom Ken had flown in from San Francisco for the holidays, lurked miserably in the other room, refusing to even go sledding.

"No, G. It's me. This is the distance she needs, the space she feels safe in. Jordan cares, but only just enough."

It was a posture of bending away from love; one I fully recognized in the shadow of my mother. Even in my stepdaughter, the denial made me ache, with Ken and for him.

I decided then that the best means to navigate this stepdaughter minefield was to remain willing: open, but undemanding. I agreed, accommodated, accepted and stood aside. The thirteen-year age difference between Jordan and me was too semigenerational to permit parenting, and apparently too great to span friendship or sisterhood.

It wasn't until Jordan routinely broke Katy's and David's hearts with missed birthdays, canceled Christmases, and forgotten weekends, that I began to carefully omit the words *big sister* from the situation. Jordan was making it clear that while she didn't object to these new members of the family, she also couldn't or wouldn't bond with them. "Big sister" was not the role, "absent stepsister" was. Jordan subtly enforced the gap between first family and second family, until for me, she became the barrier.

During the years Ken and I lived in California, Jordan fell into a pattern of appearances and disappearances that had everything to do with drinking and unhappiness, and her excesses caused us great concern. Adolescent abuses had blossomed into serious problems for her as a young woman, but her interest in our involvement remained limited to assistance in resolving her financial issues and frequent medical crises. We had visited therapists with Jordan and helped her through costly specialty clinics.

In her late twenties she finally decided on her own to enter a rehab program north of the city, and Ken followed the advice he was given by her rehab therapist. "If Jordan asks you for money for this treatment program, Mr. Grunzweig, you must only agree if she considers your help as a 'loan,' with conditions and repayment. Without major skin in the game this girl will slide right through rehab and back into trouble the moment she's tired of working life straight."

We had done as advised.

Miffed, Jordan had asked her boyfriend Kurt for the money. A few days later, Ken hung up the telephone after a particularly trying conversation with Jordan—her first angry week in rehab. He slumped down next to me on the back porch, staring into space.

"Jordan hates me. No matter what I do, or how hard I try,

she hates me. She's on a goddamned liver transplant list, for Christ's sake. It's like we're forever bound together—a wound, a thorn in each other's side."

"That's not your fault, Ken."

"No?" He closed his eyes. "Where does it begin and where does it end when we fail our children?"

Unfinished business, closed circles.

"Damn!" I blurted under my breath. I had accidentally burned myself pulling out the roasting pan. I stuck my finger in my mouth, nursing the sting. Off the deck, a white-tipped bald eagle rode the upper thermals over the broad valley.

I finished my wine, tossing a salad as the roasted chicken cooled on the counter. The sound of Ken's low laughter from the living room made my heart brighten.

"I'll call with whatever I know, Abby," I overheard Ken say. "Yes, we got the fruit basket. The pears were great."

Must be nice to have such unwavering loyalty, I thought a bit enviously, suddenly reminded of Helen. My youngest sister had called on her way to the airport just a few days ago to deliver a message from Mom.

"She doesn't need you at her doctor's appointments, Glenda. She wants to go by herself. She asked me to tell you this." Her tone of voice made sure I knew she was both messenger *and* confidante.

"She's not *seeing* a doctor, Helen," I had blurted out, exasperated. "I just made her an appointment with one she says she *might* see!"

"Just relaying the message."

All that work down the drain. My family circles wobbled on bent rims.

Holding the phone away from his ear, Ken wandered into the kitchen and sank into the comfy plaid chair. "You take it?" he asked, one thumb over the mouthpiece.

He handed me the telephone, closing his eyes.

Wiping my hands on a dish towel, I recapped for Abby what the doctor had had to say. "Yes, still coughing. No, he's not discouraged—just tired. Don't worry. Honestly, Abby." There was muscle in my voice. "We've been to the mats before."

Ken nodded from the chair.

Abby's husband came on the line, asking for Ken. Reluctantly, I handed the phone back over. I could see Ken felt overwhelmed by their questions and anxiety.

Abby's husband, an overland trucker sometimes employed laying fiber-optic line, suggested to Ken that maybe the lump was an infection, valley fever, a fungal spore from the Southwest. That could make pockets in the lungs. He should get a blood test.

Ken finally hung up the phone. He rubbed the back of his neck. "Abby's just beside herself."

Brushing his cheek with my fingertips, I called my family to dinner.

I would shelter Ken. I was the house that love built. I regretted not one moment of our life together. I had been right about the two of us.

Tree Angel

In three weeks it would be Christmas.

Christmas had always been my favorite holiday, especially now, mixed with Ken's childhood traditional celebration of Hanukkah. We lit the Hanukkah candles and spun dreidels. Ken looked up the words of the Hanukkah prayer and the songs because he just as quickly forgot them, explaining to the children each letter's meanings on the dreidel top. I treasured the look of David's face reflected in the menorah candlelight, Ken's voice reciting the old Hebrew.

We baked sugar cookies, wrapped gifts for the community giving tree, and always set up our own tree of lights, hanging each ornament we had collected as a family over the years—the red lobster sitting on a trap from Ogunquit, Maine, the sled from Aspen, and the mission bell from Taos.

Somehow the hum-along cheer and spicy bustle of the holiday not only eluded me this year, it repelled me.

We put the tree up the first Saturday of December. Ken

placed an ornament or two, and then stood back to enjoy the kids as they squirreled around the branches hanging their "collections"—David had his miniature antique cars and trains, Katy had her tiny Barbie dolls from around the world. Ducking happily in among the tree branches, Katy held in her fingers a tiny Paris Barbie, a blonde fashionista attired in Audrey Hepburn black, singing into a tiny plastic cabaret microphone.

As the kids hung ornaments, Ken uncased his flute and half-heartedly meandered through a few Christmas carols, his tone altered, unexpectedly melancholy and inward. The flute marked the landscape of Ken's quite time. Late at night, during stressful periods of work, or sometimes just floating on a lovely mood of reflection, he would play Chet Baker jazz standards on the silver keys, pacing the empty rooms. His music was both beautiful and haunting, like listening to someone dream.

Ken glanced up from an elusive high C in "Little Girl Blue," catching his breath, and our eyes met. I walked over and kissed his head, feeling the slight fever that was so constant now. He laid the sliver flute, a gift from me on our second anniversary, back in its velvet-lined case and came to stand by the decorated tree.

He surveyed our work with a smile. "Ready for the angel?"

David jumped to his feet, "Let me this year, Dad! I'm big enough!" He took off for the ladder, but Ken snagged him in an affectionate bear hug.

"No. I'll lift you."

"God, no," I protested. I wasn't sure if I thought David, at nearly ninety pounds, would break Ken, or if Ken, so ill, would drop David. But there was a funny look in Ken's eyes. He wanted to do this, needed to.

David hopped onto the piano bench and then shimmied up Ken's back to straddle his shoulders. They bobbed and staggered and I feared for the Christmas tree.

Holding my breath, I handed David the porcelain angel. "Be careful, boys."

Our family tree angel was a treasure from Katy's first Christmas visiting Leavenworth, Washington, the quaint Bavarian village nestled in the Cascade Mountains west of Spokane. No more than five months old then, Katy too had ridden high on Ken's shoulders as we explored Leavenworth's glittering ornament shops.

"Whoa!" Ken huffed as they lurched backward, recovering from an off-kilter dive toward the tree. David was laughing hysterically, his face bright with exertion as he reached toward the top of the tree.

"Almost got it, Dad! Just a little closer!"

At last Ken found purchase, nose deep in the scruffy branches, and planted his feet. David stretched upward over his head, but the top branch remained just beyond reach. Determined, he braced one hand on the top of Ken's head, lifted himself an inch or two higher, and in one swift thrust centered the angel on the topmost branch.

"Got it!"

Ken grinned, beet red in the face, David laughing and hanging on for dear life. I snapped a picture and it was done—a memory for that year's Christmas.

We put away the holiday boxes as Elvis sang sassy, bluesy Christmas carols on the stereo. This year, there would be only a few lights strung outdoors in the bare branches of the ornamental pear.

"Too bad we don't still have Plastic Santa," David lamented.

"He overpartied," Ken said, snorting.

"More like partied over, you mean." I laughed.

For our first Christmas in our Los Altos, California, house, we decked the place in garlands and bows for a company party. But maddeningly, every light on the string of outdoor bulbs blew out on consecutive nights throughout December. Even the blinking string on the olive tree took a turn for the schizophrenic. But poor Plastic Santa had fared the worst. He tipped over in a sudden gust of wind and split along the seam running from his cherry red nose to his list of naughty and nice.

"Remember later, reading Christmas stories, Mom?" Katy's eyes twinkled, alight with her new, arch "grown-up" recollection of childhood adventures.

"Yeah! After the party!" David exclaimed, and they began to fill in for each other, interrupting and embellishing the familiar story.

Ours had been the same tradition every year. The last thing Christmas Eve, I would read Christmas tales with the kids in our big bed. At the *thump, thump, thump* on the roof, we would pause in wonder as we cocked our ears, hearing the tinkle of a real harness bell. "Ho-Ho-Ho, Merry Christmas!" would belt through the window in a huffy baritone and the kids would fly off my lap, running to the window.

But Santa would be gone, and only reluctantly could I then coax them into bed to await Santa's later return when the chubby gift giver "knew they would be sleeping."

That particular Christmas Eve, after the rack of lamb and oysters Napoleon in lemon cream, caviar and chives had been cleared from the buffet table, the champagne and party glasses washed and put away, I roped the kids onto my lap and began reading *The Polar Express*, one of David's favorites. Almost four at the time, David remained a true believer in Christmas bells, although Katy had grown into a more skeptical age six.

Suddenly, the *thump!*

But a thump sounding peculiarly like a large rock lobbed at the chimney, and then harness bells jingled loudly and the three of us looked at one another knowingly. I smiled, anticipating what I expected to come next.

"Ho, Ho—*shit!* Jesus Christ! Ho, Ho, Ow! *Goddamnit!*"

We listened in horror to the unmistakable sounds of someone, or something, crashing into the back of the house, ending in the racket of gravel sprayed against the fence behind the cactus garden.

"Mommy!" Katy exclaimed, her mouth a big O. "Santa's swearing!"

"Well," I muttered, fighting for a straight face. "Maybe Old St. Nick fell off the roof."

"Let's go see!"

They flew to the bedroom window, peering out in excited alarm. Alas, no telltale sleigh wreckage on the lawn.

"Better leave a Band-Aid with the cookies, Mommy," David advised solemnly.

"And the next morning both Plastic Santa *and* the Band-Aid were gone," David finished, pleased with the story. "And all the fudge, and cookies too!"

I smiled, remembering how later that night I had kissed Santa's boo-boos—and the next day buried the remains of the barrel cactus, badly crushed by a Nike, size ten.

Domestic Saints

The frosted Christmas cupcakes had gone to school, the holiday band and orchestra pageants were penciled in, yet still, our lives hung in limbo.

It was no longer a question of cancer—but what *kind* of cancer. Ken's biopsy slides had been sent to Stanford for a second opinion. The medical team in Spokane needed to clarify the conflicting opinions among doctors on the origin of the tumor cancer cells. Until then, no treatment plan could be decided upon.

I drifted through the winter days, irritable and anxious. Lung or *whatever*—what the hell difference could it possibly make when that thing sat in Ken's chest eating his life away one stealthy moment at a time?

Downstairs in his studio, Ken was struggling with the mat cutter, trying to exactly frame a platinum print, a photograph he planned to donate to the school auction. The image was a beautiful, dreamy still life of tulips, opened just past their peak and arching over the sides of a round glass vase. The image was breathtaking, and somehow, sad. I looked away.

"Come for a walk with me?" I asked, quiet. We had always walked. And some of my favorite walks were the earliest ones. Very pregnant with Katy, I had strolled every summer afternoon with Ken, his fingers gently entwined in mine as we headed to my near-daily scoop of ice cream. Something about the slow stroll, the expectant gentleness of a baby on the way, and the wide open future we had so fully embraced, lulled me. When Ken and I walked, we fell in rhythm with each other and the world. What was important rose, even as the insignificant peeled away like winter leaves rolling at our feet.

"Come for a walk?" I repeated.

Ken stiffened. Just before breakfast we'd had a terrific row, and in the hours since, kept a civil distance. Our argument shimmered in the air between us, hard and glittery.

That morning had come on the heels of a sleepless night. Ken had a difficult time lying down and managing his cough. After exhausting hours of battling both the waking and the coughing, it had seemed easier to both of us just to rise.

Weary and hollow-eyed, feeling only a year of rest would make up for so many lost nights' sleep in a row, I headed for the kitchen. The wood floor felt smooth under my bare feet as I prepared tea for us. The furnace clicked on and sent a rush of hot air through the vents, warming my ankles. In his blue gray flannel bottoms and a soft gray Henley, Ken stood by the window near the front door, contemplating the dusting of new snow that had fallen during the night.

Finally, he made his way to the kitchen, pulling out the breakfast basics: granola, oats, hot cocoa for the kids. Holding an empty milk carton upside down over the sink, he flatly announced that there was no milk or juice for breakfast, as if he blamed me.

I bristled in frustration. No milk? *No milk?* For weeks the man had been this human vegetable. All alone I had carried the full load of the household, the kids' schedules, the holidays, while Ken wandered around in sweatpants looking like shit until noon. But if necessary, he could clean up and go to a wine party at the Art School, or fly off for a weekend executive board meeting in California.

"No milk? I'm sorry." So much unspoken frustration buried in the even tone of my voice.

Ken paused at the refrigerator. "Are you mad at me?"

"Of course not." I snatched the cereal bowls off the table, bowls that we obviously could *not* use if there was no milk. "Who's allowed to be mad at a sick person?"

"That absolutely isn't fair, Glenda." Ken always enunciated my name *Glen-dah* when he was angry—using that particular adult tone of rebuke.

"Maybe not fair, but true," I struck out in childish pain, hating myself for it. "You don't even have a confirmed diagnosis, Ken—yet for weeks you've been out of commission. Well, news flash! I'm exhausted! I'm cook, housekeeper, handyman, parent, and apparently, milk cow. You're taking naps while I'm beat!"

I marched outside to the garage fridge and hauled in a gallon of frozen milk, plunking the plastic block down hard on the counter. "Things are going to get tough soon enough. And you've already worn me out!"

Ken pivoted on his heel and left the kitchen. Down the hall I heard him throw on clothes, and moments later heard the roar of his truck, gunning down the driveway.

Ken had stayed away the rest of the morning and I told myself I was glad for the time alone. One moment, *just one moment in my life free of the presence of cancer.* But Ken had not taken his cancer with him—the beast rested right in my lap, balled up in the niggling anxiety I felt for my husband's safety. Was Ken cold? Driving too fast on the icy roads? Oh lord, I shouldn't have unloaded. I was tired and scared and confused. And he had to be that, and more.

As the hours ticked by, I stood at the kitchen sink, aimlessly scrubbing the same pot, my eyes focused out the window on the pine branches tossing in the December gusts. I felt so damn angry at the world, and I feared the absolute worst. I felt in my bones the depth of Ken's cough.

I rinsed the pot in water so hot my hands stung, and reflected back on that dream of Ken and the strange boxlike rooms. The images taunted me. What did they mean? There had been other dreams in my life before, like snowflakes on my pillow, telling me of other people's mysteries. But this dream's meaning eluded me.

I considered the dream I had the night before Ken's mother had died. I had awoken with Rose still clearly in my mind, the dream images grainy, like a black and white film. In my dream, Rose was about twenty, dressed in a saucy hat and wearing her wool coat, carrying a valise. She had climbed aboard an old steel train, and stood on the rear platform, waving. Slowly the train had gathered steam and disappeared into the white distance. *I'm going to Chicago,* she said. *Because I've never been.*

"What is it with all the white fog?" I wondered aloud, perplexed. That dream of Rose had certainly been prescient. But Ken and the dream of boxes? *Everything will be all right,* the voice had said.

It had begun to snow again.

If a plentitude of tiny, scientific miracles such as snowflakes could exist in this world—instantaneous and perfect, so beautifully unexplained—might I not hope for my own miracle? I watched the snowflakes twist and drift in the wind, spinning by like bits of fluffy cotton torn loose. My lengthening prayer list fluttered just the same, worn and tattered, a long rope of Buddhist colored flags.

Strange, this need to pray. As if my soul sought communication, touch. So alone within the body, I felt as if I knocked on walls from within, hoping for a tap from the other side.

Unexpectedly, I heard the truck rumble into the garage, Ken stomping his boots clear of snow. Moments later, the back door opened and Ken retreated straight downstairs to his basement darkroom.

He was home.

I took a deep breath, waited a moment, and then followed him down the stairs. "Ken?"

At the sound of my voice, his back straightened. He did not turn to face me but leaned forward and splayed both hands the length of the edge of the cutting table, as if he too were now made of wood, a force to be reckoned with.

Hesitant, I touched his shoulder.

He turned, took my hand, and pressed it to his lips. "Come for a walk?"

* * *

Boxing Day, the British call it.

Bags of wrapping paper and crumpled ribbon littered the living room. The Scottie hung half out of his new plaid basket, asleep, and alone by the back door, the Yorkie watched morosely as a flock of quail etched tiny fleur-de-lis footprints across the cold crust. Today was the quiet, thoughtful, sometimes melancholy day after Christmas.

But ours was not a true Christmas.

Pushed by Ken's doctors, we had pinned the holiday on the calendar a week early. The medical team had tentatively scheduled Ken for a surgical biopsy December 24, early Christmas Eve morning. The biopsy would remove the swollen lymph nodes in his sternum, and if the nodes were found to be clear of cancer cells in the OR, they would proceed with an immediate thoracotomy and midlobectomy—surgery to remove the lung tumor itself.

In preparation, we celebrated our family Christmas early in the middle of December. I arranged for the kids to join my brother, Tim, and his family in Seattle over the actual holiday the following week, when Ken would be in the hospital, recuperating. Tim and his wife had graciously offered to fold Katy and David into their own family celebration. There would be snow sports in the mountain pass, and spy movies and Xbox games.

Knowing I might not see Mom over Christmas, I left a care package of warm flannel pajamas, James Bond movies, and Drambuie in the foyer of the house on Fortieth Avenue. When I telephoned, the rings echoed in my ear until the call clicked over to the disconnect of her mobile phone. But a day later we received a holiday card in the mail, saying she preferred to remain at the farm, "The pastures are so beautiful under their new blanket of snow." She would enjoy Christmas with her coffee, watching the old horse trek through the drifts to join the deer at the salt lick.

I hadn't the heart or inclination to argue. Things were moving quickly in Ken's treatment schedule and I needed to gather my family together and somehow make it all work—the holidays and now surgery.

Our "faux Christmas" morning had been peaceful. I busied myself Scotch-taping holiday cards to the refrigerator, tucking the new gifts in their opened boxes under the tree for all to enjoy. For an hour Katy had been practicing cello, seated on her chair beneath the large windows in the living room. Something pensive lingered in the air.

Folding my arms tight across my chest, I melted out of the hallway shadows, startling her as she was putting her instrument back in its case.

"Kates? We need to talk."

Obediently, she followed me into the privacy of my bedroom. I took one of the two facing bedside chairs, Katy the other. She sat on the very edge of the tufted floral seat. Her fingers nervously worked over the end of a tassel from the pillow she pulled onto her lap and hugged close to her chest. Much had changed in my daughter since the onset of my mother's illness; Katy had put aside sketching her fashion designs and her play dolls, closed her much-loved books, and taken to spending long hours alone in her attic room, thinking.

I had wrestled all week with how to tell my daughter the truth—she was still so young and I would have to use such very scary words. But with each passing week, Ken was noticeably less himself, often fading from the room at unexplained moments for the solitude of his room and a nap, or joining us on a school project, or at the table, but too tired to leave his chair. The children had observed everything—from the increasing flurry of medical tests and whispered conversations, to Ken's untouched plate at dinner—and I knew Katy, the oldest, deserved to know just enough, and David a little less, to prepare them for what might lie ahead.

"Honey, I want to talk to you—and to David too—about Daddy. But right now, just you and me. You're the oldest and I think you can help me share this with your brother."

Carefully choosing my words, I explained the results of the medical exams thus far.

"The lump in Daddy's lung is a tumor, Katy. A cancer.

What kind, we don't yet really know, but it needs to come out. Daddy will need lots of treatments and all our love and caring for a while as these treatments might make him very sick."

Cancer was a word Katy understood. Gramma had cancer.

Katy had done her research report for eighth-grade science just months before on cancer, contacting the Director of Stanford University's Oncology Clinic to ask, "Why choose a career in oncology?" The doctor's answer became the keynote of her paper: "Because I have seen the most courageous human beings, and learned the most about life from my patients." Katy had declared she wanted to be an oncologist too. I saw thirteen in her eyes. She would save the world. Not through prayer, but science.

"So there it is, honey. Daddy's is a different kind than Gramma's—and he's much younger and stronger than Gramma—but it is cancer."

I had said the word. *Cancer.*

Katy nodded her head and pressed her lips tight, very grave. Her grandmother had cancer, and now, so did her daddy. The enormity of these facts blanketed her expression. I yearned to fold her into my arms, to erase away all I had just said, but I remained seated, letting her absorb things in her own way. I hurt at her bravery, felt her silence slice my heart. These were truths bigger than a secret now; they were the shape of our lives, and I could not promise how it would end.

She saw right through me.

"It's okay, Mommy. I'm glad I know."

Lists

Snow that had fallen the second week of December soon melted in a brief, warm, windy Chinook. Ken and I headed out for a walk, careful of the patches of sidewalk ice that cracked underfoot. I had bundled Ken up to the point where he looked ridiculous in a wool hat, thick muffler, and heavy coat, but Judy had warned me to protect his lungs, to protect him from the cold.

We followed our familiar path through the neighborhood, passing the stately houses and barren wintry yards. The last time we had taken this walk together, autumn's crimson geraniums stood silvered with frost. It would snow again soon. You could feel Canada in the air.

Holding hands, we walked in silence, as we had always walked.

"I talked with the kids, Ken." I said.

He looked at me, his face tired and gray in the light.

"How'd they take it?"

"Bravely. Katy knows more of the facts than David—she works things out in her head, that one. David, well, he just worries. It's enormous for him just knowing you're sick without having to wrestle with the details."

It was David who jumped through the house with all his young boy energy, stopping when he saw his dad to ask, "How are you feeling, Dad? Are you okay?" and Ken would then smile and say, "I'm feeling fine. Don't worry." That was their thing, their code for *you know I love you.*

Ken bent to cough, his pace slowing. "Should I talk to them?"

"It's okay for now that you don't. Especially since we know so damn little. And honestly, I think they want to be outside all this . . . sickness . . . with you."

I kissed his cheek.

Ken didn't look at me, but I sensed his expression crumple, as if he had let them, me, down somehow.

"Just be Daddy. One step at a time," I said.

*　*　*

"What's this?" I asked Ken after our walk. We were drinking tea in the kitchen and I was reading over David's shoulder. David held in his hand a list of cars.

"Only every car I've ever owned." My husband grinned.

The record of every boy's life: in Ken's case, the history of a Jewish kid from Cleveland, a teen in jeans and a grease-stained T-shirt who had rebuilt broken cars in his neighbor's garage.

I looked over the list. As the years and the cars progressed, so did their expense and variety. Ken's catalog blazed with his lifelong magnificent rubber and metal passion: the piston engine loves of a guy who read *Road & Track* magazine cover to cover in the bathroom, a subscription my mother had renewed for both him and David the previous Christmas.

Ken could tell you the make and model of any car on the road. Any.

It was a game with the kids: "What's that, Dad?" they chorused as something eccentric with twin fins and a huge hood thundered by.

And certainly, it was an odd list. Not just a history of cars, but of the times lived, the fads of the day. A list of dating, destinations, style, budgets, families, careers. Boy to man, man to Dad. *Cleveland: 1949 Ford, gray, stick—never really drove it. Cleveland: 1953 Studebaker, 2 door, stick, V-8. Leaving Cleveland: 1957 TR3A, overdrive, 4 cylinder, green. Sacramento, Air Force: 1960 Ford Falcon, green, 2 door. Living in Long Beach: 1964 Fiat 1500 Spyder, red, 5 speed. . . .*

The last vehicle purchased, after the sedate 1997 Volvo 850 GLT was upstaged by the 1999 hot red Lexus coupe, was a used 1998 Toyota 4Runner, a choice that marked the move to the Northwest. Ken had searched the Spokane area for months for the ideal field expedition vehicle. A photography adventure truck: a rugged, dependable "go anywhere" vehicle still capable of fitting into a standard garage. The symbol of his new beginning; a symbol of freedom.

Ken laughed, perusing the list over my shoulder.

"Half those rust buckets never worked—or never when I needed them to. My favorites, crotch-rocket fast! And all of them cost too much, lasted not nearly long enough, or ended up being towed. . . ."

"Or repossessed."

"So the bookkeeper forgot to pay the bills!"

This record of wheels and deals was a core sampling, exposing the geological stratification of Ken's life—in fact, a map, a "heavy metal" cultural dictionary of speed and glory: seduction, the V-8 kind.

"So why now? Why make this list?"

"The car show!" Ken and David chorused.

The Classic Car Show opened in just under a week, and the boys planned to attend, Ken's detailed record in tow. Guy time. Hours to drool over shiny hoods and gleaming silver motors, Ken handing down what he knew and loved of cars to his son in a sacred masculine tribal ritual—popping the hood.

I kissed them both.

A day later I uncovered another inventory.

Lists were falling out of Ken's pockets and belongings: slipping from his field notebooks, his slim volume of the poems of Edward Abbey, the many stuffed backpacks of camera gear. A tremendous sorting and realignment was clearly occuring within the man, and penciled lists spilled onto the counters, falling half-tucked out of boxes and drawers.

I unfolded them as I found them, reading with wonder and curiosity. The cars, the jobs he had held, the beginnings of sketching out a lifetime's key events. Each list was an intriguing piece of the puzzle; fragmented continents of the man I loved that invited a kind of cultural anthropology—translations of decisions, choices between work opportunities, lovers—which I would decipher if I could. What did the sum of these choices say? And which key experiences were the bold signatures of luck—that mysterious intersection of accident and intent?

Paper route, Plain Dealer *(age 11). Shovel walks, winter. Cut lawns. Always collect bottles for redemption (2 cents). Grocery store—carry bags, stock shelves. Pee Wee's Bike Store. Drug store—soda clerk/counterperson. Berg Toy Store—toy assembly . . .*

In the quiet of late night, I sat alone in my office, my feet propped on the corner of the desk resting on the broken spine of *The Picture of Dorian Gray*. A teacup stain encircled Oscar Wilde's name. I stared at the dog-eared book, thinking.

Instead of catching up on work, I had just spent the last hour rereading Ken's list of jobs, unconsciously marking the point at which a wife entered or exited, or a child.

The cars I understood. That list was fun, born of collecting and curiosity, I guessed. But this record appeared more serious, an evenhanded recapitulation of one man's entire history of enterprise, of ambition, of success. *The Encyclopedia of Ken.*

Pausing over the detailed pages, I marveled at the range of things: the length of the boy's reach and the man's accomplishments. What restlessness, what drive!

Yet what was Ken sieving for in these lists he was making? These private, odd, unexplained accountings?

Howl

The days between hanging Christmas ornaments and cutting out cancer had whittled down to four. In ninety-six hours Ken would have his surgery, our single best hope. Each passing day hung in the hours, was felt in every careful, hopeful word and gesture in our little family. The kids played with their new toys and then packed and repacked their bags, preparing for the car trip to meet up with their uncle Tim. I eyed the clock, counting down the days.

Folding the laundry, pressing the kids' warm clothes to my cheek, I realized abruptly how badly I wanted the comfort of my own mother. I ached to tell her how much I needed her. Her own cancer had shut her down completely; learning of Ken's might unhinge her. She was so genuinely fond of Ken . . . and becoming aware that I needed her would only drive her further away.

It was our familiar pattern. Mom wanted to be there, but

she just couldn't. And I couldn't bear to be rejected, again. Not now. I was left with my need, swallowing it whole.

The medical team had attached so many "ifs" in their discussions of Ken's treatment that I wobbled between fierce optimism and a creeping suspicion of what wasn't being said. I stopped sleeping. Lying awake, I listened through the hours to Ken's uneven breathing, his harsh cough. I mopped his brow with a cold cloth during the night when fever seized him and he tossed, damp with sweat but refusing to ask for help.

"Sleep, kiddo," he muttered.

How could I tell him I could not, might not ever again sleep? My world was in complete jeopardy, and now, finally, I knew it. I had added up all the facts and subtracted all the hopefuls. I totaled the statistics and treatments over and over again in my tired brain, factored in new possibilities, possible new treatments, any potential unexpected news from the upcoming chest node biopsies, good or bad. The Web sites listed a lung cancer patient's chances of survival between 14 and 49 percent, depending on the spread of the cancer outside the tumor. Beyond five years it just didn't seem to matter. The odds were grim.

Ken had walked into my office when I was researching the medical information and read the statistics over my shoulder. He paled.

"Remember the two percent, baby," I said. "We're the two percent that *can*."

We could be the telling differential, the miracle cure, the lucky son of a bitch. Not the percentage of cancer cells that survive, the tiny percentage that escape the surgeon's scalpel and poison the rest.

Ken squeezed my shoulder gently, repeating what he had

said in the car as we drove the country roads, "No matter what, we fight like hell, G."

That night, knowing the day after tomorrow I was to ferry the kids west to Tim, I tucked them in with a tender kiss, reminding them "no worries." I gave Ken his prescription cough medicine, laced with codeine to calm his chest spasms and read next to him in the bedroom chair until he drifted off to sleep.

The house was quiet. Everyone was asleep. In three days it would be Christmas. *Real* Christmas. Our kids would be in Seattle, and Ken and I would be in the hospital, his fate in the hands of fate itself.

I set down my book and turned off the light, kissing Ken lightly.

Unsettled, I found myself wandering into the darkened kitchen. Filling a glass of water, I crossed to the windows and stood for a few moments, gazing outside at the full moonlight, the silver winter below.

Abruptly I lifted the scotch bottle off the cabinet shelf, pulled Ken's down jacket over my pajamas, and went out onto the deck in my slippers. I tossed the water from the glass and poured in a sliver of scotch, gulping it down. The alcohol burned my throat and I winced, tearing up. Coughing, I held tight to the deck rail, catching my breath.

And then without warning, I began to bawl. Great, silent, shaking tears.

I wept as I poured another scotch, drinking because it hurt, because this was a pain I could *feel*, and then feel pass. I shook my fist, hurling the glass into the trees, aiming at the beautiful midnight light. I sank from fury to sheer shivering sorrow.

Oh God I was afraid. Afraid to lose Ken, afraid of what his illness and treatment would do to us, and afraid of the dependency I had created for myself. My man who would *never* leave me. . . . What if he had no choice?

I was about to crash land into my middle forties with no viable means of supporting myself or my family. Like my mother before me. Alone.

Where had my education and my youth—my career, pension, and paycheck—gone? Where was the young executive woman who had learned as an adolescent not to be dependent? The girl who watched her own mother desperately seize whatever sparse employment crumbs remained available as a divorcée, a mother of middle age with no recent job experience. Me, the woman who believed work was independence and a paycheck was power. Where had I gone?

Tears spent, I leaned over the deck railing nauseated, flinging the scotch bottle onto the shrubs below. Closing my eyes I fingered my wedding ring.

Sad, I thought about my parents. My dad was from a line of fatherless boys, and I myself had become fatherless before the age of twenty-one. And given the growing fear in my heart, so might my children.

Hearing the bark of a distant coyote, I stuck my hands deep into Ken's jacket, and looked up at the harsh white stars.

I thought back to the camping trips of my childhood, the almost mythical way my father had seemed to slip into the skin of another person, an easy, happier person once he was in the wilderness. He had worn solitude like a coat, an unreachable, inner loneliness filled his pockets. A fatherless boy in a grown man's body, at home only under the stars.

If history defines us, then what new lines were Ken and I laying down for our children? What would his illness, my heartbreak, do to them? I thought of Katy, with her need to love all wounded things well, and David, with his quietness, at home under the stars like my dad.

I thought about the significance of loss, in particular my dad's father, Lt. Colonel Harland Francis Burgess. I had grown up on the stories: his dress calvary sword hung on the wall of every house I lived in. Leader and hero of American men interred in Japanese island prison camps, the grandfather I had never met died in the war four years into imprisonment, on the brink of the surrender of the Japanese armada. American aircraft fighters bombed the unmarked transport, sending twelve hundred American prisoners of war to the bottom of the sea. My father was the vulnerable age of nine, just a few years younger than David.

The thought gave me chills.

Another brother of the colonel also perished in the conflict. All officers, all brave, all heroes. Every generation of Burgess had served the military tradition. The colonel had left behind two sons—my father, and his older brother, Geoff. Geoff ducked into a physics lab and stayed there, teaching at a midwestern university his entire adult life, leaving the military tradition to my father. And what enormous shoes my father had tried to fill.

Becoming fatherless was in itself a kind of destiny, I realized.

My dad commissioned as an officer in the U.S. Air Force after college. In the years that followed, perhaps he drank too much because he was so often alone; or perhaps he was just unable to face the expectation of greatness, the length of his own father's shadow. Perhaps his own failure to achieve became too much to bear. Ironically, it was probably my father's inability to live up to a greatness that would justify the enormity of my mother's sacrifice that created the harsh, sarcastic silences of their marriage.

Had Dad always had so little to say? Did he contemplate what he couldn't change about himself in the same way Ken could not speak of cancer to his kids? Does love ultimately leave us with the impossible on the tip of our tongue?

˙ The final truth was that my parents' divorce left my mother fending for herself, and cancer might do the same for me. My world was breaking apart. I had come full circle, just like my mother.

I wiped my face, standing up straight. On the day she banked her first paycheck, I recognized in the steely glint of my mother's eyes that work was an achievement, a declaration of independence, and that she was taking back control. For a Phi Beta Kappa college grad forty years of age, minimum wage on the night shift at a nursing home was a tough landing. We were strong women. I had it in me to survive.

The single, plaintive note of a barn owl echoed the length of the long valley.

Lights of Dallas

Our intake meeting at the hospital's Oncology Lung Clinic was set for December 22 at 8:00 a.m. sharp, two days before our surgical slot. Ken would meet with his oncologist, his radiologist for possible postoperative radiation treatments, and go over all the test results to date. The team was assembled, the ball in play.

Ken wore his dark turtleneck and soft corduroy slacks. He appeared stark, handsome, arresting. I parked underground at the hospital, near the elevators marked for radiation patients, hanging the special parking permit the nurse had given us over the rearview mirror. For an instant the sign hung there between Ken and me. Quiet, we followed the long septic green halls to Oncology Radiology.

Nice waiting room, big TV blaring out the prizes from *The Price Is Right,* free coffee, happy nurse with a raspy voice and loud laugh, one small old woman bowed over in a wheelchair left parked in the aisle. Her soft white hair pillowed on her hospital gown. She was snoring.

Ken walked briskly up to the counter and identified himself as if he were making a business call. The nurse with the big yellow teeth quit cracking her gum for a second and directed us to a small exam room off to one side. A moment later a tall, slightly stooped man slipped in, extending his hand in welcome. "Hear you might not even need me, but thought I should introduce myself. Solomon Dauer, Radiologist."

The meeting was swift and preliminary. Dauer needed to screen Ken and take measurements of his body tomography. The staff would then fabricate metal molds to channel the high-density laser beams precisely to the site of his tumor. Dauer led us to a secondary waiting room, sandwiched between two small changing rooms.

In this room two women in wheel chairs, their skeletal arms folded quietly across their chests, chatted quietly. I counted a handful of weathered, toothpick-chewing farmers seated in a row of chairs—men who drove the hundred or so miles into town for their weekly treatments. Brain tumor, one of them offered, field spraying. And you?

Ken and I sat down, offering faint hellos, and then lapsed into silence. The other patients chatted amiably about their tumors, how many weeks they had left under the radiation gun. Nervous, I picked up a tattered *Newsweek*, and then threw it down. 1997. The travel and cooking magazines on the table dated from 1983.

I glanced at the wall of brochures. *Pain and Cancer, What to Eat When You Have Cancer, Breast Cancer and You, Sex and Cancer Surgery, Scars and Surgery, Lung Cancer, Prostate Cancer, Cancer of the Bone, Brain Tumors, Radiation and Your Skin, Living with Final Stage Cancer, a Guide to Meaningful Moments.*

Bela Lugosi's reading room.

Determined not to be intimidated, I took one of each.

Filling a Styrofoam cup with black coffee at the courtesy pot, I sat back down next to Ken, absorbing the comforting warmth through my hands. "Let's run away," I whispered.

His lips smiled back, but not his eyes.

Minutes later a technician appeared in the room and Ken was led to an inner fortified chamber, a heavy metal capsule flanked on either side by banks of computers. Pretending to nurse my coffee, I peeked into the inner chamber, observing an enormous laser gun mounted on a rotating counterweight, the naval-ship-sized gun aimed at a floating slab it appeared patients lay on as the laser rotated around them.

Ken stretched out, shirtless, on the slab, and four opposing laser pointers defined a grid across his chest and throat, up through his sternum, and down his spine. The data fed back into the computers, and the tech assistant outside the room completed measurements of all angles of Ken's body, the computer screen building a hologram of Ken's upper torso.

Twenty minutes later, Ken returned, tucking in his turtleneck, and a nurse ushered us into yet another small cubicle. The door edged open and Dr. Daniel Drayneau walked in, the team commando, the chief oncologist.

My initial impression was that one good puff would blow the man away.

Drayneau greeted us quietly and took a seat on the edge of the examining table, pinching together the pleat of his slacks, adjusting them neatly as he crossed his legs. Nice burgundy loafers, good wool slacks, sandy hair, and light-rimmed glasses. Midwest school, I guessed. Long articulated fingers, a barely-there voice.

"First the good news, Ken."

Drayneau pulled his stethoscope loose around his neck and I couldn't help but think of Drano—of clogged pipes and caustic chemicals. Great moniker for an oncologist. We seemed to attract them, I thought. The urologist named Dr. Butler, our dentist, Dr. Payne. I wanted Dr. Feel Good.

I forced myself to pay attention, floating somewhere above the wall of brochures, looking for cracks in the ceiling, ways to slip out like a wisp of smoke.

The oncologist consulted his chart. "The CT scan of your abd/pelvic area is clear. No sign of disease, particularly in the pancreas as the pathology originally suggested. And the blood marker tests for pancreatic cancer and the other blood series are also clear. You do have one generic cancer marker in your blood—which I am guessing is from the lung tumor itself."

The oncologist smiled with a practiced, gentlemanly irony. His eyes were candid. He was clearly a scientific sort, unafraid of bad news. We would get truth when we asked for it.

Drayneau uncrossed his legs and smoothed down the pants crease. "However, there are three spots on the last bone scan that still remain unexplained, Ken." Drayneau studied his clipboard. "One on the left rib, and two on the skull." He pursed his lips. "I'd like to schedule a second MRI this afternoon to explore these further."

Reflexively Ken fingered his ribs. "I'm willing to bet the rib spot is from karate—I broke my rib. And the two on my skull are probably leftover scars from a bad bicycle accident I had twenty years ago. A car hit me and I woke up in the ER."

The oncologist blinked, surprised. "Could be. But I need to make absolutely sure they're not cancer."

I observed the nuances of Drayneau's body language, the

comments held to a minimum, his careful notes, printed neatly on the file margins. The doctor never once touched his carefully styled hair.

"And after the MRI, we'll squeeze you in immediately for a PET scan."

Ken sighed. "So the surgery date tomorrow is a maybe? Depending on the MRI and this PET exam? What's that, exactly—a PET?"

"Another nuclear medicine test, like the bone scan. A relatively new procedure, but I've found it useful. Not all surgeons embrace PET results, though, and I should warn you, not all insurances will cover it." Drayneau looked inquiringly at Ken, who, after a quick glance at me, nodded the go-ahead.

Drayneau explained the test succinctly.

"A nuclear contrast injected into your veins pools in those areas of high metabolic activity throughout your body. The theory behind the science is that cancer cells are active at higher rates of metabolic growth than normal cells, so pockets of cancer activity will measure on the scan as 'bright lights.' This test identifies cancer we can't otherwise detect through exploratory surgery, or MRI."

"In other words, I might light up like a night sky in Dallas?" Ken deadpanned.

I sat there mute, distracted, calculating the financials. Our insurance, as independent self-employed citizens, was basically "catastrophic coverage." After major deductibles of several thousand dollars were tallied, partial coverage kicked in until we reached out-of-pocket expenses that would amount to truly big dollars. At that point our medical coverage would shift into "full coverage"—with the exception of pharmacy and certain hospital supply costs.

Imagine yourself stumbling into a tea kiosk at Mount Everest base camp: helpful, if you get that far. The assignment of a case administrator by the insurance company fairly well defined "catastrophic": We were in deep enough to need an official shovel.

"A clear PET scan would indeed suggest your cancer is less advanced than was first assessed, Ken." Drayneau perked up. "Perhaps Stage II, with only local spread to nearby lymph. I would consider that a desirable surgical situation. I'll request immediate reads on these scans. Let's keep that operating team on schedule."

"And if things come back otherwise, I'm toast?"

The doctor permitted himself his first real, pinched smile. He adjusted his rimless glasses squarely across his nose. "At this point I'm accepting your cancer as lung. What you see is what you've got, to paraphrase the clinic radiologist. Given your general excellent health," he nodded approvingly at Ken, "I still hope to remove your tumor surgically—the main reason I had you complete the necessary pulmonary studies.

"In fact," Drayneau scribbled a note to himself, "I'll have Patsy make you a pre-op appointment with Harley Denton late today, so we can definitely hold on to that operating slot on the twenty-fourth. Denton is the most thorough cardiothoracic guy in town when it comes to lung cancer. You want a specialist for this, not a general surgeon."

*   *   *

Two hours later, waiting over coffee and lumpy broccoli-cheese soup in the hospital cafeteria, I rang Drayneau's office on my cell phone and asked after Ken's MRI results.

Patsy, Drayneau's oncology nurse, promptly answered. "Doctor's out, but maybe Radiology sent something up. Lemme check."

She raced back to the phone. "All clear! Ain't nothin' in his noggin' that shouldn't be there!"

Thrilled, I shared the news with Ken.

He grunted, his head gripped in his hands, battling a fierce headache that had set in after the brain scan. Abruptly, he doubled over in a sudden coughing spell, twisted to his side, and coughed so hard the spasms triggered a bloody nose.

He looked up at me, hands full of bright red blood, holding the bridge of his nose in disbelief. "Well!" And then he swore. Even, calm, precise invectives.

There was nothing else to say, so I hugged him and ran to the cashier for paper towels.

A sandy-haired woman in her early fifties in a physician's jacket walked by as we were mopping up, and seeing us, stopped.

"Glenda? Ken? What are you two doing here?" She smiled, curious.

"Hello, Rachel." I recognized her from school parent meetings. "We come for the food, don't you? Killer Jello." The joke fell flat. I shrugged. "Ken's having some diagnostics done. A PET scan."

"A PET? That's pretty serious."

I looked down at the floor, and Ken squeezed my arm gently. He explained his diagnosis to Rachel, and even though we did not know the woman well, we both assumed a broad doctor-patient confidentiality. After all, we were in the hospital, the woman was a doctor.

We were wrong. The next day news of Ken's cancer was all over the children's school as the physician's daughter whispered to her friends behind Katy's back. The news quickly spread down the grades until even David's sixth-grade friends, no more interested in gossip than grammer exercises, knew the Grunzweig kid's dad was "sick." That encounter marked the beginning of a painful public exposure for the children, for all of us.

After a four-hour wait, Ken was ushered through the underground corridors of the hospital into a semitrailer—the mobile PET unit. I waited in reception, my only company an unconscious elderly man on a gurney. I occupied the time considering the science of nuclear imaging, the use of chemical markers and radiation maps at the level of our cells. How like the darkroom image, the reversals of light and dark.

What if, as Dad had always described the galaxy to me, our cells were also bits of chaos and engineering, roped together by some impossible scheme of order? Could just one cell, one falling star, really bring the whole circus act crashing down?

Ken had pinned a cryptic note above his darkroom sink.

Where am I? It is time to stop waiting to do things. Now is the only time. I think this is what they call self-actualization, because actually, if you don't do it now, you may be too old to ever do it.

There was a story in Ken's family, which he hotly denied, that his earliest photography "lab" in the family attic set the roof on fire and nearly cost the family everything they owned. Relentless, my husband's fascination with the black and white image. And now, a black and white image of far greater mystery would reveal the essential secrets of his innermost being; pinpoint light on black. Falling stars hunted against a plane of pure cellular night.

On the oncologist's recommendation, Ken had recently been to see a cancer therapist, to put, as the therapist said, "his game face on."

At their first meeting in her office, the therapist had suggested to Ken that cancer was a disease of shame and guilt.

Talk to someone who has cancer, she said, and you will find a heart full of something unresolved: deep shame, or perhaps blind guilt, a regret held too long in the body. Something we believed should never have been said, a tragedy that should not have happened, shame that cannot be talked about, the hidden failure, the crimes real and imaginary, buried in the tissues of our body.

"Ken," she had asked gently, "what is held in the exact field of this tumor in your chest?"

"And you believe this?" I had demanded of him.

"No. I refuse to give *anything* that much power over my body."

Yet following that meeting, a new inward thoughtfulness had appeared in Ken. There was a quiet, leveling look in his eyes.

At half past four, Ken came out of the PET chambers, pale and shaky. "For an entire hour—not allowed so much as a shiver, not a sneeze, God forbid a cough!"

"Thought you might be hungry." I handed Ken a fruit smoothie.

"I prayed while I was lying there," Ken confessed as we walked slowly to the parking garage.

I glanced sideways, startled. Ken did not pray. It was not that he didn't believe in God; but a Jew with a moral code and no temple, he did not pray, he took action.

"What did you pray?"

"That there would be no light. I focused on smooth dark emptiness. *No cancer.*"

I fell silent. If Ken had begun to pray, I knew that every bit of him was in the game. He was going to God with his hat in his hand.

Private Knowledge

At the end of what had become a very long day, we took Ken's medical files to the Heart Institute.

The surgeon was a sleek blue fish, a tuna in an expensive suit. A fast-talking New Yorker with a mop of black hair and unexpectedly stubby fingers. The hands of a boxer.

Harley Denton laid out Ken's PET exam results—punching them vigorously. "All clear, buddy. Only bright spots are those we expected, those swollen lymph nodes here in the sternum area, the mediastinum. Ready to get that fucker out?"

The last hurdle had been cleared. Ken would go under the knife.

Denton laid out the procedure. Ken would be given an EKG, shaved from his navel to his chin. The OR team would lay him on his side, take him five levels under, and then strap his right arm tight above his head to expose his right ribcage. They would then saw open a cleavage midway between his ribs and insert a spring-load device to hold the ribs apart, or perhaps, they would have to break or remove one if they refused to yield. Ribs open, the surgeon would delicately pry aside Ken's nestled organs and lift the lung, removing only the affected midlobe. Wedged between its larger brothers, the upper and lower lobes, the midlobe was about the size of a small fillet.

Snip, snip, solder and seal. The surgeon would then clip one end of a chest wall muscle and stretch the muscle around to close off the removed lung's bronchial stump, a procedure performed dangerously close to the heart. Before wrapping up, the team would scrape out any and all tissue that appeared diseased or damaged.

"Sounds fun. What's recovery look like?"

"We place two one-inch diameter hoses in your chest wall, Ken, and feed them out of your body through an incision in the side." Denton seemed to relish the macabre details. "The hoses are attached to a negative pressure pump hung off your gurney to drain the blood and fluids from the lung. You keep that rig about four days, and then we yank it."

I blanched.

"Your tumor, meanwhile, heads off to pathology—they like to look at those buggers, they're sickos down there in pathology—and you leave here with a souvenir scar from your back shoulder blade to the center of your chest." Denton tapped against his own solid ribs. "Any questions?"

"Just get it out."

"That's the plan. Unless," Denton pivoted back around, eyeballing Ken as he adjusted a cufflink. "Unless we find cancer in the mediastinum we don't already know about. If that happens, we shut down, send you home, and you go through neoadjuvant therapy—chemo and radiation first. Why? Better statistical results."

"We'd prefer to take out the tumor now," I affirmed.

Duh, was the look Denton gave me.

We took the hospital paperwork and drove up the icy streets of the South Hill toward home. High on the crest of Grand Avenue, the stone of St. John's Cathedral glowed in the after light of a winter sunset, the bell tower spires a splash of orchid against the sky, a great ship of faith riding the bluff.

"Do you like them?" I asked quietly as I guided the car through traffic. "These doctors? Do you believe they can make this right?"

"Of course, G. I wouldn't trust just anyone to crack open my hood." Ken straightened in his seat and grinned tiredly, buoyed by the immediacy of action at last. "These docs see themselves in me. I'm sure they'll do their level best."

Ken said he was confident in Drayneau, absolutely at ease with his technical, carefully parsed demeanor. And the next player, the surgeon, had whisked us through discussions of chest saws and tubation as if he were cracking open snail shells. If confidence was competence, this surgeon was the Anthony Bourdain of the OR. Oh Father of Surgery, let us get a word in edgewise.

"What about a trip to a national cancer center? You know, like M. D. Andersen in Texas? Would that be a better choice?"

"This shit will be hard enough without living out of a motel," Ken said bluntly. "The technology is disseminated everywhere. Let's stay home."

After making love, we fell asleep, Ken's cheek on my bottom, my face in the pillows. My hand reached down under the sheets and held his, tightly.

Touch. A simple Braille of the heart.

Making love had always been our way to unearth the hidden. Years of private knowledge tangled within us, our lives rooted and entwined.

From the very beginning there had been something remarkable in our comfort with one another's bodies. That first weekend together, hiding away in Ken's Spokane apartment, Stan Getz had played on the stereo, something sultry and Brazilian, and we had made love all Sunday afternoon; rolling across breadcrumbs and olive oil, and the juice of fresh tomatoes left on the crumpled pages of the *New York Times*. As the hour grew late, Ken had reluctantly left the bed to pack for a business trip. He was due in Los Angeles early the next morning.

I lay stretched out across the comforter, propped up on my elbows, thumbing through Ken's jazz albums, wearing only his cast-off shirt. I looked up from the bed and smiled. Impressively efficient, Ken had taken out an ironing board and iron, a clean wrinkled shirt, and butt-assed naked, was ironing his dress shirt for the next day, humming along with the jazz.

The scene was so completely ludicrous, and charming; this unselfconscious domesticity. The geography of my lover's body so new and unfamiliar to me I let my eyes travel upward over the curve of his calves, and tight, muscular buttocks, lifting to his broad chest and square shoulders. I studied the unruly splay of dark hair fanning across his belly and chest muscles, the clean jaw, and perfect nose so classic in profile.

Tender to me, the vulnerabilities of the flesh.

We knew the precise moment we conceived our children, and spoke of that knowing in wonder. Only apart could we remain angry—were we to touch each other in a fight, the fury would fall away. Consolations, complications, consecrations. The brilliance of the beloved's touch.

Could love save us now?

Nice Shoes

One day to go.

I loaded the kids' duffle bags and presents for their cousins into the trunk of the Volvo. Ken stood in the doorway between the garage and the kitchen, his face pensive. Out in the front yard, David threw a snowball across the drive, pinging a snowcap off the street lantern. It tumbled to the ground in a little avalanche of powder.

"How're you feeling, Dad? You okay?" David called out.

Ken smiled. "I'm feeling fine, David. Don't worry."

Katy came out of the kitchen from behind Ken and wrapped her arms around his middle. They stood like that for several moments, and then Ken bent down and kissed the top of her head.

"Have fun at your cousins," he said. "We'll call on Christmas."

"Get well, Daddy," Katy whispered. "I'll miss you."

I drove the kids three hours, halfway across the state, to

meet Tim in the small town of Vantage on the Columbia River.

Braced against the stiff winds of the gorge, I hugged my brother hard and handed the kids and their gear over, smiling brightly into their anxious unsettled faces. After a flurry of hugs, they jumped into Tim's car, waving good-bye.

Tim detained me, a gentle hand on my arm.

"Are you going to tell Mom soon about Ken?"

I shook my head. "No. And I'd appreciate it if no one else did either—at least for now. I think knowing about Ken's illness would scare her more than her own does, and she's still not dealing with that."

I headed back to Spokane, suddenly lonely and more afraid than I wanted to admit of the uncertainty that lay ahead. I would need to go almost immediately to the airport. Jordan and her new husband, Kurt, the boyfriend who had seen her through rehab, would arrive that afternoon, Abby as well. All of them were planning to be present for the surgery tomorrow and stay a few days post-op, visiting.

We'd had such a fight, Ken and I, about Abby coming to Spokane. I had argued desperately that I needed these few days to be private, needed to clear the decks of all distractions to get us through what by all accounts was a difficult surgery.

But Abby had asked and Ken had said yes. Ken then invited Jordan too.

"Jordan's just discovered she's pregnant," Ken said, beaming. "I'm going to be a grandfather! This could be good, you know, for all of us."

I could tell that he hoped his daughter's becoming a mother herself might bring all of us together. I couldn't help but think of it as one problem now multiplied.

Jordan came off the plane first, on the arm of her husband, a stocky, sandy-haired young man with John Lennon glasses he thought were übercool, but gave him the slightly musty look of a librarian. In pregnancy, Jordan had grown into the full beauty of her mother's exotic looks—her wide half-moon cheeks rosy with good health. Eyes bright as polished shale, she peppered me with questions about Ken as we waited for Abby.

Her flight soon followed Kurt and Jordan's. She strode off the plane from Los Angeles in tight, silver-buckled jeans and tinkling hoop earrings, the accessories of her newly adopted "Western" style. I was not surprised, as her second husband was all things country. But, to me, on such a petite sophisticated Jewish woman, this was startling. I automatically hugged Abby, who stood half my height, and was immediately suffused in layers of stale cigarette smoke and expensive perfume.

After a cheerful dinner and much catching-up, Kurt and Jordan retired early to bed. I cleared the coffee cups, troubled, glancing away from Ken and Abby on the couch. Stacking the mugs in the dishwasher, I turned the machine on, comforted by its immediate roar, the efficient racket of water and suds churning through the scrub cycle. Why had Abby let Ken get up all evening to refresh her coffee? Did she not see how fatigued he was as she jabbered on (between cigarette trips to the porch) about her recent trip to Arizona and the goings on of the older brother we never heard from?

Three houseguests: completely dependent on me for transportation, and utterly unfamiliar with the town and its surroundings. And there was Jordan's new and surprising pregnancy to consider. Was she still sober, still ricocheting between bulimia and her endless hours at the gym on the Stair-Master, still cruising on Prozac?

At half past eleven, Ken finally sent Abby off to Katy's room, her borrowed guest room. Happy, he shut the bedroom door behind us and climbed into bed, dragging himself up against a stack of pillows to breathe easier.

I crawled over him and sat gently across his hips, gathering his hands in mine.

"I love you."

Ken gave me that little, crooked smile. "Don't worry, babe, it'll be okay."

"I know."

I unbuttoned his pajama top and dropped light kisses across his chest.

Ken sighed. A soft sound full of regret, and what I imagined he hoped he could hang on to—this, us, his life.

*   *   *

Christmas Eve morning the winds scoured the valley below our house and rattled the frozen reeds along the edge of Latah Creek. The reeds made a faint, clear cracking sound as they broke in two and fell to the ice.

As Ken was body-shaved at the hospital, a thirty-minute personal history was taken online by a second nurse typing into a portable monitor. Off to one side, a thin, slightly unsteady gentleman in his late sixties approached Ken and began to bag Ken's clothes and personal affects, taking inventory. He had a kind face, deep patience dug into every wrinkle of his yellowed skin.

Clearing his throat, he asked why Ken was having a thoracotomy, and when Ken answered, he sighed. "I've been living with cancer seven years now. You just gotta take it a day at a time. Good luck to you now. Shame, this being Christmas Eve and all."

By 9:30 a.m. Ken was on the gurney and headed up to the fourth-floor surgery, the cardio wing.

"I should get a driver's license for these things," he cracked.

"You've been on a few," I acknowledged with a smile.

I followed behind the orderly wheeling Ken along until I bumped into the guy—he had abruptly stopped at a set of swinging double doors.

"Here's where we leave you. You can wait in there." The orderly pointed down the hall to a waiting room for the families of open-heart patients, an airless lounge tucked off in a "kiss and cry" corner of the hospital, conveniently adjacent to the office of the chaplain.

"But—"

"Don't worry, he's just going into anesthesia prep. You'll get to see him again before surgery."

Ken squeezed my hand and I kissed his forehead. His eyes said, *Don't leave me,* but he joked, "So this is where I take the express elevator down?"

The orderly missed the joke, but I chuckled. "Your drugs have *got* to be better than the coffee in that room."

The glass doors swung shut behind them as the orderly pushed Ken through. Beyond, I observed operating room personnel in scrubs assembling carts and equipment. A fresh-faced balding man, dressed in a button-down shirt, edged around me, as if I had become invisible. He palmed open the double doors and disappeared.

Must be the anesthesia guy. And I don't even know who he is.

Two hours later Abby arrived at the patient lounge in the company of Jordan and Kurt. Toting cell phones and paperbacks, the three were prepared to wait things out, and sat chatting idly with a family of four from Chewelah still waiting to hear how Grandmother's heart valve repair had gone.

A telephone in the tiny room rang shrilly, and several of

us jumped. All heads swung around to face the black phone jangling on the empty courtesy desk.

I reached over and grabbed it. "Hello?"

It was an OR nurse. "Mrs. Grunzweig? You can come in now and see your husband. He's prepped for surgery."

From inside the double doors a nurse pushed a release button and ushered me in. Across the white-tiled room Ken was lying draped in green, his head in a shower cap, IVs strung up from both arms, and a contained, intense look on his face.

Reaching his side, I leaned over and pressed my cheek to his. "How are you?" I willed my warmth through his chilled skin.

"Okay!" He threw a friendly, woozy glance at the nurse. "This is Darlene, she's heading in with me."

I smiled up at the nurse. "Take exquisite care of this man, Darlene. He means the world to me."

"Don't you know it, honey. We can tell he's a charmer." Darlene cracked a big smile and another OR nurse joined in the laughter. "Now let's share a last little smooch and get this show on the road, shall we?"

Ken snatched at my hand, his plastic ID bracelet cutting into my skin.

"Glenda," he said, his eyes and tone urgent, his voice a bare whisper, "I want you to know this—no matter what, I'll wait for you. Do you understand me? *I'll wait for you.*"

I hid a surge of tears, kissing him again. How the hell did he know to say these things? We had exchanged vows on earth, but now he was giving me the afterlife too? Telling me, and himself, it would never be over, ever? Now, I was frightened.

Darlene gently pushed me out the door.

The waiting seemed interminable. Jordan and Abby

passed the time chatting on the phone with Abby's boys, Jordan's grown cousins in Los Angeles and New York. Kurt paged through a four-year-old *Sports Illustrated,* cover to cover. I paced, and then sat. Finally I left the crowded waiting room, preferring to walk alone the length of the long halls, pausing at the glass overlook of the westernmost mountains of Montana, softened by snow.

I fell to thinking about the others in the waiting room, Ken's family. Each of us had our stories, our unplanned anthologies, different pasts bound together in one skin. To deny one story would deny another part of the self. As the *next wife*, shouldn't I know this? Accommodate the necessary layering of our lives with as much grace as I could muster? I had recently come to the conclusion that all we can do is row the boat we're in. Greet each day with the best of intentions—it's not given to us to set the compass, chart the stars, or make life work for everyone we love. We aren't given that power or control. We are only given the grace of intention.

Quiet, I took Abby a cup of black coffee and squeezed her shoulder encouragingly.

Hours later the chaplain poked his head in and asked the assemblage of strangers if anyone wished or needed to talk with him. An uncomfortable silence fell around the coffee pot. The wispy guy with his receding hairline and stringy ponytail, toting his Bible under his arm, did not look like a miracle bringer to any of us just then.

The phone rang again. "Mrs. Grunzweig?" the nurse asked. "The doctor would like to speak with you."

I bolted out of the waiting room, followed by Kurt, Abby, and Jordan. Denton came out of the OR in his scrubs along with his assisting surgeon, a younger, timid doctor I had never met. Denton motioned us into the hallway.

Suddenly, I felt within me the vibration of danger.

Denton spoke, stripped down and direct in his manner. "I regret to tell you, Mrs. Grunzweig, but there is cancer in one of the three lymph nodes I just biopsied from your husband's mediastinum." He paused for emphasis. "No point opening your husband up if the cancer has spread from the lung to the middle of his chest."

Denton paused, shook his head, pulled off his surgical cap.

"Head of Pathology—guy's a true no-bullshit scope jockey—walked down and gave me the assessment firsthand."

"More cancer?" I blinked. "How much cancer did you find?"

"Small bit in the node nearest the tumor, but—and here we have a problem, Mrs. Grunzweig—it is *not* a lung cancer cell Pathology believes they're looking at. Not at all."

What—another questionable pathology?

"What do they think it is this time?"

"An aggressive signet cell—typically a cell found in abdominal cancer."

"You're saying they suspect a different primary? Again?"

Denton shrugged. "No sense removing a man's lung if the tumor is a bigger part of something else. Wouldn't do him much good, know what I mean?"

The assistant surgeon, who had nervously been watching the exchange between Denton and me, nodded in silent agreement. I sensed, no, I *knew*, there was more they were not telling me.

Poor fuck hovered unspoken in the air.

Rapidly I absorbed what Denton had said. We would have to wait for the official pathology report and then a reassessment of all the diagnostics to date, and possibly, face a stomach wall biopsy to determine what other, possible cancers, this might be. Worse case, we might be confronting an advanced cancer whose only visible sign is this tumor in Ken's lung.

Denton looked down at my feet. "Nice shoes."

Bewildered, I glanced down at my feet and then back at the surgeon. *What? What had he just said?*

"Don't worry. I'll let Ken know how things stand when he comes to in recovery." Denton offered a tight smile. "Merry Christmas."

He clasped my hand in both of his in a cheery, burly dismissal, and returned to the OR, his assistant trailing behind him.

Kurt, Jordan, and Abby turned to me in confusion. They hadn't the faintest idea what all this meant, and they waited for me to lay Denton's findings out in words they understood. I found myself protecting them, as Ken would.

"Change of plan," I said quietly, and outlined what neoadjuvant treatment involved and the reasons for presurgery chemotherapy. "Unless, as they fear, this lung cancer is actually from somewhere else."

"And if it is?" Abby asked, her pixie face gone pale.

"Well then, at least Ken didn't go through a thoracotomy for nothing."

Merry Christmas. Nice shoes.

What You Have Not

New Year's Day we gathered at Judy's in Moses Lake, Ken chugging his liter of cleansing solution to prepare for a full upper/lower gastrointestinal endoscopy scheduled for the following day. He was to be scanned by an expert, a cancer specialist instructed not to give him a routine "once over," but to examine inch by inch every dark corner of his being for cancer.

Abby and Jordan and Kurt had flown home, chastened and awkward. They had hoped to cheer on a successful surgery, but instead, the situation had taken a shadowy step toward a worsening prognosis.

A noisy New Year's crowd caroused at my sister's. There was something disheartening in the gathering of overweight men and their fishing stories, the gut-splitting buffet, and this secret, growing cancer.

I found Ken in a back room, watching the television with the kids and Judy's youngest, Mitzy, age six. Mitzy was galloping a plastic horse down the length of one of Ken's shins. He looked up as I stood behind the sofa and stroked his shoulder.

"Need anything to drink?" I joked.

Ken held up his half-empty milk bottle of solution. "Just fine, ma'am, thanks."

"What's on?"

"Geckos," David answered absently, his eyes fixed on the flickering wide-screen television.

"Did you know," Ken added with an odd spunk, "that with future advances in global data search engines, a click on the word *gecko* will not only get you a picture of the green guy, but his global habitat, zoology facts, stories of anthroiconology, gecko sounds, and songs about geckos—data in as many layers and in as many dimensions as you can't imagine?"

"Unreal."

"Yeah. And the more layered and unreal the world grows, the more we're going to crave actual reality. That kid on the television will want not the encyclopedic info-bomb, but just a damn gecko he can keep in a two-buck yard-sale aquarium."

I bent over and kissed the back of his head. "Here. That's real."

* * *

A nurse poked her head out. "Mrs. Grunzweig?"

I jumped to my feet and followed the young woman to a curtained outpatient bay.

Ken was sitting up, a teary grin on his face. "I'm clear, baby. All clear!"

I burst into embarrassing hiccups, hugged the surprised nurse, and kissed Ken all over his face. "Oh, thank God! Thank you, thank you, God."

The gastroenterologist came in and confirmed the good

news. He showed us slides of Ken's colon, his stomach walls—more beautiful pink tissue. No sign whatsoever of stomach or colon cancer.

Ken and I grasped hands, in what I can only describe as a celebration of genuine grace.

Late the next day we took down the outdoor Christmas lights. Ken stood bundled in his heavy jacket, holding the strings of lights as I detangled them from the tree branches.

"It's such a relief to begin something, anything, to fight this thing," he murmured. Tomorrow he had his first appointment in Radiology to begin radiation treatments, and an hour later, in Oncology to begin an initial round of two sessions of six-week chemo treatments.

The chemicals they would be putting into Ken's body were daunting: one week of carboplatin combined with Taxol, followed by two of Taxol alone, a repeat of the three, and then a week off if his white blood cell count plummeted too low. A repeat session followed of the six-week combo; all the chemo treatments in concert with five-day weekly radiation to the tumor area and to the center of Ken's chest and throat, the mediastinum lymph nodes.

Ken stamped his feet in the snow, and wiped his nose with a Kleenex—it dripped all the time now. His expression was closed, anxious.

"Do you think we should go for a second opinion before beginning all this?" he asked.

I looked down from the prickly branches, balancing on the ladder as I climbed down. How many times had I asked myself that same thing?

"I don't know. I just don't know."

Folding up the ladder, I hefted the decorations box and headed for the garage, Ken following. I took off my gloves, unzipped my jacket, and hung his things up with mine. "The diagnostics are done. I'm confident they're thorough, aren't you?"

"Oh, God yes."

"So, do we believe we have the best medical expertise advising us? I think so. That's what everyone is telling me—this is a medical community with cutting-edge technology and well-trained docs."

I was rambling aloud, but that was what we needed to do, run out our options. The option we both believed in, immediate surgery, was gone to us forever: We had to make good with what we had—radiation, chemotherapy. I vividly recalled Denton throwing the *New England Journal of Medicine* across his desk at me: proof, he said, of the statistical evidence favoring neoadjuvant therapy.

Ken made us tea, and we sat down at the kitchen table, watching as dusk gathered in the trees, listening to the kids playing an action movie downstairs.

He pulled out his pocket notebook and consulted his last entry. "Here's what the surgeon said on the telephone yesterday—"

"Harley Denton called you?"

"Yes. He said he had reviewed the clear IG series and had assembled a list of 'reasons to dismiss the conflicting pathology' and go with a diagnosis of lung tumor."

"So what are these reasons?" I was beyond irritated with the inability of the medical establishment to call a bean a bean. Time was cancer and plenty was passing.

"Reason one, the clinical presentation of the tumor."

"Brilliant."

Ken smiled. "Two, there are no other clinical symptoms of abdominal or pancreatic cancer. He cited the three clear CTs and MRIs, the bone scan, the brain MRI, the clear PET scan, the negative CA19 blood test which is eighty-five percent accurate for identifying pancreatic cancer, and the GI series looking specifically for abdominal, colon, and pancreatic cancer. All clear. Denton concurs one hundred percent with the oncologist and radiologist's combined plan of treatment."

"They conferred?"

"Apparently. And spoke directly with the GI guy."

"A team approach, solid analysis, and four heads talking the same plan. . . ."

"So, go?" Ken waited.

I hesitated. "It's your call, honey," I offered softly. "You have to do this. It's your call."

Ken twisted to face the window, his features chiseled in the falling light, his somber gaze resting on the distant ridge. "Well," he said after a moment, "I think the sooner we jump on this thing the better."

He turned back and smiled. "You have to like a guy who says, 'In my mind you're salvageable, Ken. We're gonna fucking cure you!' "

"Denton said that?" I burst out laughing.

* * *

Two days later Ken gripped my elbow as we walked into the oncology clinic. "However I feel after this," he whispered confidently, "at least we know it's on the way to cure."

I suppose I had been expecting chemotherapy and the "infusion suite," as they called it, to be a weird kind of science lab: the chemist, IVs and rubber gloves, hushed assistants. But we were ushered into a room with eight armchair recliners, each with a rig of IV stands, pillow and blanket, cable TV suspended centrally from the ceiling. A fish tank occupied the center next to a jar of lemon drops, one sealed lab door marking the room where the toxic chemicals were mixed. Patients snoozed, or chatted with the nurses, sunlight pouring in through the slatted blinds. An old man rubbed his wife's feet.

I glanced discreetly at the other patients. There were three middle-aged women receiving chemo through surgical ports in their upper chests. A woman in a Pucci head scarf frowned ferociously at us as we walked in. The anger in her gaze seemed both directed and diffused, as if she were too angry at too much to even be aware of the magnitude of her emotion. Her gaze lingered on me, and my face felt burnt, like scorched earth.

One of the women was quietly reading a mystery, her hand fiddling with a curl of her red wig tilted down over one ear. A third, her pink scalp glinting like a pearl under the lights and wearing large gold hoops in her ears, chatted with her husband, a burly man in greasy overalls bouncing their toddler on his lap. Near the back of the room, a man in his seventies in a hospital gown, fully reclined and nearly comatose, lay surrounded by whispering relatives.

At each station the IVs were systematically hooked, drained, and changed, rubber gloves whipped on and off, and warm water bags applied to fatten reluctant veins. The nurses followed a fixed routine—first administer the antiemetics to block nausea, then the strong antihistamine blockers to mitigate any allergic reactions. Finally, those priceless bags of chemical hope, fed slowly into lax, bruising arms. The nurses made the rounds, tucking blankets around several sleeping patients already dozing under the sedative effect of the antihistamines.

The atmosphere was hushed and intense, yet profoundly and tenderly humane. The smiles and the concern from the staff were real, I sensed. I knew, as Ken took a chair to begin his first six-week cycle, that soon, we too would be known here by our first names. Silently I hoped that whatever robust strength Ken walked in with would not deteriorate over the upcoming weeks of treatment into the wheelchair fragility of so many of those we observed.

Ken asked the nurse her first name. *Pat.*

I gave him his headphones and his book. As the first course of IV drips began, his eyelids sank closed, telltale shadows of exhaustion in the orbital hollows.

I held his hand, watching him nap for the two hours of the combined drip. I had plenty of time to drink coffee, ask questions, and comprehend the subtleties of what was not being said in the chemo suite. This was front-line care, medical triage in the fight against cellular disintegration, a lineup of recliners at the precipice. All around me were patients in some part of a cycle: a cycle of beginnings and ends, of treatment, of illness, even chemotherapy as a palliative, a merciful extension of the inevitable, a kindness. Here I finally understood the corrosion of cancer on the human spirit. Cancer was gunning for Ken in this very room.

I began the list of things to do, to be careful of, watch for, purchase at the pharmacy:

Radiation daily, 10 a.m.
Chemo weekly—Mondays at 1:00 p.m., consult with Dr.
. *Drayneau to follow.*
High protein diet, softer digestible foods, bland.
Stool softener, counter the effects of the drugs.
Supplement drinks—massive calories needed!!
One vitamin, no other supplements allowed—might block
effects of chemo.
Prescription aloe skin care for radiation burns.
Throat soothing/coating liquid medicine.
Hiccup and antispasm medications. Thorazine?? Isn't

that what they give in mental hospitals? *Counter effects
of mediastinum radiation.*

Antiemitics.

Sleep aids.

Narcotic pain medication. The inner burn of radiation
begins??

And hope.

Buckets of hope.

Treatment week two. A worse week, as they said they
would all be. The effects were cumulative and algorithmic.
Not just worse, but Richter scale worse. A magnitude 8.5
quake was occurring in Ken's body.

I stood by helplessly as he wrenched over with sudden
vomiting and gasped through spasmodic bouts of shortened
breath. And in the night, the wracking hiccups without end.
The dense fatigue; the raw, deep burning inside both his
throat and chest from radiation.

Thinner. So much thinner; his body smudged away as if
by an eraser.

The errands seemed endless.

I headed out to the organic grocery store, picking up
fresh ingredients for a nutritious quiche. Neither of us particularly liked quiche, but it went down easy.

I put brown eggs in the basket; as well as Swiss cheese,
high-fat whole milk and heavy cream (need the calories!), scal-
lions for the taste buds, and pancetta for a bit of flavor. I fingered the brilliant green leaves of fresh spinach. High in iron,
good as Ken's levels of anemia rose. This too.

I added a good chardonnay to my basket. Although I
knew Ken would not drink any, he still liked a wine glass next
to the plate. I bypassed the tough and chewy sourdough

French bread, Ken's favorite, and chose instead a soft, whole wheat roll, much easier to swallow.

I stood aimlessly in line at the grocery checkout waiting my turn, thinking of the safe, small lives of everyone around me. How normal their routines seemed to be. Bags of Oreos and school notebook paper, six-packs of beer, toilet paper, *People* magazine. I felt as if I had fallen into an internal crevasse far down inside myself.

After dinner, after the quiche was put away, largely uneaten, the kids worked with Ken to complete their science fair projects: Katy's depicted the first Moonwalk, complete with original newspaper clippings unpinned from Mom's house; and David's, a complicated display of the inner electronic workings of a radio. There was something calming and peaceful in the sight of their three heads, bent together over the scissors and glue.

Late that night, Ken and I lay close and whispered for hours.

"You are so important to me, G. I hope you know how much I love you." He rambled on, and I only half-listened as he shared thoughts on how much work and life we had left to fulfill together. My happiness was in the comforting warmth of his voice. Many times I had heard Ken say "I love you," but not spoken as if that very moment he weighed a lifetime of losses without regret—because everything had led to love.

Grace Notes

January inched across the calendar, a cold and miserable month, as northwestern storms laid siege to the valley, the vagaries of wind and ice keeping the temperatures near or below zero.

Each day Ken and I fought to stay focused and optimistic. We worked hard to manage the subtle accumulation of side effects that seemed somehow more difficult to tolerate than the actual treatments. I found it hard to stay positive in the face of the damage that radiation and chemotherapy were doing to Ken's body, and found that anxious moments would arise when I could not squelch the inner voice that had wanted the surgery first, at Christmas. Believing as I did in the principles of mass and acceleration, I felt getting the tumor mass out of Ken's chest was the logical first step to reducing the problem. As long as that much cancer lived in Ken's lung, we were racing ahead of a growing snowball accelerating down the plane of his body.

For lunch Ken and I cooked an omelet together.

Perhaps because he could not eat, the process of cooking enfolded Ken in the sensuousness of food; or perhaps by cooking for the family he felt he could nurture in return those nurturing him. Maybe cooking functioned as a creative outlet in a world where his beloved darkroom and its dangerous chemicals were, for the time being, off limits. Whatever the reasons, Ken delved into cooking.

In mid-January he began taking a cooking class with a local chef, a woman married to a symphony percussionist. A sparkling woman with a generous heart and firecracker hair, Char had followed her dream to train at the California Culinary Academy at San Francisco, returning to the Inland Northwest to open her own catering business and cooking school. The evening Taste & Technique class embraced Ken, understood his situation—the reasons for his fatigue. Once or twice I drove him to class when he was too tired to drive himself. Before leaving, I waited several moments by the door, watchful that the night would go well.

On those nights, Ken would take a seat in the kitchen rocker, exhausted, as the class tackled the rudimentary basics of French cuisine, concocting elegant international desserts. I watched as his eyes lingered on the colors of the food, his hands absorbed in the feel and motions of washing, chopping, stirring, touching the wholesome ingredients—lost in the happy chatter, the upbeat energy of the amateur chefs. Char's kitchen was a place of laughter and vitality: everything brilliant green, tangerine, pepper red, abundant and alive.

Cooking was not about cancer.

Ken and I touched elbows at the stove as we assembled the omelet. I whisked the eggs, Ken chopping spinach as he lightly seared the pancetta. I added heavy cream—just a tablespoon—to my golden swirl as he threw the diced scal-

186

lions into the skillet, flipping them as they sizzled. The odors intensified, delectable.

Ken leaned over and kissed my ear.

"I love you," I bubbled, happy.

"I know."

We took the plates to the bedroom, undressed, and snuggled in bed, eating breakfast at two in the afternoon before the kids came home on the school bus.

After lunch, Ken fell asleep. It would only be a short respite, I knew, before another coughing fit roused him. Worried, I observed the dark discoloration under his eyes, the grimness that had developed in the corners of his mouth, the way his fist clenched the comforter in his sleep. I rubbed his hand gently, freeing his grip, and tucked the blanket up to his chin. I slipped on jeans and a T-shirt, collected our plates, and tiptoed out of the room.

The dogs got the better of Ken's omelet.

* * *

My mother's weeks of retreat from the family seemed to be over. She had agreed to the appointment I made for her to see a new physician, an oncologist specializing in leukemia, and agreed to let me pick her up from the Spokane house and accompany her.

Excited, I called Judy. "Mom's going to see a new doctor today! Maybe something good will come of this. He's a specialist, from an old Spokane family she recognizes, and she seems reassured. Judy, this means she'll be able to stay in treatment with regular trips up from the farm."

"Well, don't get your hopes up. She has to see a doctor, Glenda," Judy replied. I heard her sigh. "Her prescription has expired. That chemo pill she's on is the only reason she's getting around as well as she is. Remember what the doctor here said—when that low-dose chemo becomes ineffective, it's all going to blow up on her."

Though somewhat deflated, I was determined nonetheless to capitalize on the moment. I organized myself, feeling that, thankfully, we were doing something proactive at last. I placed extra boxes of nutrition supplement in the trunk of my car, along with two flats of canned soup, and drove up the hill.

"Hi, dear," Mom said as she answered the door. She looked tired, but had made the effort to wear nice slacks and a sweater set. I stacked the food and supplement boxes in the kitchen.

"Mom, it's absolutely freezing in here." The house was still without a working furnace. She had not repaired the furnace for going on three years now, and would not allow us to do it for her. She hadn't made up her mind yet, she argued— electric baseboard heaters or a new furnace? She had just put on a new roof, and pointed out it would take a while to save up for heat too.

"I get by. It's warm enough in one or two rooms with a fire and heaters." She smiled, revealing the gap in her teeth. "Don't worry so. I'm a tough old bird. A little cold never hurt anybody. I've weathered worse."

I thought of her on the weekends she came up from the farm for supplies. She built scratch fires in the family room fireplace and huddled there with her solitary glass of Drambuie, letting space heaters warm the bedroom. There must be some deeper satisfaction in having learned to "make do, one day at a time." I could only think of how simple the solution was and how willing I was to make it happen.

"Where is this clinic?" Mom suddenly asked, brittle.

I could feel her resisting, looking for excuses.

"Right down the hill, Mom," I said firmly. "A straight shot

in the car you can make on your own, summer or winter—good roads, easy parking."

Saying nothing she climbed in the Volvo and we drove the few miles to the cancer clinic. This was not the clinic Ken was in treatment at, but affiliated with a different hospital I knew that Mom preferred. I chatted lightly, buoyed by a subdued joy she was letting me be of use. But I also felt absolute apprehension I would say or do something to set her off, or the doctor or a nurse would, and she'd bail.

We walked inside the unfamiliar building and Mom recoiled. I could see in her eyes her reaction to the somber lighting of the waiting room and the unmasked vulnerability of several of the elderly patients crumpled forward in their wheelchairs. Her glance skittered past the young women wearing bright head scarves, gray shadows under their eyes as they tended to young children, awaiting their appointments.

I drew her firmly toward a jumbled jigsaw puzzle scattered across a round table off to one side of the waiting room. The puzzle featured a half-assembled mill with a large red water wheel in a green spring forest. We sat down at the puzzle table and I tried to distract her with the thousand possible places any one piece might fit.

Mom set her piece down, clasping her hands as she studied her lap.

"I hate this place, Glenda." Her eyes looked up into mine, glaring fiercely. "This is not where you go to get well."

"Mom, it's a cancer clinic, and cancer is a serious disease. They *can* help people get well here."

Her eyes suddenly glistened and her lower lip trembled. Flecks of dried red lipstick were embedded in her chapped lips.

"It's so much like my childhood and that horrible year in the hospital. I can't do it, Glenda. I can't." Her tone was pleading, the voice of someone at the edge of the abyss. The visceral memory of hospitals, the smell of medicine and astringents, even the rustle of white coats and whispered voices, had gripped my mother by the throat.

Rheumatic fever had struck my mother at age seven. Her treatment, including a near-fatal allergic reaction to penicillin, had been followed by a year of isolation in a silent and shadowy children's hospital. Nearby schoolchildren would run over from recess and press their faces against the window glass to stare at the little girl lying alone in the bed.

Her own brother, Joe, never came to see her.

I could never piece together all the critical elements of that year, other than to understand that that experience had cemented both my grandfather's complete commitment to volunteering for the welfare of sick children and children's hospitals, and rendered my mother absolutely phobic concerning doctors. Released from the hospital, weak and vulnerable, my mother had committed herself to sports and athletics. She would ice skate, swim, golf. Achieve vital, vibrant health at any cost.

I understood. I understood her dread. But I also feared cancer—this disease was bigger than country air and exercise.

"Please, Mom. Just meet the doctor."

"For you," she said, her tone angry and childish. "Only because of you."

I sighed. I knew I had been right not to reveal anything of Ken's diagnosis. I couldn't bring myself to expose Ken to her distrust of the medical community, her caustic skepticism. Mom would simply boss him into joining her at the farm, saying, "Just breathe the fresh air!"

"Louise Burgess?" the receptionist called.

Obedient, Mom followed the nurse to an intake station and took a chair, chatting quietly as the nurse drew blood; so sweet, abruptly thankful. Her anger seemed to have melted into a worn, simple neediness as the nurse kindly asked after her weight, her nutrition.

The new doctor was a tall man with a bland but comforting face, and perfect, manicured nails. I focused on those nails as he asked questions and reviewed Mom's medical files; the three of us folded into a neat but shadowed office, the blinds drawn against the sun. More than once the doctor raised his fingers to his teeth, and then as if reminding himself not to bite his nails, tucked them firmly under the armpits of his white jacket.

The review completed, he proceeded at Mom's request to repeat the uncomfortable bone biopsy, taking the sample from Mom's hip. However, barring any contraindications from the second bone biopsy, he concurred with her first doctor at the Moses Lake clinic. Mom had leukemia. I suppose it had only been the wildest of hopes in Mom's heart to think otherwise.

Rubbing his chin solemnly, his tone remained compassionate as the three of us talked in the tiny examining room.

Unaccountably, Mom began to cry.

"It's just so hard! I'm sorry, I'm sorry. I don't mean to cry. I'm sorry, doctor," she bowed her head, choking.

I stood at the foot of the examining table, shocked and helpless, afraid that if I touched her, she would throw off my hand. My mother had not evidenced a single emotional response in the four months since her initial cancer diagnosis, and here she was, giving up an entire heart full of pain to a doctor she had met less than twenty minutes before. I held my breath.

Mom's voice sunk low over a broken sob as she rubbed her eyes with the backs of her roughened, blue-veined hands.

"I've tried to do things right my whole life. To be a good person, a good Christian, to do what was expected of me and work hard. I was Phi Beta Kappa at college because it pleased my dad and he was paying for it. As a young wife I entertained the old military biddies because that was how my husband would succeed as an officer. I bought and sold so many houses. I moved us—alone almost all the time—with four small children."

The doctor handed Mom a fistful of Kleenex, listening quietly.

"And then, my husband—" Mom bit off what she was going to say, her eyes hurt and angry as she glared up at the doctor. "You have no idea. No idea how the world treats a divorced woman. Forced to raise all four kids by myself, I worked miserable jobs. All I asked for these last few years was peace. Some time with my horses, my dogs."

Abruptly defeated, her eyes implored the doctor helplessly. "What did I do? Why is it always so . . . hard?"

Her thin shoulders shook as I placed my hand on her back, willing her body to hang together but letting her cry it out.

The doctor leaned in toward Mom and deep humanity reached through the warmth of his eyes. "My dear. You did *nothing* to deserve this. You didn't deserve to get leukemia."

He handed Mom the entire box of Kleenex. She blew her nose, balling up the tissues. I knew the anger in the twist of those hands. She had cancer: therefore, she must deserve it. She must have done something wrong, somehow been not quite "good enough," and Heaven knew. After all, God cradled the good, deserving lambs of Jesus. The Bible promised God blessed the deserving. This, then, must be the suffering of the unworthy.

I wanted to reach across and still her hands, but like the doctor, tucked my own tightly at my sides. My heart was breaking. Where in this tragedy was grace?

Mom and I drove in silence back to her Spokane house. She picked up her list of supplies for the farm and left that night. She would return, she agreed, for her next monthly blood draw in February. I suspected she might not.

The memory of her tears in the doctor's small office tightened my throat. I wanted to comfort her, wanted her to *want* me to comfort her. I missed the relationship we might have had.

Slingshot

It was impossible not to notice strange and unexpected links between points of experience in Ken's life. What had seemed simply astounding at the time, in hindsight bore even greater significance, the mark of an unsettling synchronicity. Closure at a time when closure, the settling of the details of a life, in particular Ken's life, frightened me the most.

Waiting alone in the radiation room as Ken went through his sixth week of treatment, I reflected on the shattering impact of a single telephone call and the urgency of the events that had unfolded. One unexpected call in the afternoon, nine months before Ken's cancer diagnosis, now seemed to have changed *everything*.

I remember I was folding laundry, looking out the back windows at the darkening sky. Thinking the call was Ken, I had answered on the first ring, happy and unconcerned. Visceral even now, that surge of fear, the clutch in my gut.

"May I speak with Kenneth Grunzweig, please? This is

Detective Haggert from the Oakland Police." The caller paused. "I have, uh, information for Mr. Grunzweig."

I remember I babbled something—Ken was out, could I take a number.

"Have him call me back. I believe he'll remember who I am," the detective requested, something tight and uncomfortable in his voice. "Tell Ken there is new information regarding the murder of his wife in Oakland, twenty-two years ago."

I hung up and immediately rang Ken on his cell, pulling him out of a meeting.

"You won't believe this."

Ken waited for me to be specific.

"The Oakland Police called, not ten minutes ago. A Detective Haggert."

"Haggert? Detective Haggert of the Oakland PD? That twit . . ."

That was all Ken said. "That twit . . ."

* * *

The Oakland Police Department had instigated a new search for Beckah's murderer. Why now? Why this case?

The unspoken possibilities were daunting. Were the police planning to reinvestigate Ken? Did they possess new facts, or secret proof of what had actually happened that night? Knowledge of who might have killed Beckah?

For eight years following her death, the police department had hounded Ken, scrounging for any scrap of evidence, convinced they had no other viable suspect than the estranged husband, Ken. Their investigation eventually dwindled, and over time, Beckah's homicide became a cold case. But for Ken, the fear of those years never quelled. He lived for twenty-two years as a suspect.

When he arrived back at the house, Ken loosened his tie, opened a bottle of water, and dialed the number I had written on the yellow notepad. His expression was shuttered, his shoulders set.

Detective Haggert had remained late in the office, awaiting Ken's contact. He answered on the first ring. I leaned in, straining behind Ken's back to hear the detective speak.

"Mr. Grunzweig? I'm sure you remember me. I certainly recall you. Let me cut to the chase here. We have positively identified the person who murdered your wife in Oakland, December of 1981."

I felt the tension click up a notch within Ken's body and closed my hand gently around his free hand.

"And?"

"The murderer is an African American currently sixty-four years of age, Cutter Jones, goes by 'Junior,' incarcerated in Folsom State Prison since 1982 for the first-degree homicide of a woman in Oakland Hills—a crime that occurred a month from the date of the murder of your wife. He has been positively identified from DNA evidence preserved in your wife's cold case file."

"Identified by whom?"

Haggert identified a well-known California prosecutor, Rockne Harmon, a recognized crusader in the field of cold case DNA criminal prosecutions. In the past year the Alameda County senior deputy district attorney and his team had taken the entire data bank of California felon DNA records, and using a state forensic computer program, run the collected DNA against every unsolved homicide in the San Francisco area in the last twenty-five years.

A perfect DNA match with Beckah's crime-scene evidence, a bit of skin under a fingernail, implicated a felon already incarcerated for homicide. The convict's DNA also tagged six other unsolved homicides in the area that had occurred within the same time frame: five women and one man, with potential matches expected in several more cases outside the area.

Haggert informed Ken that the State of California intended to retry the convict on the three strongest of these subsequent charges, including Beckah's case. Would Ken be willing to come down and meet with the detectives? The district attorney himself would call Ken in the morning on his way back from Congressional hearings in Washington.

"I should also inform you the Oakland PD is planning to release this information to the papers."

The detective named a San Francisco reporter, and Ken grimaced, his eyes hooded. In our private conversations, Ken had skimmed lightly over the details carried in the Bay Area papers. The stories were speculative and presumed guilt, fueled by the lurid murder, the impending divorce, Ken's stature as a successful businessman. Nearly a decade ago while packing up our office credenza for a move, I had stumbled across a crumpled brown folder labeled in pencil, "Beckah, Save."

"What's this?" I asked Ken, who was boxing another corner of our shared office.

He looked at the folder in my hands and frowned. "Things I thought I should save from the investigation after Beckah's death. Press releases, mostly."

"Can I read them?"

"If you want."

I knew he didn't really want the folder to even be in the house, let alone his life, but I opened the folder and read through the yellowed clippings. The worst report was a full third front-page story detailing the procurement of a search warrant to comb the estranged husband's apartment for evidence, as well as the family home. The search warrant indicated that Ken was the primary suspect in the case. The reporter brushed aside a successful lie-detector test Ken had taken administered through his defense attorneys, which the prosecution dismissed as inconclusive.

Seeing the reality of these accusations in print, I finally understood exactly how impossible Ken's life had become. His integrity had been stripped to the faith he had in himself, sustained by the faith of his family and friends. I put the folder in the very back of the box and neither of us revisited the subject again.

Oh yes, Ken recognized the reporter's name.

"Why that guy?" Ken demanded of Haggert over the phone. "He wrote a sensationalized search-warrant story based on allegations leaked from your office! As a reporter he ignored all the evidence. That man spit my entire life out as front-page news."

There was a delicate pause on the line.

"Yes. That's why we want him to do the story, Mr. Grunzweig. He volunteered, in fact. Everyone recognizes you were wronged—science has vindicated what our investigations could not. Everyone here wants to give you your due as an innocent man."

Ken's silent *fuck you* held the moment.

"But we need you, and perhaps your daughter, to agree to testify. If you agree, the prosecutor can immediately open a court case. Put this bastard away forever on all counts."

Ken took a moment to think.

"I need to talk to Jordan first. She has every right to decide for herself if she wishes to be involved, to testify." There was rigidness in Ken's voice. He was incapable of trusting these people, even now.

"Absolutely, Mr. Grunzweig. Cutter Jones is not going anywhere."

Ken hung up the phone and turned to me, breathing one word. "Finally."

*   *   *

It seemed to me, looking back, that these events thundered over our heads too quickly to take in.

Early the next morning after Haggert's phone call, I went out onto the porch to pick up the morning paper. Two inches of spring snow pampered the frozen ground, the fat flakes piling one on top of the other.

Standing at the bottom of our porch steps waited a cameraman and the boy-faced anchor from our local news channel.

The newsman scurried up to me, blowing into his hands for warmth. "I'm sorry to disturb you—Mrs. Grunzweig, I presume? Our national affiliate and the regional San Francisco Bay news channel have asked us to interview Mr. Grunzweig on the, um, DNA case—his former wife's murder? Do you have time for us?"

I stood frozen and exposed in my favorite ratty pink robe—no doubt there were toast crumbs on my chin.

"Right now?"

"The nationals need the story on the AP wires by ten. It's going out in *USA Today* and the area papers tomorrow."

Uneasy, I looked down the street. The camera truck parked at the curb displayed the familiar rainbow peacock, unfortunately blocking the neighbor's driveway.

"Okay, come in. You'll have to wait a few. My husband's in the shower."

I let Ken know we had "guests," and put on coffee. *Chaos and chance,* I remember thinking. *One spectacular slingshot from destiny.*

Holding my robe closed, I sat down at the kitchen table and served the journalists dark roast coffee with fresh-baked scones. Completing the knot in his tie, Ken walked into our living room upright and commanding, but nonetheless wary.

The young anchorman stood up, extending his hand. "Sir, can we talk about this recent evidence? How you feel about your full exoneration as a suspect in your wife's murder?"

"Exoneration," Ken repeated flatly. A powerful word, *exoneration*: a word that presumed evidence of innocence in the presence of implied guilt. Accusation, proven or not, that carried great weight.

I held my breath.

"No, not exoneration. Vindication, that's what I feel," Ken said. "Vindication for my deceased wife, for my family, and for justice and the science of DNA matching."

Every inch the chief executive in the crisp blue shirt that matched his eyes, Ken conducted the television interview live on camera from our living room. He downplayed the personal, emphasized the importance of closure for all victims' families, and urged greater legislative support for cold case DNA funding.

That night Ken's story appeared on the three local news channels, a longer clip on CNN, and a thirty-minute feature carried in Seattle. A neighbor stopped us in the streets. "Was that you?" the shocked man gasped. "Your former wife was actually murdered?"

The following day Ken flew down to San Francisco, met up with Jordan on her way in from San Mateo, and together they arrived at the Oakland Police Department. The two original detectives on the case had both retired. Detective Haggert, then a junior officer on the force, now served as the point person on the cold case investigation.

"How did the meeting go?" I asked Ken on the telephone that night.

"Surreal, G. I was right all along—Beckah's killer *was* a serial murderer. All those women killed by one psycho."

Haggert had produced a picture of the suspect—his prison mug shot.

"Haggert intends to meet with Beckah's sisters," Ken added, subdued.

"Even the crazy one? The one that stalked you, and then wouldn't stop calling us? No one in that farmily will believe your innocence."

"They'll believe it. They want to blame *someone* and I was convenient. But now they have someone better, a convict."

I closed my eyes. Never again would I have to answer a telephone in the night and hear that crazy bitch hiss in my ear, *"Do you know what kind of man . . ."*

I knew what kind of man.

"And how's Jordan handling this?"

"Hard to say."

"And you?" I asked. "How are you?"

"Numb, I guess. I still can't believe it. All these years—nothing. No evidence, no leads. And then a simple computer search . . ." His voice faded over the phone.

I hung up, wondering privately if hearing the man's voice, or seeing him in court, would unlock Jordan's memory of that unfortunate night. And would this, in some positive way, finally precipitate her elusive healing? A trauma therapist had theorized that Jordan's inability to remember anything of the night her mother was murdered in the bedroom next to hers was most likely suppressed memory. Jordan might have been afraid to remember. Afraid memory might expose her father as the assailant. Knowing now that he absolutely, positively was not—would that cleanse her of the last vestiges of suppressed conflict?

*　*　*

Back home the next day, Ken informed me that he had decided to face Cutter Jones in court. He needed the closure of confrontation, to stand up for the innocent life Beckah had unfairly lost. Jordan also had given the prosecutor her consent. Her mother's assailant behind bars, she was no longer afraid: freed of a life-long paranoia, fear that a stranger, who thanks to the media knew her mother had not been alone in the house, would come to find her.

She would stand beside her father in court.

The facts in the case revealed Beckah's bravery. Beckah lost the struggle with her assailant but succeeded in protecting Jordan. She never cried out. She did not call for help. She fought hard and silent, afraid to awaken and endanger her sleeping daughter. Her undaunted courage gifted Jordan with a profound truth: *I loved you this much.*

Beckah's last words in the ambulance had been "that man tried to hurt me." Not Ken, or Daddy, but *that man*. Why should it have taken so many years for the police to believe her?

The week before Ken was to meet with the prosecutor to ready the case for trial, Cutter Jones "Junior" died in his jail cell of natural causes. Heart trouble, the prosecutor said. He had lived just long enough for time and technology to expose him.

Once all the sensationalism dwindled, friends and family

202

weighed in with quiet acknowledgments of support, some of them learning of the scandal for the first time and stunned that Ken had lived his life for so long in the shadow of a major crime.

Ken walked alongside me on one of our quiet morning strolls with the dogs. He stopped at the corner of the driveway, wonderment in his eyes.

"You know when the universe hands you a big one? Well, this is a big one, and I'm grateful. I just wish my parents had lived to see this. I'm damn thankful I did."

Those words haunted me now.

My little cup of coffee had grown cold. I flipped through the pages of the three-year-old copy of *Gourmet* magazine on my lap as new patients filled the waiting room. Ken had been in the radiation chamber for an unusually long time.

F. Scott Fitzgerald so infamously said, "There are no second acts in American lives." Had Ken proven the old adage wrong?

Losing Words

Ken's journal lay open on the kitchen table.

February 6, 2003. Had the hiccups for sixteen hours straight . . . up most of the night. But with 4,500 total rads aimed at my body (180 daily through the front and 180 through the back) and enough chemistry to embalm a frog, why not hiccups too? After this third week of chemo so tired . . . my stomach aches, my throat burns, and I'm still nailed by these coughing spasms. I am determined not to take a break between courses. Blood counts are low but steady, so started Procrit for anemia, and am near end of second session.

Worst day of tiredness—couldn't even make it through the car show with David. Could barely walk with my son. Had to sit on a bench with the old men.

Last scans show tumor has shrunk by half and of the three lymph nodes in my mediastinum—two are gone and the third shrunk to 1 1/2cm. A 50 percent reduction in cancer! According to docs "prognosis is very much improved at this time . . . we've got this cancer running."

Ken's tumor, which earlier had shown no shrinkage on an MRI, had retrenched by half. The doctors were unbelievably upbeat.

The reality was tougher to navigate. Many obstacles lay ahead. Additional primary cancers could occur at any time, just as random and secretively as the first. And the effectiveness of neoadjuvant therapy, despite the surgeon's convictions, remained unknown: We would not know until surgery if the cancer was really eliminated. Dead or alive, the tumor would always display the same profile in X-ray, if smaller.

Cancer from "seed" cells posed the greatest danger, what the oncologist called *the core*—and if those cancer cells considered the tumor's "seed" remained alive, they were the most voracious and resilient of all.

Cancer had become our life, our habit, our new routine. Burned from radiation, Ken grew unable to eat or swallow, and soon lost the muscle coordination in his diaphragm, causing endless hiccups. And always the raw cough and the fatigue.

Ken still had some hair, a sweet duck fuzz like babies have. Wispy, but definitely there. We laughed—Ken sported what a friend jokingly called a free "Brazilian." There was a chiseled and gaunt Euro look about my husband now. Undaunted, those blue eyes.

What was I missing, besides everything? Sex.

The cancer literature tap-danced around the matter, using words like *personal intimacy,* focused on strategies for coping with the effects of surgical maiming (referencing breast and genital surgeries), scars that might interfere with self-esteem or "partner engagement." The brochures said it all so sweetly, "By all means live normally, and do what you feel ready for."

Barbarians.

We deeply believed sex connected us to the life force. Ken had a strong male animal nature, but with his body under siege, sharing sex was sharing energy, something he could ill afford. The cancer meds had wiped out all of Ken's robust instincts and the drugs had maimed his physical responses. I missed our intimacy, the comfort of my husband's body.

We were both of us in a deep-freeze experience: Life hung in suspension.

*   *   *

At our last clinical visit, I had asked Drayneau how we would know if any of these devastating treatments were in fact working, and his answer haunted me. "We won't. The only judge of success is how you are doing, this moment now."

A few days after that last appointment Ken awoke and sat quietly for a few minutes in his resting place in the bedroom chair, wrapped in the warm alpaca blanket. He gazed unfocused out the bedroom window. I was about to offer a "Good morning!" and suggest tea when the unfamiliarity of his expression rendered me mute.

I recognized death in his eyes.

I could see what I now knew Ken could see: His body was no longer able. His soul was embracing the inevitable need to separate. I knew it, I felt it. My heart thudded to a stop. How could I know that some part of Ken, the important and immortal part, was letting go? A decision made without doctors, clinical diagnostics, or even prayer, but through the guidance of a primitive inner wisdom.

I swallowed hard.

I could not dismiss what telegraphed between us. Unspoken but acknowledged, his soul's truth witnessed by mine. But I could not accept it as irrevocable. We all carried within us the face of our own death. Basic biology bows to the laws of physics, the degradation of matter. What I had witnessed in Ken's eyes had been simply biology in crisis, I assured myself. A glimpse of what the face of death *might* be. The pulse of his soul just traveled very close to the surface these days.

Bringing Ken his medication, I dismissed my fears. I had to.

* * *

The next week, Ken seemed especially robust, revived from several days of deep, restful sleep. He returned to work, engaging in his continued consulting and mentoring obligations both at the city arts commission and at the college. But then one night, Ken lacked enough strength for the chamber group concert soiree, his favorite music venue at the Davenport Hotel.

I hung his jacket back up in the closet.

The drugs lined the kitchen counter. For a man who had taken only the occasional Tylenol for a headache, Ken had become a chemist's contraindication nightmare; a warning label a mile long. Nausea seemed ever present in the wings, and Ken's weight slid, ever so subtly.

In my office, I paged through the stacks of dusty manuscript pages, the writing I had not faced for months now. A coffee cup sat unmoved on Oscar Wilde, the bottom dredges scummy from weeks of neglect.

Quiet, I contemplated my writing and the things that writing had brought me. I felt suddenly grateful, remembering the long weekend Ken and I had spent in New York last October. The four-day trip, just the two of us, had taken place just weeks before the photography trip to the Southwest that had led so precipitously to Ken's diagnosis. Arriving in the city, we had taken a cab to midtown Manhattan and placed my finished manuscript, the one Ken had read for me, in the hands of my smiling agent.

The trip offered a chance to celebrate, to enjoy a romantic weekend, and for me personally, to acknowledge a proud accomplishment. After years of balancing the needs of our young children with corporate moves and fulfilling my role as an executive's spouse, in completing this manuscript I had stepped back into the world. My world, the world of a working writer.

That weekend in New York was glorious, the city, beautiful—wrapped in autumn foliage and late-summer warmth. We ate in chic and intimate restaurants, and made love in the quiet of our hotel room. Carrying to-go cups of Dean & DeLuca coffee, we walked through Central Park and spent hours nosing around the art galleries. Chuckling, we whispered how we hated the blinking media exhibits at the Guggenheim. *This stuff resembled a boys' Saturday sleepover— Xbox and DVDs, CDs rapping on the boom box.*

In the afternoon we stood in silence beside the empty pit of the Twin Towers and Ken pointed out the building at the edge of the gaping devastation where he had once worked. I thought of the faux Cartier, now just a watch face with a broken band in Ken's drawer. Together we read the notes and signs, and counted the hats and flowers pinned to the chain-link fence. Thousands of broken hearts echoed and collided in the wire mesh in a collage of human grief.

Our last day in the city we ordered cappuccinos at the Metropolitan Museum of Art. We nursed our coffee, admiring the smooth marble statutes, part of a priceless Greek and Roman collection gracing the tropical palms in a botanical hall. We had just explored a magnificent retrospective of contemporary photography by Richard Avedon. Ken was glowing, swept up in the genius of Avedon's images of face and personality. We celebrated the city of arts, and each other as artists.

I was grateful. Writing had brought me this.

Spiritual Lite

Ken would be rescheduled for surgery the end of February or the first of March. Drayneau wanted to go in immediately, but to his surprise, Ken asked for clemency. Clemency: *a disposition to be merciful.*

"Why wait, Ken?" asked the doctor, his pen poised on the top of Ken's blue file. "You've finished the first round of chemo and radiation, the CTs show shrinkage of the tumor, and there are no signs you even *have* lymph nodes in your chest. You're as ready as we can make you."

"I just . . . can't. I'm sorry. I need time."

"For?" Drayneau prompted.

Ken looked uncomfortable. "I don't think I can hold it together, to be honest. I've run marathons, Drayneau. I've biked hundreds of thousands of racing miles. You have to believe me. My body has nothing left to heal itself with. Two weeks. Let me have two weeks."

I believed Ken. To delay was not a question of will, but

sustainability. Two weeks, we asked for: to focus on rebuilding Ken's immune system, put some weight back on his body, hope the rawness of his throat would heal.

It was during this time I decided to write Mom the details of Ken's illness. I had not seen her in person in a very long time. Four months into his diagnosis felt like an optimistic point, I rationalized: The worst was behind us, it seemed, surgery finally at hand. But Ken bore the unmistakable face of cancer now; a gaunt, solitary warrior. My mother had to know.

I sat in a coffee shop for two hours, struggling with the words. I had a good pen, thick stationery, and nothing to say.

> *Dear Mom,*
> *I have some difficult news to share, that if I had told you earlier I feel would only have added to the worries and concerns you are already coping with. It's Ken. A few months after your own diagnosis, Ken too was diagnosed with cancer. He has a lung tumor—of a significant size, and a stunning surprise for someone who doesn't smoke. Recently we've been going through a long and difficult process of determining what kind of cancer cell, and how best to treat, and until we really knew all the facts, I felt this would only burden you—I know how much you care for Ken.*
>
> *Tim and Judy have been available to help when needed. But lately Ken's illness has become more apparent in the aftermath of early biopsies, radiation, and preliminary chemo. He's had to go through a lot to prepare for upcoming surgery to remove the tumor. We hope this surgery will give us the cure Ken is fighting so hard for. In every other way he is in remarkable health!*
>
> *I thought you should know where things stand*

*and why I haven't made the trip down to the farm
recently. Please don't worry. You need to focus on your
own health. That's paramount. I just wanted you to
know.*

*As always, you know all of us would love to see
you. Let me know when you're planning to come up?*

*Love,
Glenda*

Mom called Tim and Judy a week later, asking each of them if the news about Ken was in fact true. Then she asked, "Why didn't Glenda tell me? You knew but I didn't?"

What could anyone say? How could I share the hardest news of my life with someone who was, by nature, unavailable?

Mom was silent and angry for a week before she came to the house to talk with Ken.

* * *

February was a month of birthdays. My mother would turn seventy at the end of the month; Ken would turn sixty a few days after Valentine's Day. How to celebrate such a momentous birthday? Sixty. Sixty, fighting cancer. Sixty with an uncertain future.

"Anything, honey," Ken responded tiredly over dinner that night when I asked him what he'd like to do. Seeing the crushed look on my face, he suddenly became teary. "I'm sorry. I love you—I hate being this burden. It's our anniversary too!"

The next afternoon, I waited on a ratty brown couch for David's piano lesson to end. David and his teacher, a stooped and reserved young man named Robert, ran the minor scales and fingered out the more difficult nuances of the Schumann piece. Schumann, the composer who went mad for love.

I drifted into exhausted tangles of thinking as the music progressed. I felt hollowed out, my energies dispersed and fragmented. Inside myself I sensed the girders shaking. What I felt was *hopeless*. A stalled-out exhaustion edged with an unshakable fear. The significant and the mundane collided at random every waking moment of my day. By the minute I stretched to get us to appointments, to unclog the kitchen drain (again), vet the dogs, meet the school bus, and somewhere in the collapsing hours, address the really enormous issues—our draining financial reserves, Ken's grim and unexplained levels of pain, our uncertain future.

Listening to David play Schumann, I made little notes on the back of an envelope I pulled from my purse. Numbers. Numbers of dollars.

There had to be a way out of our looming medical debt. The estimate for Ken's upcoming surgery was the equivalent of an open-heart surgery, plus a week's ICU—more than one hundred thousand dollars. In this instance our insurance fit our needs like petite pantyhose stretched over a queen-size butt. The night before Ken and I had argued over money, something we had never done before. Ken exploded over the proposed cost of summer camp for David, and stubbornly, I had refused to yield. I couldn't. Camp represented the kingpin of all that we were, or once had been. A normal family, making normal summer plans.

I leaned back against the frame of the old couch, closing my eyes. I was forty-six years old. My life, a life of cancer care and patient advocacy, my problems, the problems of cancer— my spouse crippled with illness, my children troubled and uncertain, looking to me for answers and small wordless assurances.

During the last months the provider's role seamlessly shifted from Ken's shoulders to mine. I admitted to myself that I was frightened. What work would I resume in Spokane, who would care for my children, who would care for my invalid husband? Deep down I felt like evaporating. Just to be gone—a whiff in the sun, a faint mark feathered in the sand.

I paused, listening to David phrase a particularly delicate melody in the Schumann. I breathed in the music. Another day, I told myself. Just finish another day.

Valentine's Day. We arrived at the clinic for a final pre-surgery CT.

On the TV in the waiting room, the United Nations was in session in New York to discuss the arms inspectors' reports on Iraq that disputed the Bush Administration's claims of what was actually hidden in Saddam Hussein's desert vaults. War brewed and nations dissembled. Private citizens were instructed by CNN to lay in emergency supplies. Osama bin Laden was on the run, hunted in the foothills of eastern Pakistan.

Ken's exams were taking a long time. I waited as nurses rolled several elderly women out in wheelchairs from behind the radiology doors, their chins drooping on their chests, their tiny, swollen ankles tucked neatly together. I saw in their shut-down expressions how the old and ill tried to not be a burden, tried to grow small and inconspicuous, folded away, neat. One sad woman looked up and smiled at me as she tugged at her oxygen hose. I smiled back, awash in sudden tears.

Ken finally came through the swinging door, walking slowly as he buttoned up his favorite Hawaiian shirt, the one imprinted with old Woodies and surfboards. It was twelve degrees outside, but today he had sun in his soul.

"Happy Valentine's Day," he said with a smile.

The Radiology nurse chuckled, having thoroughly enjoyed the red "I Love You" boxers. To know Ken was to love him, to laugh and be part of his pranks. He knew how to have such fun.

Ken had taught me the meaning of Masahide's line of Zen poetry, "Barn's burnt down, now I can see the moon." With Ken at my side, nothing was ever *that* bad.

* * *

Ken came into the bedroom with a hopeful yet worried expression on his face. He looked odd, but handsome. His skull was unadorned, but newly grown charcoal eyebrows framed his eyes. He had dressed all in black, in a merino wool turtleneck and pressed flannel slacks.

"Jordan wants to come back to Washington for the lung surgery," he said. He came up close and hugged me tight. "She doesn't know what to do, but she needs to do something. She says this time she might be able to stay as long as ten days to help look after the kids."

I looked hopelessly at Ken. He was asking the impossible of me a second time. But in his eyes was such a lost and tender feeling, I knew this request came from a special place inside him. The Daddy Place. After all the years of rejection, Jordan was seeking Ken out.

"She's showing you she loves you."

Ken laced his fingers in mine. "So?"

"She's welcome."

"Kurt too?"

"Sure."

I lifted the laundry basket in my arms and headed off with our sheets and towels. I laundered almost daily now. After the doctors' dire warnings concerning Ken's radically compro-

215

mised immune system, I was taking no chances that the kids' school colds or winter flu germs would take hold in the house.

Stuffing the washing machine full, I poured in a generous splash of bleach, still thinking about Jordan. There was a new and painful awareness in her voice as we chatted quietly about Ken's pain, his steady loss of weight. Her father, that steady and constant presence she had so foolishly spurned, was in clear peril and she was frightened.

I left the laundry and made Ken and I a pot of hot green tea. Green tea had a taste like cut grass to me, but was claimed to contain antioxidants primed for the body's defenses, support I was sure Ken could use.

Moving stiffly, my husband joined me at the table, having just hung up on another telephone call, this one to the petite and endlessly optimistic Karla Ann Luffe, his psychologist, scheduling his next cancer therapy session.

"What will you talk about, the surgery?"

"Cellular empowerment." Ken grinned. Karla Ann wanted to discuss his body's acceptance of surgery at the biomolecular level. Engage the process of psychologically "granting permission": embracing the invasive injury of major surgery for the higher purpose of ultimate healing.

This made a kind of simple sense to me. Who wasn't damned afraid to lie on that operating table?

Outside, late February winds blew hard across the roof, making an eerie singing noise as they sheered across the cedar shakes. Thin patches of ice and dirty snow still clung to the ground. Late winter, the season Spokane looked its worst and felt worse than it looked. Even the grand pine forests seemed depressed, their feet jammed in the cold snow and frozen mud.

Ken and I sat near each other, gazing out the windows at the flat skies. He seemed to read my thoughts when he leaned over and kissed me. "Don't worry. I've already covered a lot of distance with Karla Ann, and this session is really about closure."

"Closure?"

"Not that way, kiddo. I'm not quitting the game just yet." He grinned, running a hand across his bald scalp. "I mean, putting to rest some lifelong things, laying down the years of grief and disappointment. Karla Ann says we lock pain away physically in our cells. That we cripple our own immune systems and program our bodies to endure years of accumulated pain and damage."

I listened hard. Ken was opening up to something in himself, and within it, a new paradigm.

He twisted his mug around in his hands. "I've experienced some pretty lousy crap that I've never been able to shake free of. Beckah's death was the biggest chunk. I want to unload the rest."

"You'd be entitled."

There was no denying the synchronicity of recent events with Ken's diagnosis. If there was something to the cellular pain theory, Ken was walking proof. I noticed early on that Ken radiated a particular intensity regarding the work he and Karla Ann were doing together; and he never missed a session if he could help it. These were private sessions, bordering on the sacred, and so I never intruded.

"I've thought about this—how we carry shame and disappointment in our bodies, how cancer may be *the* disease of shame." Ken's gaze was clear, reflective.

"You really believe that?"

"I'd rather not. I'd hate to carry responsibility for generating my own sickness—who wouldn't? It certainly feels better to blame Dad's lifelong indoor cigars for creating secondhand cancer." He tapped his own chest. "But I've felt *physically* under siege since childhood, and every lousy thing has made me think I was at fault." He snorted. "This is absolutely so Jewish."

"Funny, but you sound like Mom."

"I see precisely how I absorbed guilt, internalized responsibility, accepted fault, shame, all of that, and made my body sick."

I bit a fingernail thoughtfully. I couldn't see that Ken had done anything wrong but fight to survive; battle hard against the odds.

"Easy, girl," Ken pulled my finger from my teeth. "Your brain's smoking. No, I don't mean I intentionally caused my tumor. But I do think if we live in a persistent state of inner turmoil, suffer shame or failure or conflict, we set ourselves against ourselves—and this becomes the seed of disease. Disease. Toxic guilt."

I frowned, wanting to separate psychology from illness: to box symptoms in an orderly, systematic, logical index. The body politic sounded a little too New Age for me. Pass the chakras, please.

"So you and Karla Ann aren't working 'wellness meditations' and all that? You're discussing your parents, and work, and Jordan?"

And me? I left that unspoken.

"All of it." Ken shifted on his seat bones, and wrapped his hands around the teacup for warmth. "Karla Ann calls me on all the rational bullshit I've used to defend myself for years. Seems I can't disengage that part of my brain that is all ego and control, the 'guy in charge' part of me. It's so easy to be a CEO in response to cancer—to charge ahead, delegate, do the risk assessment, execute Plan B." His smile radiated a gentle self-mockery. "But I *have* to deal with it emotionally, like it or not. It's happening inside me, not *to* me."

"Well, I personally refuse to believe you caused your cancer."

"Did or didn't." He shrugged. "Doesn't matter. I'm mad as shit I'm sick."

"So what is Karla Ann's advice?"

"She asks me to answer simple but logical questions. Were you, or they, doing the best you could at the time, the best that you knew how to do? Were you in charge of all the issues? Were they even your issues to be responsible for? Is this part of your journey or someone else's?"

A break in the overcast sky cast an intense square of yellow sun across the blue tablecloth. Ken rubbed his hands, kneading veins that often ached from the chemo infusions.

"Those questions made me realize a lot of the shit I carry is not even mine. And some of it, especially where Jordan is concerned, is collateral damage. But still, not mine to resolve. Knowing that, I can let go."

Tranquility eased the lines in Ken's face, and a calm gentleness had anchored deep in his gaze. "Jordan and Abby need to know I can't carry their troubles anymore. I can't fix everything." He stopped, obviously pained. "It's important Jordan understand I'm not letting go of her, just the troubles we've had. That was then, and this is now. I want to be clear and heart whole, that's where I'll find the will to live."

"What? The will to live?" I set down my tea, startled for a second time. Wind shook the windowpane and the outdoor chime clanged wildly.

"Life force. I'm talking life force."

"Oh." I seemed to have lost my voice. "You're letting *all* the crap go?"

"Yes."

Ken held up his hand, ticking his list off on his fingers.

"One, I love my parents for their wishfulness and forgive

them their incompetence. Two, I love Jordan and understand her grief has been this particularly unpleasant journey for me, but now that's over. Three, I'm grateful for my career. I respect myself for all the noble things I wanted business to be and it wasn't, and I fully celebrate the moments it came close. Four, I love myself as the artist I've felt unworthy to be. And five, I respect myself for surviving. Just surviving when it was so damn hard."

He offered a loopy grin. "And, I love you. I love you for giving me my only experience of pure and unconditional love." The smile fleeting, Ken reached across the table for my hand. "You and the kids are the single reason I go through this. It would not be worth it, would not be bearable otherwise."

I knocked my knee gently against his.

"And then? When you've let the mental crap go and cherished yourself for surviving, then what? How does any of this help?"

"Peace, it brings peace. I go to this place in my mind—a cabin set in dappled sunlight near the sounds a river makes. I go there and focus on *not being cancer*."

I reached out and pressed Ken's chest with my fingertips, feeling the broad hard bones of his sternum through his sweater, absorbing the heat of his heart, knowing without listening the exact music of its beat.

"And heart, baby. You have heart."

A moment's silence stretched between us as the clock ticked insanely on the kitchen wall, beating minutes and seconds out of nothing but space and light. I stood up and gathered our teacups, bumping his shoulder playfully with my hip.

"I forgive you the penguin, by the way."

Ken's eyes widened and he laughed. "Anything else?"

"Isn't that enough?"

The "Penguin of Shame," a stuffed bird in a red bow tie, was the secret icon of shabby romance, the remnant of a brief affair Ken had with a baby-faced airline stewardess before he met me. The blonde from American Airlines had insisted on the penguin, and indeed the bird had gone on shameful romps through Napa Valley, Barbados, New York. The orange flippers and plaid bow tie of that stupid stuffie said it all. The great men of the world, even my great man, could be idiots.

"I forgive you the penguin." I grinned. "You aren't the only one practicing spiritual *lite*."

Old Flannel

Ken and I invited my mother and Uncle Joe to lunch at a nearby diner on her seventieth birthday. Mom arrived wearing an oversized Go Cougars sweatshirt. She had hand-chopped her own hair, and it clearly needed another color as it had grown out half brassy blonde, and half pale, natural white.

Uncle Joe sat at the table, his flat moonface expressionless as he polished his ancient trifocals. He was wearing my grandfather's plaid jacket, which was badly stained, and on his thinning sandy hair, the new tweed jockey cap Ken and I had given him for Christmas.

Ken's tuna melt sat untouched.

Mom ate half of her meal silently, intently. She had processed the shock of Ken's cancer, wearing on her face her lingering resentment that she hadn't been informed from the beginning. But over lunch she came out of her pout, both barrels loaded.

"Just skip that terrible chemotherapy," she urged Ken,

chewing through her hamburger with her good remaining teeth. "Look at you. So thin, all your hair gone! You need to do what I do. Come down to the farm. Let good fresh air handle the rest."

"I've got kids, Louise," Ken said gently. "And, I really do believe in the technology. I believe in the medicine. I intend to do every single thing they think might work."

"Ha!" she snorted, fully disgusted. "You don't know doctors. They think they know it all, but they know almost nothing. They had me so tanked up on drugs in Moses Lake, I could hardly stand on my own two feet. Always pushing you around and testing for this and for that and still telling you nothing for certain."

"Louise, I know you have reason to be bitter."

"I'm not bitter. I just refuse to be sick."

"Right on." Ken reached across the table of the diner and wrapped his hand around her thin, gnarled one.

Uncle Joe had yet to look up from his plate, forking through his Denver omelet and the stack of silver dollar pancakes with intense concentration. He was there because Mom had insisted, demanding her brother check in on her from time to time. I suppose Mom had determined Joe would be her backup if she were too sick to fend for herself. She knew she could bully him to her terms and conditions, but I worried she had neglected to take into full account the absolute uselessness of the old bachelor who had lived off his parents his entire life.

Mom minced bacon into small pieces, favoring her left jaw. The dental abscess had become a scarred mass in her right jawbone and the doctors recommended this too be biopsied, which she refused.

Ken liked my mother. She evidenced the same frustrating do-it-my-way stubbornness of his eastern European relatives.

Stupid I may be, as the saying went, *but I'm in charge of me.* Living in the solitary company of seven dogs, three horses, weird cats, and strays of all persuasions had clearly exacerbated Mom's unanimous Rule of One. The animals didn't contradict much.

"Thank you for the crates of Ensure," Mom said softly, pouring a second cup of coffee, black. "You and Glenda are good to me."

"Tastes like shit, doesn't it?" Ken grinned. "I gave you mine."

They chuckled. Somehow they had achieved an odd bond: Mom was rooting for Ken, flagrantly oblivious to her own needs, and Ken tenderly guarded her vulnerability, respectful of her need to remain independent.

"Take care, Louise." He kissed Mom on the cheek as we got up to leave. "Call if you need anything. Anytime, right? The only thing you *can't* have is my teeth."

"Oh, I fixed that." Reaching into her ever-present Rite-Aid bag, Mom pulled out a vampire set of wax Halloween chompers and popped them into her mouth, grinning madly.

"What? It's Halloween?" Uncle Joe asked, confused.

We kissed good-bye in laughter.

*   *   *

"Update check. When did you see Mom last?" Judy called from Moses Lake.

"Last week. She just dropped by—and stayed four days."

"No kidding."

Ken had rallied himself for an important board meeting and flown down to California the same evening Mom arrived, unannounced, on my doorstep. It was snowing hard when the doorbell rang. Mom stood under the porch light, her skin blue with chill, eyes red-rimmed and watery from the stinging snow.

"Brought you some candy," she offered with a smile, proffering a grocery bag of Snickers. She coughed hard then and I drew her in, petrified she had come down with pneumonia. The savory smell of vegetable stew simmering on the stove and homemade garlic-mashed potatoes kept her with us through dinner. The worsening roads dampened her plans to leave. There was more ice and snow in the forecast.

"Stay here tonight, Mom," I said. "Keep us company."

That night we watched movies together in the family room, warmed by the fire. David curled in against Mom in the sagging La-Z-Boy, and her face grew soft and relaxed. She hooted with pleasure as the pod-racing sequences in *Star Wars: The Phantom Menace* shot onto the screen. She coughed, and wheezed as she tried to catch her breath.

Discreetly, I gave her a Drambuie-laced hot tea and sat in the shadows, basking in the quiet pleasure of my mother at home with me.

"Four days? She stayed four days?" Judy's voice was shocked.

"Sick with bronchitis, Jude. Too sick to argue, if you can imagine it. The storm hit and no way she could stay warm with those crappy space heaters in the Spokane house."

"She could leave the farm animals that long?"

"I don't really know. God, Judy—she looked terrible."

"Well, of course. She's got leukemia."

All through that first night, hoarse coughs wracked Mom's stooped frame. I helped Katy set up the humidifier in the guest bedroom and brought out a jar of mentholated cream to rub on her back. As Mom lifted her shirt, I confronted the harsh reality of her illness. Her middle was swollen like a gourd from leukemia's effects on her abdominal organs. She had wrapped herself in loose sweats, but as my hand rubbed the heating cream gently along her ribs and spine, those bony protuberances evidenced erosion of her sturdy, muscular build.

I could count each vertebra, each skinny rib. My mother had dwindled, fragile as a bird under those many layers of clothes. Her skin felt slack under my hand, loose and dry, each bluish vein and thin muscle visible around her bones. Her hollowed cheekbones, the "slender" arms she was so proud to have now, were marks of cancer.

I helped her slip on old flannel pajamas and tucked her into the big bed. I kissed her forehead like a child's, and she looked up at me.

"Thank you." Mom teared up. "You're taking good care of me. Thank you."

"Oh, Mom." I heaved a deep sigh, pained that she should thank me. "You're my mother. I love to care for you. I love you."

"I know you do, sweetie. And I love you and your great little family."

As snow covered the streets and blanketed the trees, we cooked soups, watched movies, and baked bread. Slowly Mom's cough responded to sleep and warm food. We three—David, Katy, and I—nursed her back on her feet, and in return, she offered to see her doctor while she was in town.

Encouraged, I helped her organize her medical files, make new appointments, pick up more medicine and food.

"So, do you think she's still taking her medicine?" Judy inquired.

"I think she ran out and came to town to refill her prescription. She's buried in piles of stupid paperwork from Medicare. We tried to straighten it all out when she was here. And I think she's been splitting pills for a while . . . her abdomen is so swollen, I suspect her white blood count is really high again."

"Her nutrition?"

"She eats what doesn't upset her stomach. She seems so fatigued, Judy. She trudged up the front steps."

"And you say Uncle Joe agreed to come down to the farm to visit?"

"He did. Mom even bought him a warm coat and sturdy shoes. What is he, seventy-four now? I know."

"Her choice, I guess." Clearly bemused, Judy said goodbye and hung up.

When the roads cleared, Mom departed feeling her cough had improved and anxious to see her animals. The next weekend she drove the eighty miles back to Spokane for her Monday morning checkup at the clinic and stayed by herself in the Spokane house.

Sunday night, home from his California trip, Ken made turkey sausage chili with fresh tomatoes and basil—the best chili on the planet—and Katy whipped up pans of honey cornbread. I rang Mom to invite her to join us, but her cell phone switched over to message and rang unanswered. I bundled up in a jacket and snow boots and ran a bowl and a plate of bread up to my mother in her little house on the hill.

"Why, thanks, sweetie!" She smiled from the doorway, three layers of socks on her feet and a blanket around her shoulders as the little radiator clicked and groaned behind her.

I kissed her.

Our unfinished business was never really finished, but we had found a way to be kinder.

Chest Plumber

We sat down and faced the oncologist, who began rhapsodizing over market fresh cherries, smiling benignly at Ken. "Your prognosis is much improved at this time." Drayneau nodded brightly. "You're in good hands with Denton. He's known to be careful and takes his time."

"Meaning?" I asked, puzzled. For a fee of a hundred grand, wouldn't you take your time?

"Well . . ." Drayneau paused, choosing his words. "Not many surgeons take on surgery after massive radiation. Radiation turns tissue to mush, which leaves little to suture or repair. And a good cancer surgeon can determine what cancer remains in various stages of viability."

Ken and I fell silent. No mention of this before. Tissue destruction could be considered a serious downside risk to neoadjuvant therapy, thank you. So Ken's insides were cantaloupe, and some guy with a scoop was going to scrape the rind and try to find a good chunk left to sew him back together? I thought about Denton's fancy technique to suture the stump after the lung was removed. How would Harley Denton anchor a chest wall muscle in destroyed tissue? And after all that scraping, wouldn't there be internal scarring? Would Ken's insides be pulled out of alignment as he healed?

"See you post-op, Ken." Drayneau popped a cherry pit into the can.

We drove to the Heart Institute, taking our turn in Harley Denton's full waiting room. I found myself jealous of the portly men in their midsixties bouncing out of the office as they got the all-clear on their heart post-ops. "Ticker's fine!" Armed with Viagra and a new day.

Denton ushered us in, bullish on Ken's scan results. He clipped up the "before" and "after" CT scans, reading to us from the report filed by the radiologist: "Patient evidences a remarkable response."

"Which your entire team concurs on, Kenneth." His cheeks swelled with pride, Harley the Puffer fish.

Great, I think. Happy, happy docs.

Denton meticulously detailed every contingency of surgery, all the possible collateral damage. But, he reminded us, if there was evidence during surgery that more of the lung was cancerous, he might be forced to remove more tissue than just the tumor. He would not remove the entire lung however, as postradiation Ken was no longer in robust health.

I absorbed this. It seemed with each discussion our options narrowed.

Denton explained that any living cancer cells found during surgery would mean a back-end round of chemotherapy. This, he warned, would be more difficult postsurgery, as Ken's physical reserves were drained and his internal organs already likely damaged from chemotherapy drugs, his susceptibility to infection high. Finally, Denton outlined the risks of the actual surgery: chest drainage tubes, danger of pneumonia, danger of infection. Danger, danger, danger.

I concentrated on Denton's face, ignoring the flakes of dandruff skimming across the shoulders of his expensive gray suit. His work—holding hearts, the pump of human life in his hands—must seem simple, given the confidence of his gestures, the snap in his eyes. A *cardio thoracic surgeon*: not a nine-to-five skin technician, not a chemistry man, not a slide jockey. Harley Denton was a hands-thrust-deep-in-your-chest human plumber.

Wrapping up, Denton pumped Ken's hand up and down as we left his office. "Don't worry, Ken," he growled. "We'll cut that goddamned fucker out."

* * *

Denton came out of the OR at about four p.m., trailed by another unfamiliar assistant surgeon. Both men were distracted, still in their green OR scrubs and masks. Denton hopped around on both feet as he looked from my face to Jordan and Kurt's. He clapped his hands together, warming up for action.

"Okay, we've got good news, and some not so good news."

I heard Jordan's swift intake of breath.

"The good news, Mrs. Grunzweig, is that the tumor is gone. Cut that sucker right out of your fabulous husband. One point three centimeters of tumor wedged in a lung sandwich that pathology now says is, *for certain*, lung cancer."

The surgeon loosened the neck of his scrubs and glanced out the wall of windows behind us as he spoke. With that black bushy hair now flattened under his surgical beanie, Harley Denton looked neither blusterous nor impressive: he looked half the man.

His eyes flickered toward mine and held an instant.

"The not so great news is that once we sectioned the midlobe away from the upper and lower lobes, I found viable microscopic cancer in the margins, in the border where the lobes touch one another. And, cancer cells where the midlobe joins the trachea."

"Microscopic cancer? How viable?" I asked tightly. "Viable sort of? As in 'damaged by radiation and dying' viable? Or 'damaged but recovering' viable?"

Kurt and Jordan listened, their faces immobile.

Denton heaved a sigh.

"Any viable cancer is *not* dead tissue, period," he said, his voice measured. "We can't call Ken's surgery a CR, a 'complete response.' No, not a cure, Mrs. Grunzweig. Something less, I'm afraid, which makes another round of radiation and chemotherapy the conservative, correct follow-up."

Kurt put an arm around Jordan, pulled her near.

"Mop up chemo?" I echoed. "We need mop-up chemo? And more radiation? I thought Ken had already received the maximum lifetime radiation you can give anyone—how can he do more?"

"Already checked. Radiology assures me they can target just that tiny area of the stump, and that your husband can receive enough rads to make a difference there."

"But not to his throat and chest? Not the mediastinum," I faltered, *no more burning*. "He couldn't take more of that."

"No. Those central nodes are all removed, in the bucket. Pulled 'em out like a string of pearls. No sign of cancer there."

"You didn't consider a complete removal of the lung?" *If there's cancer take it all. Give us a chance.*

Harley Denton shrugged, looking over at his partner impatiently. *I told you she was a talker. Wants the details.*

"Losing his lung would be extremely difficult for your

husband to adapt to at this point, post-treatment. Recuperation is extremely difficult and he's far less resilient. We removed the tumor with the midlobe. A complete lung removal wouldn't have given us any more assurance than that."

But why?

And then it hit me. Mitigation. Medical treatment fell somewhere between complete cure and degrees of mitigation. Cancer had been found in the stump adjoining the trachea. And if cancer had made it there, cancer was out of the lung and on the blood and oxygen superhighway. Removing the entire right lung wouldn't stop the cells from where they were already headed, throughout Ken's body.

I looked at Denton. *You sonofabitch. You will not tell me what your eyes say you know.*

The white spring light from the skywalk windows seemed blinding suddenly as Denton plowed on. He described a successful closure of the stump, securing the bronchia with a twist of chest wall muscle to keep the seal tight and strong. He congratulated his assistant, the faceless Doctor Whoever, on that nice piece of work.

His words receded in the white blindness.

"We cleaned the damaged tissue out well, I must say, Mrs. Grunzweig. Your husband will heal beautifully—won't even know he lost that midlobe." Abruptly jovial, and obviously tired after six hours of surgery, Denton appeared anxious to wrap up and get out of the OR. "Ken's en route to the ICU. All good there. His lungs have successfully reinflated, and his vitals are good."

Denton and the assistant disappeared back into the OR.

Jordan and I stared at each other. We repeated everything just said.

The chaplain with the gray ponytail, on Christmas duty when I had waited in this exact same place three months previous, skirted by and then paused: He looked as if he might inquire, but then changed his mind and moved on. We were those people past the input of faith: We were post-op, possibly postmortem. I couldn't blame him for not wanting to know which, or care, for giving in to that evasion which is human nature.

I hugged Jordan gently. "Listen, guys, we're done here. Would you go home and help the kids on their homework? Order in a pizza? I'll call in a bit to tell everyone how your dad's doing in recovery. The good news is the tumor is out."

Jordan nodded, bravely masking her uncertainty.

Before he left, Kurt touched me, offering a comforting squeeze of the arm. I smiled blankly into his plain, good face.

We had just ripped Ken's body asunder and put it back together again no better than it had been before. Science and God, science and God. When Ken opened those beautiful eyes, what would I say?

I went upstairs to the ICU.

Mortimer Snoo

Fat tissue-sized flakes of snow were falling. Beautiful and insane, this snow in April. Little geometries of science, crystal chains pierced through by sunlight. By day's end the snow had changed to a grim, thin sleet.

It was Monday, and Harley Denton gave Ken his final surgical release, took a new X-ray, and announced Ken "clean as a whistle." He noted a pocket of accumulated fluid still present in the right lung, but dismissed it. And he seemed unconcerned by the twisted angry welt of Ken's scar, and the formation of hard nodules along the seam, none of which seemed right to me.

"We're just watching this guy for reoccurrence now!" Denton exulted to his assistant.

Observing Ken, Denton recommended he take another two weeks to recover his strength before beginning the "mop-up" treatments. "After all," Denton joked softly, "we don't want to establish cure on autopsy!"

I watched Ken walk out of the doctor's office, unsteady, frail. *O my love.*

We should feel optimistic—yes, we should be hopeful, upbeat. We had finally conquered this thing! But without question the last stint in the hospital had taken Ken to ground zero. He was fighting to walk, to just eat and breathe without pain. "Watching for a reoccurrence," Denton had said. Cancer in the rearview mirror. You were given only one good shot at beating cancer, the medical people said. Not because the disease was impermeable to "repeat" therapy, although it could be; but because each one of us can endure the devastating therapies only a limited number of times. The body stripped of its resources, immune system, and biostasis by multiple assaults from radiation and chemotherapy was left with permanent residual damage, lingering chronic debilitation. Treatment for cancer had made Ken a very sick man indeed.

Everything in me wanted to hide him away and nurture his body back to health.

Silent, Ken and I acknowledged the upcoming treatment. One final, new, and different chemistry—and God only knew if it would be enough. All we knew was that Ken had reached his limit.

* * *

Ken returned home, determined to tackle his desk.

There were three telephone messages, all from the board of the new technology company he advised. They were a plucky group, these Ann Arbor engineers and scientists; operating with big ideas on a shoestring budget. They knew that Ken had cancer, and why he had been unable to attend recent board meetings, and they knew his ability to work had been compromised. Ken kept them apprised of the facts of his illness as treatment evolved, and contributed by teleconference when he could, hoping those contributions already made would successfully play out.

On the day Ken sat down to face the mounting bills and chaos of his office, the company president called again. The board had voted unstintingly to continue to pay his retainer, to stand behind him and support our family in this one small way.

One minor human gesture, born of community and friendship. Ken put his head in his hands and cried.

In so many ways I had learned the geography of human caring was far more complex than the simple topography of the family or love affair. And one gesture's reach, far greater than any of us could imagine.

* * *

Four weeks later, Drayneau laid out the second protocol, explaining the potent new mix of chemistry.

"Your blood work indicates some anemia, Ken. You have to focus on enhanced nutrition." Drayneau glanced at me.

Frustrated, I nodded. Getting Ken to eat was not something I could force: He remained nauseous, unable to swallow well, disinterested.

"What are the risks of *not* pursuing more treatment?" I asked, hesitant.

Drayneau frowned over the top of his reading glasses. "The probability is *very high* the cancer will reoccur. Cancer was discovered outside the tumor, remember? In the margins of the midlobe. You've taken four weeks for recovery, but we still have a good opportunity to successfully retreat any unchecked cancer weak from the previous treatments."

I looked the man straight in the eye.

"What if we're flat out of reserves?"

Drayneau said nothing more, his gaze resting on Ken.

What choice did we have? How could I keep Ken alive? How could we make it? Thin, thin, thin. I couldn't believe how the scale had dropped, each week eight pounds at a time. I yearned for Ken's old smile, his strength, the solemn thud of his heart under my ear. Now his struggling heart jittered and shimmied, banged hollow at double the speed.

Ken rose to his feet, unaware of a slight tremor, a new whisper of motion in his hands.

"We'll be here Monday," he said to Drayneau, shaking the oncologist's hand.

I stood back and watched Ken leave the office, his shoulders held erect, the shadow of his old drive and purpose in his step.

Drayneau's hand closed on my shoulder; a fleeting grip as he rose and closed the door behind us.

The truth, the fidelity and rigor of the science I loved, had become more than I could bear. What I felt now seemed both unreasonable and foolish. Standing at the nurse's station, surrounded by staff in grape and green jelly bean–colored smocks of zoo animals and storybook landscapes, I was flooded with images of Ken's made-up stories, the tales he invented when the kids were small. The incredible, unlikely adventures of a purveyor of balloons: the elderly, stout Mortimer Snoo. Bowler hat in one hand, the other wrapped around the ties of his enormous bundle of brilliant helium balloons, Mortimer Snoo rose nightly above the world and solved the dilemmas of lost and frightened children, brought treats to the animals in the zoo, cheese for the man in the moon.

Magic, oh, God, give me magic.

Hang on tight, Ken. Don't let go of those balloons.

Survive, Ken, survive.

Visitation

I tossed through a restless half-sleep, attuned to Ken's erratic breathing as he slept propped up against the pillows beside me. Without warning he caught his breath and held it for countless seconds as he struggled to sit upright.

I rolled over, rising in the dark on one arm. I anticipated a coughing spasm, a cry for water. But Ken simply tensed, alert. He exhaled softly. He raised his chin and cocked his head slightly to the left as he listened, his hand abruptly extending toward the window, palm open.

I felt suddenly alarmed as I too sensed someone with us. I could *feel* but I couldn't see anything unusual in the dark.

I held still, waiting out the moment, feeling what I could not observe.

"Ken?" I whispered, touching his extended hand. "Ken, are you all right?"

His head turned, the strong planes of his face distinct in

the shadows as he faced me. His eyes were open, wide and clear. "Did you see her?"

"No, who?" I sat up, flinging off the bedcovers. We were alone in the warm dark, just the two of us, whispering.

"She came," he sighed, amazed. "The angel. She came in through that window there." He pointed to the bay window on the other side of his nightstand. "She touched me awake. I held her hand, Glenda. She came to tell me everything's going to be all right."

"You're sure it wasn't a dream?"

"I'm sure."

I accepted this. I myself had sensed someone speaking to Ken and holding his hand. I had felt a presence as surely as I could not see one.

"Do you know who it was?"

My husband permitted a soft smile, full of lovely melancholy. "So tall and lovely. That lovely, lovely brown hair."

His hands made the shape of a woman in the air.

"Who, honey?"

"Diana. My first wife, Diana!" His eyes shone. "She said it's hard to come through, difficult to make herself strong enough for me to see her and know her, and that she could only be here a moment. But she wanted me to know she's there, that she loves me, and that everything will be all right."

"Is she still here?" I whispered, confused.

"No." Ken eased back into the pillows. "She left as she came, through the window." He remained silent for a moment, and then said simply, "Her hand was warm."

I looked over at the illuminated clock. 2:57 in the morning. Ken had had his last pain meds at 8:00 p.m. the night before and he was long overdue, probably suffering now, but most certainly not drifting through any drug-enhanced haze.

"Do you hurt?"

He nodded silently.

I got up to get his medicines, still shaken by my own physical sensations, the weight and presence of something I knew to be real but could not verify. All my body alerts had registered an "other," and yet there was no other to identify.

Diana, bride of Ken's youth. The soft-spoken girl from Lincoln, California. Ken had held Diana as she died in his arms on the side of the highway. And now thirty-eight years later, Diana had apparently made a singular effort to return to Ken's side, to offer Ken the reassurance of her hand and her love, her faith in the comfort of the future.

It was extraordinary. Real or imaginary, it was extraordinary. I could not shake or excuse the moment away.

Alone in the empty kitchen, I filled a glass of water and counted out Ken's pills beneath the solitary kitchen light. When I returned to our bedroom, Ken was fast asleep. His face was peaceful, at rest.

Ever You Fall

Ken's second radiation was going well, according to the radiologist studying the X-rays. But the irritation from the renewed radiation was tremendous. Ken slept upright in the chair most nights; the only position he could breathe and rest in.

A few days into treatment, Ken broke out in shingles, an angry rope of painful blisters wrapping one side of his body from his spine to the center of his chest, entwined around the purple welt of the surgery scar.

Drayneau abruptly started Ken on antidepressants. All of us had noticed that Ken's smile, his dry wit, had begun to fade away. In cooking class he spent most of the night in the chef's kitchen rocker, his lips set tight against waves of unrelenting pain.

Ken's anemia levels had improved in May, but were still shy of normal. The white blood cell count stayed excellent. This was important, as the chemo in his next two cycles was known for whacking white blood cell counts and platelets flat out.

"Will Ken be able to stay the course, be strong enough?" I asked his nurse, Pat, as we took our place once again in the "infusion lounge."

She consulted his chart. She had a kind face. The face of a woman who had probably raised a few troubled kids, stuck by a difficult husband, endured unemployment, and accepted a future lacking the lake cabin they once hoped to own.

"I don't know," Pat said simply. "He's had a lot of radiation and chemo."

We watched Ken take his chair. From the back, my athletic husband had shrunk and bent into the slump of an old man. His beautiful, solid musculature was gone. His bones bumped out from his skin, and Ken stood oddly now, wrenched slightly sideways to the right over his gnarled surgical scar. His hair, just a shadow really, had grown in battleship gray. Gone, the thick dark hair I had loved to thread my fingers through.

Ken bent to gravity. His mind wandered. He left for meetings with toothpaste on his glasses. And when he became tired, his voice grew small and querulous. The doctors said all of this was chemistry, cancer, surgery, radiation. The symptoms would be gone when the cancer was gone. I didn't believe them. I saw an irreversibly damaged body, the final language of loss. I felt terrified of what Ken's body, and some part of Ken so riddled by suffering, had become; a wasted body lying next to me in the bed. I could not hold him at night anymore—his side ached if my arm rested anywhere near him. His hips were tent poles, and his shoulder blades jabbed through his shirt. I could not find cotton soft enough to comfort those bones.

Ken wavered in the shadow of himself, a maimed, bewildered soul. And I stood in the shadow too, living within Ken's cancer. I was losing the love of my life. This space, this new geography of inadequacy and regret, of fear caught between sorrow and rage, shredded my heart. My prayer flags flapped away, abandoned—the small prayers cut loose in the wind. So many parts of us snapped on the line, but most of all, Ken.

* * *

The male oncology nurse, a dark Russian in a billowy animal smock who resembled nothing so much as a Brothers Grimm fairy-tale giant, weighed Ken in. He marked his chart: June 4, 2003. He expressed shock, rechecked his numbers. Two days—six pounds.

I looked at the scale and cried. Six pounds lost. I looked wordlessly at Ken and before Drayneau came in, I fled.

After his appointment Ken came out into the parking lot. He found me sitting outside the clinic on the stone bench, tears flooding behind my dark glasses. I couldn't stop crying. The sun beat down on us, hot and relentless.

Ken laid his hand on my shoulder. He just stood there, quiet, comforting.

Sobbing, I pulled his hip near my cheek and held on for dear life.

"I hate this," I whispered.

"I know."

"So what do we do?"

"We don't quit."

* * *

Summer blew in under the wings of returning geese. Warm June days, and on this morning, the rhythms of rain showers.

Jordan continued to report in that she was doing well, her pregnancy good, and the baby due sometime in July. "I want to name the little one, our girl, something after Dad. Do you think he'd be pleased?"

I wanted to hug her. She had no idea how the arrival of this first grandchild had become a signpost on the map to survival for Ken.

The past week had marked a noticeable increase in Ken's pain. When I mentioned this to the clinic team, worrying aloud about what this new pain meant, pointing out that the radiation doctor had felt hard, unexplained nodules developing behind Ken's surgical scar, Drayneau remained noncommittal, but increased the potency of Ken's narcotic meds. He suggested we try different medication strategies.

Silently I stared at him.

Drayneau reassured us Ken's last X-ray remained clear, and it was unlikely any tumor mass could reestablish itself in under two months. Ken's bouts of shortness of breath were likely related to waves of uncontrolled, intense pain.

Late in the night after our clinic visit, I stood at the kitchen sink, my fingers gripped around a mug of tea. Ken's two a.m. pills were measured, ready in the pocket of my pink robe.

Closing my eyes, I prayed for a miracle. A miracle that was *just Ken*. That's all. Ken. The tea mug slipped from my hand and shattered in the sink, dark amber tea swirling down the drain. Suddenly I understood. Prayer was not a question seeking an answer. Prayer was emotion. A song in the face of loss.

Ken had been fighting cancer for months—his nature was to fight to survive—but cellular biology existed in chemical disequilibrium: Only death represented equilibrium. Mom had figured right after all: There was no second-guessing biological crash. She opted to ride life to the ground. Her decision to not squabble days bartered or lost through medical intervention meant freedom to spend the present sipping coffee in the front yard, watching deer come down from the spring.

Not my Ken. His body held together damaged elements in organic survival. What, then, if we just surrendered to this illness? Existed within that space as best as we could, scanning for that break in the fence? All these days of worry felt like a betrayal of the present moment. And there were so very few "present moments" left to waste.

"No, I do *not* pray," I announced quietly to the dark forest beyond the kitchen windows. I had learned to pray all wrong. Childish petitions, fear laid wishfully at the feet of some imagined being more powerful than me. Real prayer, I understood, functioned in a unity of situation and awareness, a commune between the head and the heart. When I closed my eyes, I found myself in that unity. Found Ken, found the world of invisible energies, and slipped my fingers into the mystic codes that made whales sing and hydrogen bond to oxygen.

I would let faith be its own vessel. The way out of and back into the truth of this world. The power was in knowing prayer was *listening*. I would listen, and not waste any of what I heard of the truth. I would wait on the echo of small answers.

* * *

The kids stashed sun block and tennis shoes, hats and toothpaste in their duffels, packing for the few weeks away they enjoyed each summer at camp. This summer Katy chose an East Coast university science camp and David joined a student ambassador trip to Australia and New Zealand. Torn between wanting the children to feel secure in their regular routine and our own wish to keep them close by, we discussed the camps again with Drayneau, who gave the "all clear." Ken appeared in stable condition and would benefit from a few weeks of quiet rest. Drayneau promised he would warn us if for any reason we needed to bring them home. So I apprised the camp administrators of the situation and the kids began to pack, knowing that until they heard otherwise, "all was well."

Before the kids left, we celebrated a quiet Father's Day. Ken laughed, said he loved the high-tech electric razor he wanted. For what beard? we laughed. He admired the fine wooden watch case for his collection of antique watches and smiled when he opened the gift certificate for the second International Cooking class, tucked into a handmade card of tissue and gold stars.

Barn's burnt down, now I can see the moon, I had quoted Masahide. *You, you are my moon.*

I kissed his bare skull. "My dad once told me all the galaxies are magic and chaos. Physics at play."

Ken looked up at me, his eyes somber.

"Stars," I whispered. "A star is the art of mathematics. And when one falls . . . poetry." *I'll catch you, if ever you fall.*

We slipped David's small bear into his suitcase, handed Katy her licorice and flip-flops, kissed their noses, and took them to the airport.

* * *

The CT scan was astoundingly bad. Fluid had filled both of Ken's lungs, and there were many new "spots," as Drayneau called them, in both Ken's right and left lungs. Cancer spots.

The surgery scars, especially where the chest drain tubes were removed, had not healed but knotted, thick and dimpled. Ken's internal organs showed evidence of being pulled severely to the right by extensive inner scarring. All that expert scraping, Denton's fabulous new stump technique, had made a wrenching knot of Ken's right side.

Ken sat in Drayneau's office absorbing this report.

It was the twenty-third of June, twelve weeks since the surgery.

Ken had trouble breathing. The fluid in his left lung needed to be drained immediately. Brusquely, a nurse led us into a room that only three people—Ken, the radiology doctor, and the nurse—could fit into. From the hallway, speaking through the closed door, I begged the nurse to *gently* ease Ken's shirt off, to not let him grow cold. He shivered constantly. *Did she see?*

Ken's voice, low and pleasant, chatted easily as the nurse swabbed his back with iodine. The doctor arrived, pulling in behind him a sonogram machine to map the exact location of the pockets of trapped fluid. He would then insert a long needle through Ken's ribs and withdraw this fluid, careful not to collapse the lung or damage the lung tissue and risk infection.

I paced the narrow hallway, beside myself with the physical need to protect Ken. He was now my child, my wounded, my cause.

The doctor removed a liter and a half of fluid that would be sent immediately to pathology.

Shivering, Ken complemented the doctor on his expertise, assuring me when I squeezed into the room, that it really hadn't hurt too much. I wrapped my sweater around him. He was trembling and damp with sweat, gray with pain. The nurse watched us with silent, skeptical eyes.

Immediately Ken could breathe easier, but he had become absurdly fragile, easily thrown out of breath and unable to talk.

The second lung was drained the next morning. The

same nurse assisted, but this time she did not bristle at my anxiety, my interference. While I waited outside the small room as the doctor finished up, she slipped out to speak to me. Her tight expression, long set in lines of middle-aged disappointment, softened suddenly.

"Your husband is a remarkable man." Her pale green eyes had turned curious, thoughtful. "He told us in there he could only go through all of this because of his family—that you've given him the strength of unconditional love. He said he never knew what that was before. That because of you, he knows what it is to be fully loved." She touched my shoulder, a fleeting compassionate gesture. "I thought you should know he said this. In there, when he could barely breathe."

I jammed my hands in my jeans. "I love him with all my heart."

"He lives on it."

* * *

We met with Drayneau the next morning in his office.

The lung fluid contained cancer cells, millions of them.

Ken and I caught our breath in dismay. The cancer had not been eradicated, burned out, or incinerated by the months of toxic chemicals. Just the opposite had proved true: Cancer had spread rampant through Ken's lungs, and in the wash of oxygen and blood, swept to every corner of his body.

"How long?" I choked.

"Three to five months." The doctor lay both hands flat on Ken's file. "Less, if the lungs fill with fluid, if we do nothing."

Drayneau's tone was precise, with the coolest hint of regret. He addressed Ken with the utmost respect. This was Ken's call now. There was no protocol to suggest.

Ken and I locked glances. We had children. We had each other to care for. We had things we must know.

Drayneau assured us that Ken would be able to spend his remaining days comfortably at home. He mentioned there was in the oncology trade a "last ditch" chemo, known for its favorable results in delaying the inevitable. But, Drayneau explained, according to the insurance practices of the time there could be no hospice support or home care available to us as long as Ken "actively" undertook "therapy." In other words, accepted further chemo treatments.

Drayneau estimated a 25 percent chance this last drug might "arrest" the cancer's continued spread; and then, perhaps, one of the new trial drugs might be able to hold the cancer at bay for a matter of months.

"I want to do it," Ken said firmly. We would be among that lucky 25 percent. We had to be. We were the percent *that could.*

The doctor prescribed oxygen to help Ken breathe, and standing just outside his office, Ken and I had a knock-down drag-out fight. Ken refused to put on the mask, refused to use the portable air pump.

"Damn it, Ken!"

I knew the oxygen tank reminded him of his mother. The hose hooked over his ears and the nose inhalator represented stark, gut-wrenching images of "dying" to him, the last portrait he photographed of his mother smiling through her oxygen hoses, her white head close to Katy's and a big, faded smile on her face that didn't quite reach her eyes. She was waiting out her time to the beat of the hiss of compressed air.

I hooked the hose firmly over his ears and fit the ventilator plug to his nose.

"Please," I begged, my eyes stinging. "For me."

That night Ken cooked a gourmet meal of broiled and herbed halibut and buttered paprika potatoes served on a beautiful white plate beside a rosebud from my garden. He put the meal on the table, his own act of apology and grace. Food was nurturing, nurturing was love, and Ken loved me.

Hour after hour that night I sat through the dark, propped against the head of the bed, holding my husband and listening to the breath crackle deep in his chest. Ken rested peacefully and slept late into the morning. His eyes, when he awoke, were the darkest blue, nearly translucent. Light itself.

Where the
River Runs

The next morning we drove out to Riverside Cemetery, where my grandfather and grandmother lie. We chose four plots in "Remembrance," a corner of green bluff overlooking the Spokane River, near where the blue heron nest.

Subdued, the cemetery salesman drove us out to view the plots. Ken got out of the car slowly, his oxygen tank hanging off my arm as we walked to the edge of the bluff and looked down at the cool green water rushing below. It was hot, the sky a hazy blue. The July breezes smelled of corn husks and dandelions.

Ken and I clasped hands, remembering the purchase of Katy's first nursery, picking out the knotty pine twin beds, her dresser, and a nightstand with a white porcelain swan nightlight. How far and strange the journey from there to here: choosing not a nursery, but a granite headstone, going carefully over the spelling of our last name.

The salesman served us tactfully, but we could see in his

eyes how frightening to him that we should do this together; talk about death, with the near-dead still present, standing on the very ground he would be buried in. I imagined the middle-aged man in his sweat-stained discount suit felt secretly frightened Ken might drop dead on the spot, so continuously did his eyes flicker from Ken to the oxygen to my steady clasp of Ken's hand.

Ken finalized the details, direct and simple, still his humourous self, choosing the veteran's plaque for a grave marker. "After all," he half-smiled, "it's free. What else will the government ever give you free of charge?" And of course he insisted on the airtight vault: He intended to wear his best black cashmere jacket through eternity.

Ken and I returned alone to the river bluff, and parked the car, resting in silence with our thoughts.

Who does this? I wondered. Who chooses a place of rest even as they hope for miracles? Who squabbles between burial or cremation, vault or niche, the monument—what size, color? Who buys adjoining gravesites for their kids? Some bizarre idea to keep the family together?

"How do you feel?" I asked.

"Good," Ken said, sighing. "This is a natural, beautiful place. Look right, down the river canyon. See the train trestle? We can see the wishing trains from here."

It was our tradition to wish while passing under trains crossing the trestles. How many trestle wishes I had made in vain driving under the thundering trains.

"This feels like home," Ken acknowledged simply. "I know you'll come visit me. I can imagine you reading on the bench." He fell quiet for a moment. "Best of all," he winked with a sly, mischievous smile, "we finally have that vacation spot with a view!"

I squeezed his hand. The last thing that had needed doing was done.

We drove home slowly, me taking Ken's place at the wheel. Ken wanted me to learn to be comfortable with his truck, and meticulous, he took this time to show me the quirks of his beloved 4Runner, explaining all her eccentricities and surprises. I would have the taxes to learn, the computers, maintaining the quirky chemistry of the spa, the furnace . . .

I placed my hands on the steering wheel, finding the exact grooves in which Ken's hands had rested. I willed myself into him, into shared atoms and energy and all the mystery of Einstein's world where we might dance seamlessly, one light and the light of the other, all one.

*　*　*

Friends came by, traveled in, sat with us and drank tea or rubbed Ken's feet, quiet and accepting. Abby and her husband arranged to arrive over the weekend of the Fourth of July as they would be in Washington at that time, visiting friends. They said they would borrow a car, come over, and stay a few days with us.

Ken slept more now.

It became each day's task to rise, dress, greet the sun.

One late afternoon, Ken sat in the kitchen chair, reading his notes from the last cooking class. I came over, and stroking his shoulder gently, looked down and read the scrawled recipe.

Tuscany Pizza
  Quality mozzarella
  Flour board on table

Spread from middle out
Spread fresh garlic on top of pizza

Dough
Baker's yeast—touch of maple sugar syrup
3 cups of flour, salt to taste
1 cup warm water
A little olive oil
*Smooth small amount olive oil over finished dough, let
  rise*

Topping
Rosemary mixed with caramelized onion
Need pizza stone
Turn oven to highest setting
Coat dough, after forming pizza, with olive oil
Put on mozzarella, pancetta, onions, more oil
Dust cornmeal on top of pizza stone
Cook fifteen minutes
Sprinkle truffles on top after removing from oven

"Sounds delicious! Shall we make this for dinner?"

"I can't make it to class, G." Ken looked up. Tears filled his eyes and rolled unchecked down his cheeks. "I just can't."

"It's all right," I assured him, stricken by his vulnerability. "I'll call and explain. You can always make class up later."

"No. No—you don't understand," he protested brokenly, bowing his head. "This was the only thing, the only thing left that wasn't about cancer."

I crossed my arms around his shoulders from behind, resting my hands on his heart. "Come with me, then," I said. "I have some yard work to do. Keep me company."

I helped Ken outside to the deck, as McDuff, the puppy,

frolicked in abandon at his feet and then bounded away. The older dog stayed near his side. Oddly, the garden had never looked so gorgeous, blooming in a riot of delight. Ken's arms browned in the sun as he rested in the chaise, and contentedly, I weeded the flower beds. Ken's hands nestled deep in the ruff of the small dog.

Rising and leaning against the hoe, I looked at Ken's hands in a moment of simple awareness. The broad, square-tipped fingers: capable, strong hands. Broad of bone, sturdy, Ken had always been my safe place to fall.

His silhouette shimmered in the bright sun.

Breath

Ken touched me urgently awake.

"What's wrong, sweetie?" I asked, groggy and confused. I had fallen asleep late, around four in the morning. The clock said six.

"I want to—I need to go—to the hospital. I can't breathe," he rasped out softly, apologetically. "I waited, to let you sleep. But I, I really can't breathe."

I heard the harsh liquid crackle of each shuddering breath and I glanced at the oxygen tank, it was low.

Jumping out of bed, I refilled the portable tank from the frozen reservoir of oxygen kept in the garage and yanked up the meter. But the flow indicator was already set to maximum air flow and I had done nothing more than break the gauge. Running back inside, I brought Ken the fresh tank.

His hands clasped the tank loosely. His eyes were desperate.

"Okay. Okay, babe," I chattered as I threw on jeans and a shirt. "Right now. We're off right now. Let's get you dressed."

Rapidly I folded Ken into a button-down shirt, his favorite Hawaiian, and then into loose khakis, slipping his feet into sandals. In a matter of minutes, I had the car keys, the oxygen pump, and we were darting down the hill to Emergency.

Handing over our insurance information, I urged the young assistant, her young face caked in acne scabs and blots of drugstore makeup, to pass us immediately to the triage nurse. Ken perched on the edge of the hard vinyl chair, his head bowed, his chest shuddering with the effort to breathe. I gave the nurse a bullet summary of Ken's medical history, and we were shown to an examining cubicle.

Listening for a second to Ken's lungs, the duty physician suggested checking for a pulmonary embolism and sent Ken to Radiology for a CT scan. Half an hour later, the scans came back. No embolism. Ken's lungs were completely full of fluid. Only then did the ER physician note Ken's cancer history and contact Drayneau.

I held Ken's hand tight as we waited. His forehead was beaded with perspiration, his skin a peculiar white and gray as he struggled to breathe upright on the gurney.

Karla Ann, the cancer therapist, was on duty that morning in the ER. She came in and gently squeezed Ken's hand. "Can you go to your quiet place?" she urged.

Tears pressed out of the corners of Ken's eyes.

ER sent us back down the hall to Radiology to have one lung drained immediately.

"Look, my husband needs pain meds—and he needs them now," I requested from the physician. "We didn't bring any with us."

The radiologist explained he was technically unable to order Ken any pain meds unless he readmitted him to the ER. As he prevaricated, Ken doubled over, his eyes screwed shut. I took the radiologist outside the room.

"Please, you have to get pain relief. Look at him."

"Uh," the doctor looked over his shoulder. "The drain procedure is only fifteen minutes or so long. . . ."

"I don't care—*get morphine now!*"

A second doctor pushed open the double doors, laughing, his last words cut off as he assessed the tension, observed Ken on the gurney in the room behind us.

"Let's get something to help this man, shall we?" the older man suggested pleasantly. "I'm Dr. Martin. I'm going to drain your lung now, Mr. Grunzweig."

Moments later the junior radiologist returned. "It's on order."

"Enough?" I questioned. "They won't be used to the dosage on the ward—I've been through this. Are you sure you ordered enough?"

"Come in here, G," Ken gritted through clenched teeth. "Meet Dr. Martin."

The radiologist was squinting at the sonogram.

"You can do this, right?" *Where was the morphine?*

Martin launched into an explanation that I cut off short.

"Yes, yes. My husband can't breathe, and it's freezing in this room. Let's just get this done."

Ken touched a finger to my lip. "Here, hold me and we'll get this over with."

He leaned his forehead on my shoulder, and I tucked my face into his neck, trying hard not to cry in frustration. I kissed his cheek, whispering encouragements. Ken's chilled skin tasted of something chemical and strange.

Swabbing Ken's back with iodine, the doctors began to

insert the long needle between his ribs. Ken's muscles spasmed, and he shuddered, trying for short intakes of air. He was suffocating, his nerves and brain on fire.

They pulled a liter of fluid off the stronger left lung, and immediately Ken was able to breathe easier, his powerful chest heaving.

The doctors departed to authorize the paperwork for the transfer upstairs. We arrived on the ward, and within minutes an older nurse in a jungle-print smock stopped by Ken's gurney to inform us she had pain medication, but not in the necessary dosage. The nurses had been surprised, and questioned the order.

"We're not used to that dosage on this floor," the wide-eyed matron remarked.

Exercising great self-restraint I put my hand firmly on her arm. She recoiled slightly.

"Pain meds and I mean *now*."

Her face froze. Moving briskly, she injected what she had into Ken's IV and then ran down to the pharmacy herself. Out at the main desk, Drayneau was on the phone, chewing out the senior staff nurse for questioning his original order. We had been in the hospital for seven hours at this point without so much as an aspirin.

Shortly after, Drayneau himself appeared in the room. He assessed Ken quickly, his expression grim. "Let's see if we can't get you some relief, Ken."

Ken nodded tightly. His hands tremored on the white coverlet.

Drayneau took Ken's pulse and listened to his heart. He added another medication, which in combination with the correct morphine, he told us, would calm the tightening chest spasms and allow Ken greater oxygen intake.

Ken could not breathe enough to respond. His eyes

shone in narrow pinpoints of panic above the edge of the plastic oxygen mask. Drayneau adjusted the air flow to high, and gradually Ken's chest muscles relaxed and the heaving gentled.

I looked at my husband, strapped within a hissing, pumping oxygen mask, his skin an unearthly blue pallor. Our eyes met. We were both frightened.

Ken slept then for several hours, his breath a rough roar grinding through his chest. I waited by his side, breathing for him, with him, warming his hands with my own.

When he awoke, Drayneau had reappeared, Ken's chart folded against his chest.

The oncologist walked near to Ken and touched him affectionately, his hand lingering on Ken's arm.

"Rough day?"

Ken smiled weakly, pulling the oxygen mask to one side.

"Things aren't feeling so good."

"I'm afraid the news isn't so good either, Ken." Drayneau's eyes flicked swiftly to mine. "Your CT shows fluid has returned in both lungs. And the fluid report shows aggressive cancer. There are new tumors throughout the right lung— many of them, Ken. I honestly can't believe how many. And, I'm fairly certain there are signs of new tumor growth in the left lung as well."

Drayneau rubbed his chin, leaning back against the heat register, his back to the hospital window's view of the eastern mountains. He smiled then, wry regret twisting through his voice. "Ken, Glenda . . . we need to talk about 'coding' instructions." He hesitated, studying his shoes.

" 'Coding' instructions?" I asked.

"These are my—our—instructions to the staff, regarding emergency intervention." He let the words sink in. Drayneau's voice grew very soft. "It has been my experience that resuscitating a patient who has terminal cancer from heart or lung failure, responding to a 'code' as we call it, never works out to the patient's long-term advantage."

"Because there is no long term. Because the cancer's terminal," I filled in dully. "The patient's going to die anyway."

"Yes," Drayneau acknowledged. "Emergency intervention doesn't extend much quality of life at this point. Heroic efforts might only be traumatic, and of little value. I recommend a DNR, 'Do Not Resuscitate' order."

He wrote something in Ken's chart and then looked up first at Ken, and then at me.

"We are agreed? A 'no code' instruction in the advent of a failure?"

"A failure?" I reached for Ken's hand.

"Heart failure," Drayneau said. "Ken, your heart is under enormous pressure from your lungs and the burden of pumping through this fluid. And with the damage to your body sustained from the cancer, I worry about your heart the most."

I ran little circles across the back of Ken's hand with my thumb.

"All right." Ken struggled to sit upright, his gaze holding Drayneau's. "Yes."

The doctor talked briefly about available measures for keeping Ken comfortable and out of pain, measures to breathe—quality of life treatments.

"I want to do everything and anything that will make a difference," Ken insisted. "I want to be here long enough for my kids to come home, and for my granddaughter to be born. I need as much time as I can possibly have."

I looked from one man to the other, the doctor and his

patient, acutely aware of the shared trust and care. I stroked a wrinkle smooth in the hospital coverlet.

"Would you like some time alone with the doc here, Ken? To discuss things you want to know but might not want me to hear?"

Ken turned to me slowly, and nodded.

Drayneau appeared surprised, and as always, uncomfortable outside the box. I could see he felt he had done his piece, had jotted down the "no code" instructions. What more was there?

But I knew my husband. He would want to know how he was going to die, what dying was going to be like, and whether his death could truly be managed at home if he went home, so his family would not be traumatized in the process.

Drayneau called me back into the room a short while later, and we talked about stabilizing Ken over the next few days. His body hovered dangerously close to congestive heart failure, his breathing was 80 percent compromised, and he certainly faced a great risk of pneumonia and kidney failure. But, Drayneau stated, if we could get Ken back on his feet, and if he could be brought back down to a level of meds I could administer by pill at home, then Drayneau would agree to release him.

Drayneau crossed his arms. "We'll see how it goes, Ken."

Ken requested the last chemotherapy treatment be administered on schedule, here in the hospital.

"More chemo?" I asked, shocked.

"More time," Ken answered simply.

Outside Ken's room, I met with Drayneau in the tiny family waiting room. A consulting surgeon joined us and Drayneau asked the specialist to give us his opinion on inserting into Ken a permanent shunt, a lung drain. After some debate we agreed that the procedure wasn't worth the trauma to Ken. The team would drain his lungs as needed, at least for a while longer. Without saying the words, the two physicians made it clear that time was not on Ken's side. The chest surgeon excused himself.

Drayneau and I stood alone.

I stared down at the scruffy indoor carpeting, a kind of brown-blue beige that blended into the dark undecorated walls.

"How bad is it?"

"Not good. I couldn't believe the scan, Glenda," Drayneau admitted, shaking his head. "I counted at least seventeen good-sized tumors in the right lung. Unbelievable they could grow this fast. And there are tumors taking shape in the left lung as well. Cancer in the fluid means the lungs, the bloodstream . . ." His lips folded, his eyes sad.

"I can't believe how unfair this is," I breathed, shattered. "Ken has worked so hard! This is so hard on him." All I could think of was hard. *Hard, hard, hard.* This life was too hard, dying too hard.

Drayneau rested his hand on my shoulder for the fleetest second. "And hard on you."

"Can I really bring Ken home?"

"Only if we succeed in stabilizing him, and can lower the levels of drugs he requires to breathe, to survive with this pain. Ken needs to get on his feet, Glenda. At least sit up. If he can't, he can't leave the hospital. I'm sorry."

"He has to come home. We both want that."

"I know." Drayneau held my gaze. "Glenda, Ken just told me that he doesn't want anything to traumatize you and the kids. I'm trying to get you guys there."

Somehow we had to support Ken's body this last length

of the marathon. We needed our children home, and, I promised myself, Ken must live to see his oldest daughter become a mother, to celebrate becoming a grandfather. The two of us would crawl across the days on nothing but heart and will if we had to.

Presence

Ken's family gathered at the hospital. Abby and her husband, and Ken's older brother flew up from Los Angeles. Lon, Ken's ex-brother-in-law, flew in from New York. It was Lon's idea to throw a party.

On a borrowed hospital cart, Lon trolleyed up a complete gourmet menu featuring wine and catered entrees from Luna, Ken's favorite restaurant in the city. Jazz played on a portable radio and savory smells filled the ward: charbroiled lamb, peppered salmon, Steak Diane. I gave Ken small bites of the lamb, touched by the contagious joy of the gathering, the smile on Ken's face.

The family dug into blackberry cheesecake as Ken was hooked up to his last chemotherapy.

Later in the quiet hours, Ken told Abby good-bye.

"I can't take care of you anymore, Ab."

Abby held his hand, her mascara running down her face.

She nodded, unable to speak. They sat together like that for a long time.

Eventually, the nurses came in to remove Ken's chemo IV, and everyone tiptoed out as Ken had fallen into a light sleep.

Standing by the wall of windows in the seventh-floor hospital lounge, we watched the Independence Day fireworks flare upward into the dark sky over the Spokane River. Medic-flight helicopters swooped in at regular intervals, touching down on the heliport on the floor above us.

I held Abby's hand as we watched the fireworks. Divided in our love for Ken, it seemed we had at last united in our impending loss.

* * *

Tim and Judy had driven over to Spokane and brought their families to visit Ken in the hospital. Ken talked with Tim privately about his memorial and Tim reported Ken was very clear about what he wanted done, and he had volunteered to be his lieutenant, to see that everything was accomplished. Given the immediacy of the crisis, it didn't seem strange that no one mentioned Mom. If I told her the truth, asked her to come see Ken, I suspected she would find it impossible to do so. As we hugged good-bye, I saw on my brother's and sister's faces their determination to do whatever was necessary. I was so proud of them, so grateful.

Within a matter of days, Tim had spoken to the three men Ken had chosen to lead his services: Alec Drummal, Jonas Holland, and Enrico Ellis. Two were colleagues from San Francisco, one man coming in from Colorado. All three were close friends from a past "Leadership and Spirituality" seminar they had participated in at Santa Clara University, led by Alec.

Alec Drummal, a theological academic, was both Ken's spiritual adviser and friend. Enrico Ellis, a European raised in Latin America and a Jew, was a fellow technology executive and long-time confidant. The third man, Jonas Holland, former physicist and ordained Episcopal priest, had become a close friend through the experiences of their shared executive peer group. Alec had been preparing to leave with his wife on a journey to France when he got the call from my brother. My brother explained what Ken asked of him, sharing that Ken was in the hospital.

Alec put his bags down and booked a flight to Spokane. A burly, older man with elegant white hair, he arrived with his notebook in hand and spent the afternoon. They laughed and shared in the bonds of old friendship as Ken expressed what he envisioned his memorial to be. He wanted the service to be held in our home, he wanted everyone he loved and respected there, and he wanted specific ideas and spiritual truths to be shared. Ken wished to acknowledge the presence of a universal god, the truth of all religions. He wanted to celebrate both his identity as a Jew and his sense of himself as something more: that we were all *something more*. The rest he entrusted to his friend.

"You know me," Ken assured Alec quietly.

Alec wrote it all down. Together, he and Enrico would lead the memorial and Jonas would direct the private graveside service. In conclusion, Enrico would lead the Kaddish prayer. Then they meditated and prayed.

I drifted in and out of the room, astonished and grateful Ken was taking the lead planning something I could not even begin to confront—his memorial. I had no words for that.

When Alec finally took his leave, we hugged for a long moment in the hallway.

"I am so angry with God," I muttered through my tears.

"Of course you are," Alec agreed soothingly. He spoke quietly about the wisdom of God's will.

"God's will? God has no right to take Ken from me!" I interrupted fiercely. "I refuse to give *anyone* the right to say this outcome is better. My heart is breaking, Ken's heart is breaking. What God would do such a thing to such a good man?"

Alec Drummal touched the journal filled with his notes of Ken's thoughts with a gentle smile. He sighed.

"Ken accepts, Glenda. He is ready. And his journey, his life, has closure as he sees it. Your anger, that too God can accept."

So tell me, tell me, God, what do I do with the enormity, the vast agony of what I feel?

No way out but through.

Time hollowed out, no seconds, no beats. I felt sheer as glass. Our souls struggled, yoked in a steady rowing rhythm through each breath, through each day toward our goal of going home.

One night, in the hospital bed, Ken stroked my hair as I lay curled in beside him, a Mariners game on the television, his mind dreaming in and out of time. His summer blue eyes had grown a wintry gray.

"I have given you my life. This old soul is entrusted in your hands," he murmured in the night.

I touched him, and strength coursed through my hands even as the breath stumbled in his chest. I infused Ken with all the life force I possessed, holding him close, lying next to him on the narrow hospital bed and whispering to his heart.

Ken and I lived within the small moments now, and love had become the very breath he survived on. Love flowed as a life force—as biology and mystery and time. Love had become our absolute, the gravity of the heart, with its own rules and order and unknown provenance.

And somewhere in this union flowed an unobserved subset of deep-current facts, the hidden mathematical equations that constitute the gridiron mechanics of the world. Not the measure of metastatic mass, the rate of cellular destruction, or blood cell counts, but the will of the heart, the sweep of the mind, the fusion of spirit.

"Do you know what I love best about life?" Ken drowsed as we lay together. The Seattle Mariners were entering the seventh inning, the sound turned down low, punctuated occasionally by the sharp crack of the bat followed by the muted noise of the crowd rising to its feet. A boy from Cleveland, baseball was close to Ken's heart.

"No," I smiled at him. "What do you love best?"

"Our family life."

I hugged him close.

Walking the silent hospital halls through the late hours, I had become very aware of one room at the end where an elderly man lay on top of the covered bed, wrapped only in a diaper. He lay with his back to the corridor, completely alone. And then one morning he was gone, and I heard from the nurses he had passed away in the night.

Only then had I realized we were in the wing of the hospital where people came to die. Ken's refusal to do so had made us a curiosity on the ward. Throughout the day staff gravitated to his side, uncertain but following some clear inner impulse. Quiet, they unburdened their hearts.

The nurse whose father was dying on a floor above, asked, "What should I say to him?" The breath tech, a failed minor-league pitcher who had not spoken with his mother for ten years, talked instead with Ken, oxygen pumping softly through the hospital hoses. And Dr. Hanson, the new surgical resident, dropped in twice during her shifts to chat about children she had cared for on her last medical mission to the Congo.

Ken listened to every one of them, patient and gentle.

On and on, I walked the abandoned halls, gathering life, stuffing as much heart and breath and humanity as I could in my pockets. I gathered sighs, and slivers of hope, and fallen prayers and dreams all mixed together and thrown out in the laundry cart, anything of life. I hated this, hated the hospital, the smells and numbness, and yet all of this was to *still be alive*. And so I did not let the least sigh on the ward go unanswered. *I hear you. I hear you in there.*

*　*　*

The night Ken told Abby goodbye, I fell asleep, exhausted, by his bedside. The late-shift nurse pried me out of the chair I was dozing in and pointed me toward the other empty bed in Ken's room.

Could I actually rest there? The nurse nodded.

It was against hospital rules to let anyone use an empty bed, but this was his shift, and aware of my exhaustion, the endless days of caring for Ken, of working our way toward first sitting, and then standing, he gently dimmed the lights and closed the door.

Grateful, I stretched out and fell hard asleep to the hiss of Ken's oxygen.

Sometime in the night, a sound awakened me.

My eyes flew open, staring into the dark, disoriented. I realized what I had heard was Ken's *voice*. He had just spoken. I raised myself to get up and go over to check on him, to give comfort, when he spoke again. Quite clearly.

"God?"

I held my breath. A very dark and heavy presence had unfolded within the room; a chill and immutable condensation of energy.

I knew only that it was *not* God, and Ken seemed to know this also, as he stirred, impatient.

I felt death.

Death was in the room. Death bore the face of this grave angel, the dark-winged messenger. The angel waited and held open the door of Ken's death, patient there between us.

Afraid, I felt an intense urge to break in between Death and Ken, to leap over Ken's chest and force the Dark away; draw Ken back into my circle of life, my warm breath, my strong love. But I froze, knowing the moment was beyond me. Death, the crossing of death's door, was absolute, distinctly holy and personal.

Ken began to talk then, an exchange I felt permeate the room but could not understand. He drew upright, alert in the bed: engaged and unafraid, clear. His energy astounded me, his presence vibrated within the darkness that surrounded the messenger. Somehow, I knew to keep silent. That I was to honor spirit, allow Ken full confrontation with this moment.

But please not now, I begged silently. *Please, not here.*

The moment of Ken's death had arrived.

He bargained. He extended the moment. He asked for time.

And for reasons unknown to me, Death granted the wish.

I shivered on the opposite bed, feeling the lift of the messenger's weight depart from the room. I heard Ken sigh, and then the simple human night closed back around us, seamless once more.

A few moments later, the night nurse arrived on rounds to record Ken's vital signs. He flicked on a low light. Surprised to see Ken awake, he asked if he needed anything.

"No, thank you. Absolutely everything's fine."

I hid my face in the pillow and wept.

Homecoming

The next morning, after listening to Ken's lungs, Daniel Drayneau informed me privately that the time had arrived to bring
Katy home. He knew David was headed home that afternoon
on a two-day flight from Australia.

It was the day of my daughter's fourteenth birthday.

Katy called me from a pay phone, somewhere on an island in the Chesapeake Bay.

"Happy birthday, honey," I greeted her, making an effort
to be cheerful.

Katy bubbled on about the Sponge Bob cake the crew
had procured on a sneaky row to shore, the Happy Birthday lettering "To Mike" crossed out to read a messy "Katy."
How much she loved learning to sail, her study of the blue
crab.

"Baby," I took an audible breath. "Time to come home."
"Daddy?"

She knew instantly. I damned the distance between us

when I most needed to hold her safe from the world cracking beneath her feet.

"Yes. Daddy's in the hospital."

There was no moment of truth that would ever be so present in our lives again.

"Time to come home. The counselors will get you off the boat and to the airport, and I'll meet your plane."

"Okay." Her voice had grown as small as something invisible.

"Katy?"

"Yes?"

"I love you."

I felt her falling away.

"Katy? Believe in me. I'll take care of us and Daddy. And Daddy would very much like to hear you play your cello for him. Could you do that?"

"Will he ever come home?"

"That's our hope."

I picked Katy up the following afternoon at the airport. She had grown an inch taller, freckled and sunburnt. She hugged me, hollow-eyed and silent. We took her suitcase home and retrieved her cello.

She paused to take a deep breath before walking into the hospital. Smiling, she wheeled her cello case into Ken's room, hugged her daddy, and for the next four hours filled his room and the entire seventh floor with the sweet and uplifting sounds of Bach, Vivaldi, Rachmaninoff, and Saint-Saëns. Ken sat in a chair placed beside the bed as she played, and his face relaxed into an expression of rapt peace.

The next morning I returned to the airport and met David's rowdy school group at the arrivals gate. They had been in the air twenty hours, carting home Australian music pipes, all kinds of souvenirs, wearing happy, tired smiles.

David flung himself into my arms. Too excited to speak, he unbuckled his backpack on the floor, pawed through it, and still on his knees, opened a small velvet box.

"For you, Mommy," he offered proudly. In his hands lay a tiny opal on a gold chain. He had spent his entire savings on this gift for me. Unable to speak, I hugged him. David then fished out a pair of tiny earrings he had bought for Katy. "Do you think she'll like them?"

He babbled happily as we collected his luggage, and I paused to say good-bye to his trip leaders. The pair of teachers, a man in his early thirties, and an older, sandy-haired woman, looked inquiringly at me. I subtly shook my head.

The man cuffed David gently on the head. "Well, David was the best of the bunch. He's going to be voted most popular guy in high school some day! There wasn't one thing he wouldn't do—from rock climbing to karaoke. We all loved him."

David skipped off to hug one of his new friends goodbye.

The older teacher paused, and then said softly. "He was always very brave, Mrs. Grunzweig, even when we knew he was thinking about his dad."

David and I drove into town and pulled up at the ice cream store. I didn't know where else to go. Sitting cross-legged on the lawn in the July heat, eating mint ice cream, David finally asked me as I knew he would, "How's Dad?"

I looked down the hill. Beyond the spires of St. John's Cathedral, we could see the top floors of the hospital. Ken's floor.

"He's in the hospital, David. There." I pointed, and then rested my hand on David's knee. "Dad's not going to get better, honey. His cancer can't be stopped."

David stared at me in disbelief, and then broke down in my arms. Over and over he repeated through his tears, "You're sure? He's going to die? There's nothing we can do?"

I held him, hating everything. Hating the heartbreak I was handing my son, a heartbreak that nothing would ever mend. David was of Ken, soul mates bonded the moment of conception. "I always wanted a son," Ken had so often said. "A son named David." Something pure was being broken.

When David and I arrived at Ken's bedside, David did not say a word. He crawled up next to Ken and cozied in under his arm, burying his face in his dad's neck.

I would always carry the image of the two of them—the frailty of the father looking up at me in wide-eyed dismay, heart simultaneously full of love and breaking for his son—and the boy, cleaving to his side.

* * *

We had been in the hospital for nine days. On the afternoon of July 11, we received a phone call from Kurt in San Mateo. Jordan was in labor.

"You're sure?" Her delivery was supposed to be almost two weeks later.

"Totally!" Kurt laughed.

I raised my eyes to heaven, blinking back tears, handing the phone over to Ken.

Ken spent the entire glorious day talking Jordan through her labor. And when he heard the first cry of his granddaughter over the telephone as she was born, he cried his congratulations to Jordan, and to Kurt, the new Daddy. He repeated over and over how proud he was of Jordan, how much he loved her. This new soul joining their family had healed a great rift. Jordan could step forward and become someone new, a mother. His dearest desire was fulfilled: Jordan had a family of her own, her broken self made whole.

The joy in his eyes was contagious.

That day, Ken turned his morphine drip off. He refused to stay in the hospital another day.

In the morning I helped Ken into his Hawaiian shirt, the nurses removed the many IVs, and Ken walked the few steps on my arm to a wheelchair. Home health aids—a bath chair, and a bedside commode—would be delivered to the house, as well as extra oxygen and a walker. The nurses discharged us, their eyes misty. David carried balloons.

We went home.

*   *   *

I tucked Ken comfortably into our bed after a light meal of homemade chicken soup and administered his late afternoon medications. Exhausted, I retreated to the bathroom to wash my face and freshen up, leaving the door cracked open so I could hear Ken if he needed me. I could see him resting, reflected in the angle of the bathroom mirror.

Surprised, I saw David tiptoe in and climb up on the bed, curling in under his dad's arm. They had been so silent together now that "How are you doing?" could no longer be answered, "Fine, don't worry."

The two boys relaxed in the pillows, watching something on the television, the early news.

"You are going to have a lot of responsibilities for the family after I'm gone," I heard Ken say, taking David's hand in his.

David nodded.

"You have to be the man of the house. Try to do that well."

"Yes, Dad."

"Be good to the family, David," Ken continued, his words soft and rounded, gentle. "Stay strong."

Again, David nodded.

"Don't get into any kind of trouble. . . ."

I immediately thought of Jordan, understanding in Ken's words his worry his younger children would struggle after his death as Jordan had after her mother died.

"I won't, Dad." David promised, his small face serious.

"Your responsibility is to the family, David. You'll be the man now. . . ." Ken repeated. He fell silent.

"I know, Dad."

"I love you."

"I love you too, Dad."

A moment or two longer they held hands tightly. But before I could turn off the water and dry my hands, David had slipped off the bed and disappeared. Ken had dozed off.

* * *

I couldn't sleep that night and paced the house, roaming the darkened rooms. I found myself downstairs in Ken's studio. Aimlessly I sifted through the loose prints, images of David fishing in Montana, the wedding party in New York. On top of his darkroom files, and the arrangements for sending a portfolio to the museum that had purchased "Persimmons, 1998" at auction, lay a sheaf of handwritten pages.

What's this, another list?

The list ran for several pages, and appeared to have been begun and then discarded many times, picked up and begun again. I read through the list slowly, recognizing my husband in every line, every memory, every harrowing ache, heartbreak, and goofball screwup noted in his cribbed handwriting. On those spiral notebook pages were personal notations of abandonment and pain, of a larger courage, and slowly, the making of a man.

In this chronological collection of memories and events, Ken revealed a character of relentless self-honesty and indomitable determination. Ken was a code breaker, a generational maverick: the kind of kid who faced limited beginnings and determined for himself a better and different end. Beyond that, he survived. He survived to demand of the world a chance to engage: to learn what greatness he might be made of.

Ken's memories made me think. What had I learned by the river as a child so many years ago, looking up at the stars? That all of life was story: every smallest moment, chapter and verse of an unfolding tale of mystery and revelation.

A man or woman's life was given back to the world cached in small memories. Our stories in poignant recognition of unexpected role models, the engineering and design of our most secret losses, and the eloquent, sanguine grace of the most modest gesture. All of us made a life in the same manner, our roads bricked with choices and consequences amid the stunning interventions of fate.

Just these few lines on schoolboy paper carried the story of Ken. I read them, and listened to the cadence, hearing in the writing the ancient themes of struggle, courage, the undying craving for love.

Boys with bottles.
Sister act/brother relationship.
Girl with wallet. Broken window. Junior High violence.

Paddling at school.
Father beating, fighting, Mother love.
Grandmother, Father, Julius.
Playing at the shul, temple love. Grandfather Goldman.
Standing up for yourself and not standing up. Taking
  what is parents.
Fighting the goad. Park gangs.
Not understood by parents, and not understanding.
5,6,7ʰ grades—8,9,10ᵗʰ grades.
Irma, Sue, Naomi, fire-escape love.
Louis, Johnny K., & Tony, my mentor. Working on cars.
Electronics. Orgasm. House Fire.
High Bar Mitzvah.
Bike shops—Pee Wee, my mentor.
Fat to thin.
Your life is a work in progress! What are you working
  toward?
Night of running away from home.
Value of the man. Making choices.
USAF—oh my God—radio training.
Grandfather, death.
Electronics school.
Louisiana, the great cab accident, my night in jail.
Off to Iceland—adventure, just see what happens.
Being lonely.
Learning to be subordinate. Green spam. Learning to
  comply and not always fight.
Girlfriend in Iceland.
Sue and back to Cleveland.
And off to California in my TR3. . . .

I folded the pages carefully, humbled. Why does it take a lifetime to learn the truly simple things?

Traveler

I feel like I'm traveling all the time now—on a spiritual plane. There is no sense of time or place. I come to consciousness a stranger, asking Who am I?

Ken's journal, July 13, 2003

Ken was weak, and he lost balance easily, but there was about him a laser sharp energy, as though every second served a purpose. His body lived at the command of his mind.

In the still, warm afternoons, Ken sat on the back deck, breathing in the lavender-scented air tinged with pine bark and late summer grasses. Once, he opened his eyes, and turned to Katy, reading her book quietly next to him, "You can be anything you want to be. You know this?"

"I do, Daddy. I love you."

"And I love you, Katy Bear."

Ken was speaking a language that seemed to be the language of stars, as if all things, life itself, were revealed. He traveled in an open-ended parenthesis. As if this moment and the next, however different or altered time might appear to be, were a single temporal passage—one long endless loop through the universe. Ken evidenced neither worry nor fear. Gone was the aggressive resolution, the fight: and in its place floated a profound gentleness.

I was seeing a man at ease with his own life, and in mirror of that truth, death.

Our third night home we lay in bed, gazing at the forest beyond the bay windows, sharing the peace of the late summer twilight as it deepened to violet indigo night.

"Ken, what is God?" I asked, shy. I was sure he knew.

"A feeling?"

His eyes were half-shut, but he placed his hand on my solar plexus. His hand was warm and I relaxed into the physical connection. He held his hand steady, concentrating on the touch.

"Do you feel warmth?"

"Yes."

"Do you feel safe?"

"Yes."

"Do you feel anxious?"

"No."

"Do you feel love?"

"Yes."

"God is that feeling."

* * *

Enrico Ellis arrived from San Francisco accompanied by Jonas Holland. A large, outgoing man, Jonas arrived unusually subdued, aware of his twin roles of friend and priest. Enrico, perhaps Ken's closest friend, climbed the front steps slowly, his warmth bridled by sorrow, his eyes dark and solemn. The two men had already spoken with Alec Drummal and agreed to Ken's request to serve as his own missing voice at a thoughtful and philosophical memorial.

The two men joined Ken on the back deck. I brought tea, watching over Ken from a distance. He made the difficult seem easy, this talk of dying; as natural as his smile.

At the end of the day, the three men stood and shared a long, heartfelt hug. Saying their farewells on the doorstep of our house, Ken turned to Enrico. "My friend, you are standing in a meteorite shower of spirituality." His eyes glowed. "Such a *good* man."

There was benediction in Ken's presence. He had become a living, breathing presence bridging this world and the next.

*　*　*

After Ken's visitors departed, the late afternoon light settled in the corners of the quiet rooms, pooling on the scuffed wood floors. The dogs lay at Ken's feet, stretched out and dreaming, the old Yorkie making odd grunts and squeaks in his sleep. Ken sagged into the chair and I sensed a profound ebb had occurred in his energies. I encouraged him to rest as I cooked a savory meal.

That night, Ken assured me he was determined to eat well, and did so. It was as if the afternoon with his two dear friends had carried his soul to a place above pain. Sighing repeatedly, he enjoyed the small meal I prepared of grilled shrimp, slices of avocado, and fresh raspberries tossed on a butter leaf salad.

Over dinner we quietly toasted each other with our bravest smiles. Quiet, everything we did now was so quiet.

"I still want to believe I can get well, G," Ken said slowly as he gazed with enormous appreciation at the sharp fresh colors of his salad. But then he closed his eyes slightly, as if the words hurt. "But I know that spiritual insight is not given easily. God is not some Diamond Jubilee achievement."

"What do you mean?"

"Enrico and Jonas, they wanted so much more revelation than I could give. I could only tell them . . ." his eyes, grown so old and quiet, "I could only tell them to work at life. First, based on the learned traditions, and then, to offer whatever life required. To give of themselves whatever might be asked to create change, to gift back to the community." He smiled slightly. "God is not castanets. God is about being human, serving and leading humanity. God is in the work, in the mortar of the building. Easy to find but without which, the structure will surely collapse."

"You know this?" I blinked, stuck on the metaphor of God and castanets, swirling images of flamenco skirts and smoky lanterns.

"Yes." Ken stroked my hand, his fingers so frail they brushed my skin like moth wings. "The real mystery, G, is the transition from one side of life to the other. If I am given the chance to work on that other side? I will continue this work, serving and leading humanity. They may laugh at my naïveté, say, 'Oh, you puppy!' but in a few hundred thousand years, I'd like to be a *human* venture capitalist, working to leverage the capital of humanity. My chance to work on the Big Team."

I laughed. How perfect.

After our meal, I helped Ken to the bedroom on my arm, and assisted him as he changed into a soft cotton tee and fresh boxers, rubbing healing ointment into his stubborn bedsores. The skin on his buttocks hung in pleated folds, the lost body he once possessed, perfectly folded away like a Japanese fan.

Tucked up against the bed pillows, I handed Ken the relaxation tape Abby had brought from California with her. He put on the headphones and listened for a few minutes with his eyes closed to the music, his hands aimlessly dancing in the air.

Sighing, he took the headphones off.

"Well!" he concluded with a twinkle. "That's about as much California as I need!"

* * *

Time danced in a gentle waltz, with gifted moments of awareness. In the morning we lay close, our breath mingling.

Are you waking, honey? It's time for meds.

One of me woke at seven.

Who?

The physical being. And one of me woke between seven and ten.

Who?

The one who took his medicines—the protein-based being. One of me will wake between ten and eleven.

Who?

The one who loves you.

The day began with a long hug. Ken seemed so tired. I held his hands, his entire body in my arms.

Later, I came back into the bedroom with Ken's tray of medicines and found David cuddled in his arms. I smiled. Two boys in their underwear. They were making long casting movements toward the foot of the bed.

"What in the world are you guys doing?"

"Fishing!" David announced, his eyes full of playful delight. At twelve, he certainly knew he was not really fishing from a four-poster bed, but there he was, loving every minute of the imaginary game with his dad.

I climbed up beside them, nestling into the pillows.

Ken smiled down at David in the curve of his arm and then at me. "We're up at Flathead Lake, G, where David and I took our 'Dad and me' trip last summer? Since we couldn't get there this year, we're going now, on our own."

"Caught anything yet?"

"Not yet," groused David.

David cast his hands out and reeled his imaginary line back in slowly. Ken joined him, doing the same, their shoulders touching. On their faces the bliss of Montana: the wild blue lakes and white mountains, the early-morning mist rising off the waters.

Pretending, we listened for the faint *plink!* as the lures hit the lake and felt the whir of the reel as the lines came slowly in.

I leaned tenderly against David, my arm stretched around my two boys. Our house had vanished into the expedition truck: at their feet a tackle box. A father and son on a dock, casting in the reeds from shore.

I watched them fish awhile, until I noticed Ken's lips had drawn together, a pale suppression of pain and fatigue. I wanted desperately to preserve their moment of sharing, but also knew Ken needed to rest. Maybe I could spin for them a new story, carry the burden awhile.

"Honey, where is the one place in the world you most wanted to go and haven't been?"

"Alaska!" Ken replied immediately, his eyes dancing.

"All right then, my two pioneers. Fishing's done for the day. Climb on board my twin-engine Cessna for a private pilot escorted trip to the Alaskan wilds!"

David snuggled in closer to Ken. "Is she nuts, Dad?"

Ken winked at me, and shrugged.

"Close your eyes," I instructed firmly.

Arms out, I concentrated until I became pure energy, a twin-engine plane poised for flight, headed north toward the Denali wilderness. Launching skyward, we flew inland from the rocky coast through bumpy coastal rain bursts until we reached blue skies. The little plane hummed smoothly, following a ribbon of silver river. Below us three grizzlies fished in the salmon run, their great tawny paws raking the tumbling waters. We swooped low over a moose and her two calves, laughing at the great clumps of lake weed hanging from their mouths as they fed along the shore, and waved gaily to two canoes crossing a rivulet between lakes as blue as David's favorite marbles.

The tipping of gold on the snowy peaks signaled the setting sun, and lost in the silence of the wide Alaskan skies, we turned our tiny Cessna back toward home.

"So beautiful," Ken sighed softly. He was drifting asleep, his chin resting on David's head.

David kissed his father and then our eyes met. We had been someplace together that neither of us would ever forget.

*   *   *

Lying in bed next to Ken, reading late into the night, I noticed his hands dancing again in the air.

"Okay, now what are you doing?" I had to ask, too curious to resist.

"Pouring soup," he replied, grinning boyishly. "You've made this wonderful soup, you see, and I'm using these ladles to pour bowls from one to the other."

"I swear to God, you're hallucinating."

Ken chuckled, cracking open one eye. "Oh most definitely, but it's nice."

"I guess." I grunted. "Don't spill the soup."

I closed my book a bit later as Ken dozed beside me, wondering about the range of playful and serious reflections rippling in waves against the shores of his mind. There had been so many of these "flights of fancy" lately. I couldn't help but wonder if many were drug induced. But some tender part of me wondered, could they not also be lighthearted mental diversions? Invented to ease the grim and overwhelming pain?

Yes, all of that.

I was witnessing the sweetest separation of soul from body: a stepping out, partly in but nearly gone—Ken's mind slipping away from his physical being.

Ken had found for himself a way to be free. His mind mused and explored, and he shared this with me, offering us both a fragile, comforting counterreality. He lived in the fullness of his imagination, or perhaps, within the fullness of his spirit—unencumbered by his destroyed and damaged body. Free.

Embraceable You

Katy and David went downtown with friends to go swimming. The day was hot, over a hundred degrees outside.

Ken's brief rebound from the hospital abruptly crashed that morning. His breathing tightened and he seemed to be drifting occasionally into a nearly semiconscious state; and when surfacing, requested only pain meds. He had stopped talking, refused anything but water.

Irritated, he pulled at his oxygen hose. He hated it, it bothered him. His arms appeared more bruised, a sign his circulation had begun to fail. Anxious, I massaged both his feet and legs, noticing the spreading purple stains under the skin that refused to go away.

As I rubbed Ken's feet, I mused over our conversation the night before. Waking sometime in the endless nighttime hours, we had discussed letting go. Softly, we had agreed that surrendering to the body's fatigue was not the same as giving up. It had seemed important to say this—both of us recognizing Ken had been a lifelong fighter, a warrior of great heart. Neither of us felt it was necessary to hold on because of fear or doubt, better to let life take its natural course.

In a dry whisper Ken recounted the dream he'd just had. He was checking and rechecking his sailboat at the dockside, he said, making sure the boat's equipment was onboard, ready for a long voyage.

My heart grew numb, stunned at the beauty of what every element of his being seemed prepared to do.

* * *

Using the walker with David's assistance, Ken navigated the long hallway to join us at the table for dinner. Katy helped him to his chair, we sat down, and then, unaccountably, fell silent.

Before a meal we usually shared gratitudes and blessings for the day. But tonight, the kids spoke straight to Ken, acknowledging one at a time what they loved most about their father.

"I love your creativity, Dad," David began. "Your photography and the way you create beauty." He sat straight in the chair, unshed tears brimming in his eyes.

"And I love your bravery," Katy whispered, her eyes cast down. "You're fighting this illness with bravery for us." Her face held still, but I knew from the tremor of her lips she simply refused to cry.

Ken looked at each child as they spoke. His breath came lightly, his shoulders bowed in like the wings of a resting bird.

My turn. I sought Ken's gaze down the length of the table. "I love your ability to express love, Ken. I love you for the gift of our family and I love you for the legacy of your values as a father. I love you for loving me."

Ken's hands rested in his lap. "And me," he offered with the shadow of his old smile. "I love myself for my family. Family is what I love the most. And for how you unconditionally love me. God is family."

Shabbat Shalom. We broke bread.

After dinner, Ken and I sat on the back deck in the warmth of the summer twilight. It seemed too much effort to talk, so we rocked together, content in silence. We shared tea listening to Chet Baker on the stereo playing "Embraceable You," and my favorite, "Little Girl Blue." The music drifted away and the forest grew quiet.

I lit a candle against the growing darkness. Ken sat with his eyes shuttered, his chest barely moving with each breath. I sensed he had gone someplace far away. But it was his physical reality I was clinging to: the mark of his breath, the sounds of our music, our love. Him.

Ken opened his eyes and looked over at me. His expression tender, confident.

"They're waiting for me."

"Who?"

"My family."

Time felt very short now.

* * *

That night I called Jordan and Kurt. Their baby was nine days old. "If you want one last visit, now is the time."

They booked a flight for the morning, all three of them.

No Way Out
but Through

I took the dogs out for a long walk. Under the hot July sun, their paw pads stung from the heat radiating from the cement. The two animals drifted off the sidewalk and stayed on the grass, sniffing the posts and plants along the way. The Yorkie looked back often toward the house, questioning. Ken and I had walked together, always. To not walk together confused the little dog.

I trudged along, indifferent to the heat. I had not heard from my mother in three weeks: I had no idea how she was faring. Mom had not come to see Ken, I was not even certain she knew he had become so gravely ill, or had been in the hospital. The last few weeks had swept across my life like a white storm, obliterating the shape of everything—even the face and fact of my mother.

Caring for Ken, I had the odd epiphany that Mom's aloof reserve was not to her way of thinking an emotional rejection, but a gift. Her commitment to be independent forged long ago in the hard years her own mother cared for her grandfather and in the burden of caring for her parents. Mom's love was expressed by her determination to stand, and fall, alone. My mother remained the same woman who had held together a disintegrating marriage for seventeen years and sustained four children the years after. Her driving need was *to take care of her children.* Despite all appearances to the contrary, mothering was her prime directive, her instinct, her private pride and her way of love. In our adult lives, taking care of us had come to mean asking *nothing* of us. Even battling leukemia, Mom demanded we remain children. Cared for, not caring for her through what days remained of her life. My mother was permitting herself to fade from our topography, erased.

How different, she and I, in our needs. I needed tactile, familiar love. I needed the smell of her hair breathed deep in a long tight hug. I needed to look into those eyes I had known my entire life; especially now, when I felt cracked wide open, the terrain of my childhood and my marriage about to be obliterated by something I could neither control nor contain. Her death would be mine. And the man I had always known I was meant to love, whose geography belonged to me, his death too would be mine.

I thought about Ken's word, *unconditional.* Love offered without any condition of reciprocation or merit. No quid pro quo, the presence of genuine love defined by nothing more than *value.* Ounce by ounce, the more love the more suffering. How would I survive without my partner, my only love? Inside of me loneliness loomed, huge and terrifying. My days and sense of time unmoored. Marriage was my faith, my practice. Who but me would ever know how perfect we had life for a while, how good our marriage had been? I would not have even my best friend to relive the memories; for Ken was everything—best friend, lover, father. My living map of the known world.

I turned at the end of the loop and headed back once again toward home, our house, the cottage at the end of the block. With each step, I felt the full weight of walking alone.

I needed that old red wagon. *Back to how we were before.*

I reached the cool shade of the front porch and unleashed the dogs, scratching behind their ears the way they liked. I had an unsettled feeling about tomorrow, the twenty-second of July.

* * *

Kurt and Jordan arrived in the afternoon, and on their heels, hospice.

"Sorry, we've just gotten the paperwork." The nurse and social worker apologized, flustered, shuffling papers and assessing Ken's vitals. "I can't believe we've just now been called in." The nurse shook her head as she listened to Ken's heart, apprehensive.

Kurt and Jordan sat with Katy and David, admiring the new baby in the other room. They were giving the chaos in the bedroom a wide berth.

"I truly can't believe he can stand," the male social worker muttered as he thoroughly checked Ken out. He spoke as though Ken were not even there. And perhaps he was not. Ken stood within himself as though he waited alone, removed from his own body.

I was suddenly reminded of my dream, of the white fog and the small boxes. Was this invasion, this collapse, his moment in the smallest box? I wanted the medical support gone, but craved their expertise. I hated this frantic, frontline triage, the chaos deeply unsettling after the gentle calm of our last days at home.

The hospice pair left shortly after arriving, promising equipment and leaving behind a paper bag they identified as the "emergency kit." Morphine, antipsychotics, all the end-of-life emergency relief potent pharmaceuticals might provide. I clutched the bag in my hand, finally setting it down on the night table by my side of the bed.

Jordan tiptoed into the bedroom and apprehensively kissed her dad on the cheek, kneeling at his side in the bedside chair where he labored to breathe, exhausted and weak. Cuddling the baby, I leaned near Ken and placed the tiny bundle in his arms. He seemed bewildered at the arrival of company, the tiny bundle in his lap.

He looked down at his cradled arms in surprise, his grip tightening instinctively.

"Do you know who this is?" I asked softly.

Ken's eyes opened to slim slits, his consciousness struggling toward us.

"Yes," he whispered. "Of course. My grandbaby. Little Kendra."

Jordan and I exchanged gasps of pure joy.

* * *

Darkness fell around the neighborhood, but the lights from our bedroom window burned bright into the night, spilling outside through the black silhouettes of Ponderosa pine.

Ken began to grow increasingly agitated, fighting the oxygen mask and yanking it off his face with iron strength each time I begged him to let me replace it.

Over the telephone, the after-hours hospice nurse advised

me to hold the mask near his face from a distance—suggesting that perhaps the mask made him claustrophobic. I tried again, dodging Ken's fists as they swung out furiously, as if he were fighting off an assailant or taking a powerful breaststroke for breath. Jordan and I took turns holding the mask a few inches above his nostrils, keeping Ken constant company, uttering soothing, gentle words. But he fought our efforts to restrain him, and all our efforts to assist him. He refused cancer. He refused it.

Growing desperate, I called hospice again, and the nurse sighed compassionately, saying that sometimes an increasing lack of oxygen to the brain created a kind of paranoia of the mind. "Sometimes they just go as they've lived, honey, and he sounds like a fighter."

The nurse directed me to open the paper bag emergency kit, and to administer one of the antipsychotic drugs I would see clearly labeled in the bag. I opened the bag and dumped out suppositories, strange bags of dry powder.

"What's this? There's no morphine, there's nothing!" I cried into the phone in alarm. The nurse gasped and apologized for the mix-up. She assured me a courier would bring over the correct emergency medical kit as soon as they could open a hospice pharmacy. *Time*, I cried inside, *there is no time.*

Near midnight the kids slipped in to say goodnight. They had kept their distance in the frightening flurry of nurses and hospital equipment, equally afraid of Ken's flailing outbursts. But for the moment Ken lay still, breathing in labored exhaustion, his eyes closed. He lay in a hospital bed assembled by hospice at the foot of our own bed, a thin sheet covering his legs, the oxygen pump hissing rhythmically at his side.

Katy brushed his cheek with a kiss, and David leaned over, the tears welling. " 'Night, Daddy."

At the sound of his son's voice, Ken stirred, thrashing up from the bed. "Up!" he gasped out. "Let me up. *Please!*"

"Look! Look, you've disturbed Dad," Katy scolded David, frightened. The children looked at me, their hands instinctively reaching to soothe their father's flailing arms. I hugged them both.

"No, no. It's okay, you didn't disturb Daddy. Far from it, your kisses mean the world. Daddy loves you." I turned and stroked Ken's cheek, calming him. "Right now is just very hard for Daddy. Don't worry, I'm taking as good care of him as I can."

The kids crept out of the room, uneasy and deeply aware.

Ken was refusing oxygen for more than minutes at a time. Breath roared in and out of his chest with harsh, popping sounds, a fire consuming a dry house. His grip on my arm remained tight as a vice, and his sudden thrusts to raise himself upright were both startling and unpredictable.

Jordan kneeled at the head of the bed, near Ken's pillow, and began to sing a tune from the Eagles, "Hotel California."

"Remember, Daddy?" she whispered in his ear. "Remember how we used to blast that song on the radio driving up the 101?"

Ken turned his head toward Jordan as a blind animal turns toward warmth, and I tiptoed out of the room, giving Jordan and her father a last privacy.

At two in the morning, the hospice delivery pharmacist banged on the front door, the headlights of his minivan beaming brightly into the darkened front room where Kurt and the baby had fallen asleep on the sofa. Wordlessly, he handed me the new bag of medicines.

I called the nurse.

Ken's levels of pain had begun to overwhelm his body in

waves, harsher and faster, one wave crushing through the other. He no longer uttered any intelligible sounds. His teeth clenched hard, his jaw pulsing with tension.

The nurse listened to Ken's harsh and gasping breath over the telephone. "Oh, my. That's terrible. You're sure you don't want an ambulance? No, not much they could do. Let's help."

The nurse talked me through each item in the kit, instructing me to assemble the two differing narcotics. First, I was to administer a syringe of antihallucinogen by slipping the syringe into the corner of Ken's mouth, between his cheek and his clenched teeth. "This is relief, baby. I promise. This is help," I murmured in his ear.

Next, a half syringe of morphine: the second half to be delivered in two hours, if necessary. I held Ken's head firmly in my hands, fighting him as he tossed the syringe off. Concentrating, I succeeded in getting a precious bit into the corner of his mouth. I remembered what Karla Ann had said as she hugged me after her last visit. "Don't parse kindness," she'd urged in a lowered voice. No pain relief was "too much" now.

I whispered in Ken's ear the meditation cues, offering the comfort of his "quiet place." He twisted away, his jaw taut, and I bent over his bed, weary with exhaustion and frustration, fully devastated by my inability to help.

Jordan stood mutely, rubbing her dad's foot through the thin sheet.

"You go to bed, honey," I said with a sigh. "I'll take the night watch."

Jordan nodded and kissed her father on his forehead.

Silent, I observed her tenderness, her sure maturity. This child, this rebellious heartbreaking child, had grown in a matter of months into a brave and courageous woman. She was here right where she needed to be, finally and fully here for her father. Their circle joined, unbroken.

"I'm so proud of you, Jordan," I whispered.

She met my eyes, blinking back tears.

I turned to Ken. This was our journey now. No way out but through.

Wings

During the night the moon rose outside our bedroom window over the dark ravine and the summer grasses flamed white through the trees. I pulled the drapes wide open, bathing the bedroom in moonlight.

Eased at last from his pain, Ken relaxed into the raised pillows, his breath evening into long rower's pulls—shallow, easy inhalations that barely disturbed his ribs. Sitting beside the bed near his shoulders, I lay my ear on his chest and felt his heart still thudding, lightly, with long pauses. His body relaxed beneath the long stroke of my hand from his cheek to his chest.

With a warm cloth I wiped the cold sweat off his skin, smoothing the lines of pain away, humming that stupid Barney song the kids had loved so much, "I love you, you love me, we're a happy family. . . ."

Abruptly Ken's face turned and he lifted his cheek toward me. I kissed him and his relaxation deepened. With a large sigh that was both effortless and sweet, Ken rolled over onto his side and curled up contentedly, his legs drawn up to his chest, his cheek resting in the cup of his hand.

Startled, I stroked the light down of his hair. He seemed suddenly blissful.

I knew how much he had missed resting on his side. His wracking cough, and the pressure of the fluid in his lungs had meant he could only, ever, rest sitting upright. But he had settled lightly on his side cradling his cheek, his breath barely there.

I held his hand and, drawing near, whispered softly of our family, our lives together, the gift of his love that had so changed my world. I told him of my profound gratitude, my endless devotion, the amazing joy I had thought I would never know. The happiness he had given to me.

Humming the sweet melancholy notes of "Little Girl Blue," I stroked his beautiful face. How still his body had become, how serene the softness of his lips.

Quietly, I began to recite the Twenty-third Psalm and then stopped. The familiar words did not fit. There was no Valley of Death here, no fear.

Each breath slowed as his body surrendered into soft lines of rest.

One last, long contented breath slipped out.

Sure, sure in my heart.

Bless this great man. Take his soul home with grace and our gratitude, for there is none so fine as this man, Kenneth. The ordeal is over, his battle is done, his great heart stops. Go with love, Ken. Go with joy. Homeward angels.

The time was 3:45 in the morning.

I reached behind me and turned off the hiss of the oxygen and the room tumbled into stillness.

Ken's cheek tucked in the palm of his hand. His chest, still. The blue eyes emptied white. I closed the lids gently.

I kissed him, and then drew back, abruptly aware of an enormous intensity rising in the room. A great swelling of energy infused the space, a vibrant rushing, a wave that surged upward even as I felt Ken within Ken rise, spread open his arms and soar from his body.

Yes. This then, the flinging of his fists outward. How hard, the work of opening to death.

Free, Ken's spirit plunged past me and out through the bay windows. A triumphant, joyful vibration bursting into the sky, his soul answering the call of the morning birds gathered in the trees. In a spontaneous drumming of wings hundreds of birds took flight over the valley, filling the dawn with their beating thunder. Dark ribbons rising in loops and circles, aloft on the pink horizon.

I bowed my head to Ken's chest and rested there. No heart beat for me. He was really gone.

It was done.

The house dreamed. Quiet, sacred quiet.

In the bedroom I lit three candles. And in the glimmer of their glow, I began to gently bathe and anoint my husband's body.

I woke the children, and held each one. Let them cry, helped them witness the peace of their father's body, stroke his hand and kiss him a final good-bye. I wished them to hold in their hearts more than just sorrow, but a sense of grace. Ken had been ours, had loved us enough to fight this hard to live, but now, finally, his struggle and pain were over.

His face, so still beneath the touch of their small hands, radiated grace.

Coda

A few days after Ken's funeral, my mother appeared on my doorstep, mounting slowly up the steps in the early August heat.

"Gramma!" the kids yelled, racing out to fold her into a giant bear hug.

She held David and Katy for a long wordless moment.

"Oh, kids, I just came to tell you how very, very sorry I am." Her eyes were full of regret as she looked down. She handed me a bouquet of four pink roses. "One for each of you," she said.

Fresh roses, I thought. An enormous cost to an old woman without much money.

Facing my mother for the first time in weeks, I stood inarticulate and numb. I felt if we touched, I might flame to ashes. My mother. On her face cancer's death mask burned brightly within her withered, drawn expression. Her thick glossy hair, once a sunny golden blonde, hung in lank dry chunks.

You as well, Mom, I thought in a shock of dispassionate sadness, seeing everything, all of it: the distended belly, the bone-thin arms. Spirit, running out of body.

"Can I come in?" Mom fanned herself wearily in the heat. "I just need to cool down. I swear I won't get in your way."

I nodded.

Helping Gramma up the steps, Katy led her in. Filling a large cup of iced tea for her, she made her French toast. No mention was made of Mom's absence during the days of Ken's hospitalization, or the funeral she had not attended, no reference to the wilting, browning floral displays drooping eerily throughout the corners of the house.

"Gosh, that tasted good," my mother murmured, mopping up the last drips of syrup with a toast crust. She sat propped up on her elbows at the kitchen bar. "My stomach is horribly upset all the time now," she muttered, bewildered. "There's not much I *can* eat. Thank you for the extra Ensure, Glenda. I found the cartons on the doorstep."

"That was Ken's."

She winced and looked down.

"I mean, I just knew it would do you good too, Mom."

"I don't know why it had to be Ken—he had so much to live for!" She burst out suddenly in a childlike wail. "Why not me? I've lived my life." She buried her face in her hands.

"Gramma, you can't say that," Katy protested.

"But it's true. It should have been me." Her shoulders shook.

Katy and David silently wrapped their arms around my mother, but I stood apart. I wanted to reach out and enfold her in a hug that would cocoon her, spare her what lay ahead. I wanted to, and I didn't. I wanted to, but I couldn't. I had sunk into a hole of sorrow so deep I could not climb up to comfort my own mother. Even when I knew, could see in her

303

exposed vulnerability, that she needed me. I had nothing left. Nothing to give and no cup to receive.

I busied myself at the sink as my mother wept at the counter. After a moment Mom heaved herself off the stool and lifted her purse onto one thin arm. She blew her nose.

"Time to go, kids."

At the bottom of the front steps, Mom turned away and her body shimmered in the heat. Watching her make her way to her car, her gait slow and painful, a strong feeling overcame me, a fierce need to step forward and carry her back inside. I felt compelled to answer the unspoken call in the lifelong dance between us, knowing, absolutely *knowing* this was the final good-bye.

"Ken was a good man," my mother called out as she reached the side of her car, not looking back. "He was good to us. So very good." She hesitated, then shook her head with harsh finality and lifted one hand behind her in a half-wave good-bye.

The voice inside me called out, *Please, Mom. Please stay.*

Slowly I raised my own hand and waved good-bye.

Ten days later on August 20, 2003, my mother called an ambulance to the farm as Uncle Joe busied himself washing the old poodle in the back room. She died three hours later at the hospital, her brother somewhere around, yet nowhere near. Judy was the only one of us who reached Mom's side in time, holding her hand through her last, silent moments in a coma.

Unspoken regrets were my mother's legacy.

The Geography of Love

The Spokane River embraces Riverside Cemetery in the crook of a cold winter morning. The sun shines bright, but without warmth this February day. I sit alone on the stone bench. Bending down, I sweep the frosted pine needles off the flat marker and read Ken's name, so familiar, so important. It is only by reading his name, with dates of birth and death, that I can absorb that he is gone.

I look away toward the river. Below the bluff, the river plunges through the black rock of the basalt canyon, risen from the spring surge and drowning the last of fall's hollow cattails. A great blue heron stands near the rocky shore, gazing at the swaying pine and the metallic sun.

Overhead, five or six low-flying Canadian geese shadow the pines, drawn by the early spring. They honk and beat the air with their wings, shifting for position in an imperfect V. I could reach up and stroke their pearl bellies, they loft so low. They have returned home.

Have I returned home? The question haunts me. Our beginnings and our endings intersect in such particular, intimate geography. My husband lies buried here in the latitudes where we first met. And twenty miles away, in the rural farm country of her mother's people, my mother lies at rest.

"You and me, here and now, we tell one another the story of our lives," my father had said to me by the banks of the Lewis River.

Life distills in the elements of chaos and chance. Vagary, arcane and capricious, hints at destiny and confounds God, adumbrates the fragile human landscape.

Only now, in the wake of loss, do I truly understand. Dying is a part of the dance, marking the shift of gathered dust from form to light, from shoes by the side of the bed to memories caught on the laugh of a child. I once heard the phrase "a parenthesis in eternity" used to describe mankind's existence. The here and the not here. What hurts so very badly is to exist on the opposite side of this parenthesis.

Our stories are not easily brushed aside.

I have brought red silk roses for our eighteenth anniversary. I tuck them into the ground vase and lightly caress the chiseled letters of his name. I have not forgotten Ken's warm kiss, the woodsy vanilla-bark smell of his skin. In quiet moments I sometimes hear the swelling notes of his jazz flute, wandering down the sad accidentals of "Little Girl Blue."

The past is the only place my heart doesn't hurt.

But each day I get up, make my bed, prepare tea.

Tucked in my pocket are a few lines of writing, crumpled and worn, scrawled across a child's sketch of a fat sun. *G, Thanks for all of your love and caretaking of this old body. Love you, Ken.*

I turn around, and face the sun.

Oh what have I learned of atoms and love?

They dance.

This book is dedicated to
Kenneth Alan Grunzweig, b. 1943—d. 2003

Acknowledgments

There would be no story if not for family, and I thank each of you. Especially in memory of my mother, Louise—the toughest life lessons often teach the most greatly.

To friends, colleagues, and medical practitioners who stood by our side, this story honors you. To Don and the corporate team in Ann Arbor, thank you for your steadfast support when it was most needed. To Andre, Ric, and John, three wise men who upheld the pillars of Ken's life in friendship and in memorial, the gratitude is profound.

In memory of Anne, no doubt in search of a decent coffee and bagel, and Brian, who never gave an inch in the fight and shared all that he knew first-hand with Ken, from "build the black box and then forget it," to "trust the technology." And for Cordell, who had the best job and hence the best cars to ever hit the 280, Ken as co-pilot.

Special recognition belongs to Rockne Harmon and the dedicated experts in the field of DNA forensics. We are so grateful. Every victim and family deserves closure.

I wish to express my deepest appreciation to my early readers Patricia Rogers, Julie Loudon, Bridget Burgess, Joyce Lekas, Christine Molina Maxwell, Ricardo and Noella Levy, Barbara Braun, John Baker, and most importantly, Kimberley Cameron, long-time friend and guiding star, for encouragement and constancy when the work was raw and heartbreaking. Thank you to Elizabeth Lyons and Debra Gwartney of Editing International, who pointed the way from experience to memoir. And most especially, to Elizabeth Evans of Reece Halsey North, my brilliant and devoted agent and writing guru, who brought the story to radiance.

My appreciation to a first-class cover art and copyedit team at Broadway Books.

My greatest gratitude rests with Christine Pride, my editor at Broadway Books, for her faith, vision, and unfailing championship of what was so clearly to her "a love story."

The Geography of Love belongs to my beloved Ken.